# MINERS, MILLHANDS, AND MOUNTAINEERS

ᔍ *Twentieth-Century America Series*

THE UNIVERSITY OF TENNESSEE PRESS / *Knoxville*

# MINERS, MILLHANDS, AND MOUNTAINEERS

*Industrialization of
the Appalachian South,
1880–1930*

# By Ronald D Eller

*Twentieth-Century America Series*
DEWEY W. GRANTHAM, GENERAL EDITOR

**Library of Congress Cataloging in Publication Data**

Eller, Ronald D., 1948–
    Miners, millhands, and mountaineers.

    (Twentieth-century America series)
    Bibliography: p.
    Includes Index.
    1. Appalachian region, Southern—Economic conditions.    2. Appalachian region, Southern—Social conditions.    3. Appalachian region, Southern—History.    I. Title.    II. Series.
HC107.A127E4            330.975            81–16020
ISBN 0–87049–340–X                    AACR2
ISBN 0–87049–341–8 (pbk.)

*To*

**BEC**

*Who has come to love the mountains as I do.*

# ACKNOWLEDGMENTS

THE EVOLUTION of this book began with the author's own personal odyssey. Almost two hundred years ago my ancestors migrated into the Blue Ridge country of North Carolina and Virginia, where they remained for almost four generations, until at the turn of the century they were drawn by the promise of a better life into the coal mining camps and timber mill towns of southern West Virginia. In the 1950s, they joined the great outmigration of mountaineers to the industrial centers of the North, settling in Ohio among neighbors and kin forced out of the hills by unemployment and economic despair. After a few years, they returned home to Appalachia, but not before I received a scholarship opportunity to attend a northern college. It was during those years as an undergraduate that I became interested in my people, in their distinctiveness, and in their experience as Americans. Being the first of my family to attend college, I became at once proud of my heritage and embittered at the inequalities and exploitation I found in my region. When I could locate no scholarly histories of the mountains and little in the published literature to help me understand the mountain experience, a friend and teacher encouraged me to pursue my interest and to begin the research that has culminated in this book. To Professor James A. Hodges of the College of Wooster, a master teacher, I will forever be grateful.

During the past twelve years my research has been guided by many friends who have provided advice, information, assistance, and encouragement. George Brown Tindall of the University of North Carolina at Chapel Hill guided my research through its dissertation stage and remains one of my most helpful critics. The knowledge and suggestions of many colleagues have contributed immeasurably to my understanding of the mountain experience and of the impact of social change and modernization on the region. Among those whose ideas and support have been invaluable are Donald Anderson,

Dwight Billings, Edwin Cheek, Richard Dillingham, Richard Drake, Steven Fisher, Jacquelyn Dowd Hall, Helen Matthews Lewis, Gordon McKinney, Donald McLeod, Thomas Plaut, Kenneth Sanchagrin, Henry D. Shapiro, George Stephenson, John Stephenson, Ken Sullivan, and David Walls. Professors Lawrence Goodwyn and Peter Wood of Duke University provided constant encouragement and helped me through several difficult periods of writing and research, and Professor Dewey W. Grantham of Vanderbilt University provided substantive and valuable suggestions in the editing of the final manuscript. To them and to the Rockefeller Foundation and the Community Research Center at Mars Hill College, which supported my endeavors, I owe a special debt of gratitude.

As in every scholarly work, there are many individuals who contributed to this book but who, for lack of space, must remain anonymous. I would like to thank, however, the hundreds of mountaineers who have given freely of their family histories and oral memoirs to the region's libraries and oral history projects. Their value is not adequately reflected in the pages that follow, but the time spent in reading these transcripts (over four hundred to date) has provided me with insight into the broad range of social experiences of average mountain people. Without this insight, this study would have been considerably weakened. Especially useful were the oral history projects at Alice Lloyd College, Marshall University, Emory and Henry College, Appalachian State University, the University of North Carolina at Chapel Hill, and Mars Hill College.

The staffs of the region's libraries also provided assistance that was too often unacknowledged in the heat of research. At the outset of my work, materials on the Appalachian South were obscure and widely scattered, and without the aid of determined and cheerful librarians I would have been unable to locate many resources. In recent years, these same librarians have begun to pull together the vast materials on the Appalachian region, and today Appalachian collections are housed in almost every regional library, making the scholar's research considerably easier. For their help in earlier days, therefore, I would like to thank the staffs of the libraries at the University of North Carolina at Chapel Hill, Duke University, Appalachian State University, the University of Tennessee, the University of Kentucky, the University of Cincinnati, West Virginia University, Marshall University, Mars Hill College, Berea College, Emory and

Henry College, the Highlander Research and Education Center, and Western Carolina University. Special thanks are extended to David Perkins, an aspiring Appalachian scholar, for his research assistance on the maps included in this volume.

Several sections of this book have appeared previously as articles in regional journals and books. Portions of the introduction appeared in Helen Lewis, *et al.*, eds., *Colonialism in Modern America: The Appalachian Case* (Boone, N.C., 1978), and sections of chapters 1 and 6 were published in the *Appalachian Journal*. I would like to express my gratitude to the editors of those publications for their assistance, cooperation, and permission to reprint these selections.

Finally, I want to thank my family for their years of love, encouragement, and patience. My grandparents, Elsie and the late Miskel Eller and the late Reverend Earl and Thelma West, were themselves part of the inspiration for this study. Their mountains and their lives are described in these pages. I hope I have done them justice. My parents, Oliver D and Virginia Ruth Eller, taught me to love the mountains and the mountain people. Their love of family and their determination to survive have given me the strength and confidence to write. I hope I have fulfilled their faith.

One person more than any other, however, is responsible for the completion of this work—my wife, Rebecca Jean Gaeth Eller. Throughout the past nine years she has been my chief editor, critic, and typist. She has prodded, encouraged, and sympathized with me through hard days and nights of writing. She has sacrificed and delayed her own plans, and, above all, she has understood my obsession with this research. For her constant help and assurance, I dedicate this book with love to her.

RONALD D ELLER
*Mars Hill, North Carolina*
*1 April 1981*

# CONTENTS

# ILLUSTRATIONS

## PHOTOGRAPHS

## MAPS

## TABLE

# INTRODUCTION

## *Industrialization and Social Change in Appalachia: A Look at the Static Image*

WE AMERICANS have faith in progress. Throughout most of our history we have assumed that the present is better than the past and that the future will be better still. This reassuring notion is periodically bolstered by statistical evidence of rising production and other measures of improvement in our standard of life. Progress, we believe, is occurring, and the future holds yet unrealized possibilities. For the historian, this faith in the inevitability of progress presents a problem. Since historians necessarily understand the past from the perspective of the present, our unconscious assumptions about the progressive present cast a shadow of contemporary condescension across our view of the received heritage. Our confident belief in progress leads us to depreciate the value of the past or to consider history as merely the ideological defense of the present.

Since the late nineteenth century, our idea of progress has become intertwined with the concept of modernity. We have come to believe that progress means technological development, industrial expansion, and growth in material wealth. Modernization has become synonymous with progress, and we tend to measure the improvement of any nation, society, or region in terms of its modernization. "Backward" and impoverished areas like Appalachia and the Third World are thought to exist because of a lack of modernization. The forces of growth and development appear to have passed by these regions. They seem to have been set off by history or geographic isolation from the rest of our progressive world.

The belief that time and geography somehow set the southern mountains off from the rest of the American experience has been part of our understanding of Appalachia for almost a hundred years. As early as the 1870s, writers for the new monthly magazines which flourished after the Civil War had begun to develop and exploit a literary image of the region. Initially drawn to the mountains in

search of the interesting and the picturesque, local color writers such
as Mary Noailles Murfree, James Lane Allen, John Fox, Jr., and
others were quick to turn the quaint and simple lives of the mountaineers into grist for the literary mill. Between 1870 and 1890, over
two hundred travel accounts and short stories were published in
which the mountain people emerged as a rude, backward, romantic,
and sometimes violent race who had quietly lived for generations in
isolation from the mainstream of American life.[1]

Implicit in this literary image was a sense of otherness that not only
marked the region as "a strange land inhabited by a peculiar people"
but defined that strangeness in terms of the process of American
historical growth. To the urban middle-class readers of *Cosmopolitan*, *Harper's*, and *Atlantic*, the apparent persistence of pioneer-like
conditions in the mountains seemed to reflect not merely the normal
patterns of rural life but "an earlier phase of American development
preserved, like a mammoth in ice."[2] Because metaphor was more
interesting than reality, the Appalachian present came to be linked
with the American past, and eventually the analogy was accepted as
fact. By the turn of the century, according to historian Henry David
Shapiro, the idea that Appalachia was "a discrete ethnic and cultural
unit within but not of America" had become a popular convention.[3]
For Americans of the progressive period who had witnessed the
passing of the western frontier, Appalachia became "the frontier we
have left within," and the mountaineers were "our contemporary
ancestors."[4]

Succeeding generations have periodically rediscovered and rein-
terpreted the region in the context of their own day, but the static
image has remained the standard perception of mountain life. In
1913, for example, Horace Kephart found "our Southern highlanders
. . . still thinking essentially the same thoughts, still living in much

1. See Henry David Shapiro, "A Strange Land and Peculiar People: The Discovery of Appalachia, 1870–1920" (Ph.D. diss. Rutgers Univ., 1966), 250ff.,
Cratis Dearl Williams, "The Southern Mountaineer in Fact and Fiction" (Ph.D.
diss., New York Univ., 1961), 1605ff.
2. Henry David Shapiro, "Introduction" to John C. Campbell, *The Southern
Highlander and His Homeland* (Lexington, Ky., 1969), xxvi.
3. Shapiro, "A Strange Land and Peculiar People," v. See also Henry D.
Shapiro's *Appalachia On Our Mind: The Southern Mountains and Mountaineers in
the American Consciousness—1870–1920* (Chapel Hill, 1978).
4. Woodrow Wilson, "Our Last Frontier," *Berea Quarterly* 4, no. 2 (May 1899),
5; William Goodell Frost, "Our Contemporary Ancestors in the Southern Mountains," *Atlantic Monthly* 83 (March 1899), 311.

the same fashion as did their ancestors in the days of Daniel Boone. The progress of mankind from his age to this," he claimed, "is no heritage of theirs."[5] James Watt Raine traveled the "land of saddlebags" in 1924 and again in 1942, and a decade later North Callahan made a similar journey into what he believed was the "happy" but "static society" of the Smoky Mountains country.[6] With the outbreak of the War on Poverty in the 1960s, the mountaineers became simply "Yesterday's People"—part of that "other America" of which Michael Harrington wrote.[7] More recently, the rise of the new ethnicity and the counterculture movement have brought attention to the mountain people as just plain "down home folk," and a flourishing minor industry has developed to fabricate such oddities as dulcimers, quilts, log cabins, and "Hillbilly Chicken." Of late, we have also seen the introduction of courses in Appalachian studies and the proliferation of symposia aimed at diagnosing the "unique" qualities of mountain life. But this revival of interest has done little to alter our traditional views. According to one leading student of the region, Appalachia can still be seen "as a vanishing frontier and its people as frontiersmen, suspended and isolated, while the rest of the country moves across the twentieth century."[8] Marooned on an island of hills, the mountaineer has seemed shut off from the forces that have shaped the modern world. He has lived, we are told, in a land "where time stood still."[9]

Arnold Toynbee may have offered the most callous assertion of this view when he suggested that the mountain people of the South were little better than barbarians. "They have relapsed into illiteracy and witchcraft," he wrote. "They suffer from poverty, squalor, and ill health. They are the American counterparts of the latter-day white barbarians of the Old World—Rifis, Albanians, Kurds, Pathans, and

5. *Our Southern Highlanders* (New York, 1913), 211.
6. Raine, *The Land of Saddle-Bags: A Study of the Mountain People of Appalachia* (New York, 1924) and *Saddlebag Folk: The Way of Life in the Kentucky Mountains* (Evanston, 1942); Callahan, *Smoky Mountain Country* (Boston, 1952), 74.
7. Jack E. Weller, *Yesterday's People: Life in Contemporary Appalachia* (Lexington, Ky., 1965); Harrington, *The Other America: Poverty in the United States* (New York, 1962).
8. Cratis Dearl Williams, "Heritage of Appalachia," address to the Southern Appalachian Regional Conference (13 May 1974), reprinted in *The Future of Appalachia* (Boone, N.C., 1975), 128.
9. Bruce and Nancy Roberts, *Where Time Stood Still: A Portrait of Appalachia* (New York, 1970).

Hairy Ainus." But whereas these latter seemed to be the belated survivals of an ancient barbarism, "the Appalachians," Toynbee argued, "present the melancholy spectacle of a people who have acquired civilization and then lost it."[10]

Cast in the static role, mountain people have thus rarely appeared as conscious actors on the stage of American history, and almost never on center stage. They are acknowledged to exist somewhere in the background, as subjects to be acted upon, but not as people participating in the historical drama itself. As a result, our efforts to explain and deal with the social problems of the region have focused not on economic and political realities in the area as they evolved over time, but on the supposed inadequacies of a pathological culture that is seen to have equipped mountain people poorly for life in the modern industrial world. Having overlooked elements of movement and change that have tied the mountains to the rest of the American experience, we have blamed the mountaineers for their own distress, rather than the forces which have caused it.[11]

Blaming the victim, of course, is not a uniquely American phenomenon. Rather, it is a misreading that takes international form. French intellectuals talk about the Alps and Spanish intellectuals talk about the Pyrenees in much the same simple if condescending way as urban Americans talk about Appalachia.[12] Indeed, all over the world, the terms applied to rural people by urban people have implied either contempt and condescension, or—and this is the opposite side of the same attitude—a romantic admiration for the simple, hardy virtues of rural life.[13] Since the southern mountains were among the most rural areas of eastern America, the Appalachian people have suffered exceedingly from this type of urban provincialism.

Ironically, it was during the same years that the static image was emerging as the dominant literary view that a revolution was shaking

10. *A Study of History*, II (New York, 1947), 312.
11. See Dwight Billings, "Culture and Poverty in Appalachia: A Theoretical Discussion and Empirical Analysis," *Social Forces* 53 (Dec. 1974), 315–23; Stephen L. Fisher, "Folk Culture or Folk Tale: Prevailing Assumptions About the Appalachian Personality," in J.W. Williamson, ed., *An Appalachian Symposium: Essays Written in Honor of Cratis D. Williams* (Boone, N.C., 1977), 14–25; David S. Walls, "Internal Colony or Internal Periphery? A Critique of Current Models and An Alternative Formulation," in Helen M. Lewis, *et al.*, eds., *Colonialism in Modern America: The Appalachian Case* (Boone, N.C., 1978), 319–50.
12. Roland Barthes, *Mythologies*, trans. Annette Lavers (New York, 1972), 74–76.
13. Robert Redfield, *Peasant Society and Culture* (New York, 1960), 38.

the very foundations of the mountain social order. In Appalachia, as in the rest of the country, the decades from 1880 to 1930 were years of transition and change. What had been in 1860 only the quiet backcountry of the Old South became by the turn of the century a new frontier for expanding industrial capitalism. The coming of railroads, the buildings of towns and villages, and the general expansion of industrial employment greatly altered the traditional patterns of mountain life and called forth certain adjustments, responses, and defenses on the part of the mountaineers. This transformation varied in scope and speed, but by the end of the 1920s, few residents of the region were left untouched by the industrial age.

The effects of this transition were great. Mountain agriculture, for example, went into serious decline. While the size of the average mountain farm was about 187 acres in the 1880s, by 1930 the average Appalachian farm contained only 76 acres, and in some counties the average was as low as 47 acres.[14] This decline occurred throughout the region but was most pronounced in the coal fields and other areas of intense economic growth. Significantly, while the total number of farms increased during these years, the total amount of land in farms actually decreased almost 20 percent as a result of the purchase of farm properties by timber and mining companies and for inclusion in national forests and parks.[15]

Farm productivity and income also changed. While farm production had been the major (and usually the sole) source of income in 1880, by 1930 most mountain farms had become part-time units of production, and the major source of income had shifted to nonagricultural employment—mining, logging, textiles, and other forms of public work.[16] In Knott County, Kentucky, for example, the income per farm from farming in 1930 averaged only $215, while the income per farm from nonfarm enterprises averaged over $342.[17] In 1880,

14. U.S. Department of Interior, Census Office, *The Tenth Census: 1880, Agricultural Statistics*, III; U.S. Department of Commerce, Bureau of the Census, *Fifteenth Census of the United States, 1930: Agriculture: The Southern States*, II, Pt. 2.

15. U.S. Department of Agriculture, *Economic and Social Problems and Conditions of the Southern Appalachians*, Miscellaneous Publication No. 205 (Washington, D.C., 1935), 16; Lewis Cecil Gray, "Economic Conditions and Tendencies in the Southern Appalachians As Indicated by the Cooperative Survey," *Mountain Life and Work* 9, no. 2 (July 1933), 9.

16. U.S. Department of Agriculture, *Economic and Social Conditions*, 3, 16.

17. Gray, "Economic Conditions in the Southern Appalachians," 10. See also W.D. Nicholls, "A Research Approach to the Problems of Appalachia," *Mountain*

the mountains had been a major producer of swine in the South, but by 1930 swine production in the region had declined to only 39 percent of its former level.[18] Such data suggest that the traditional image of the preindustrial mountain farm must be altered, and that the small, marginal farm usually associated with the stereotyped picture of Appalachia was in fact a product of modernization—that is, a more recent development not associated with the purported isolation of the region.

Along with the decline of agriculture came subtle changes in demographic relationships as well. Whereas mountain society in the 1880s had been characterized by a diffuse pattern of open country agricultural settlements located primarily in the fertile valleys and plateaus, by the turn of the century the population had begun to shift into nonagricultural areas and to concentrate around centers of industrial growth. Between 1900 and 1930, the urban population of the region increased fourfold and the rural nonfarm population almost twofold, while the farm population itself increased by only 5 percent.[19] A few of the burgeoning urban centers were destined to be temporary communities, such as the big timber towns of Sunburst and Ravensford in the Great Smoky Mountains, but most were permanent settlements that had a lasting impact upon mountain life. It is important to.point out, moreover, that the majority of these new industrial communities were company towns. In fact, over six hundred company towns were constructed in the southern mountains during this period, and in the coal fields they outnumbered independent incorporated towns more than five to one.[20]

This rising urban population provided a base for the emergence of a more modern political system in the mountains, one increasingly dominated by corporate interests and business-minded politicians.

---

*Life and Work* 7, no. 10 (Jan. 1932), 5–8, U.S. Department of Agriculture, *Economic and Social Conditions*, 41–57.

18. U.S. Department of Interior, Census Office, *The Tenth Census: 1880, Agricultural Statistics*, III; U.S. Department of Commerce, Bureau of the Census, *Fifteenth Census of the United States, 1930: Agriculture: The Southern States*, II Pt. 2.

19. Gray, "Economic Conditions in the Southern Appalachians," 8; U.S. Department of Agriculture, *Economic and Social Conditions*, 120–21.

20. U.S. Congress, Senate, *Report of the United States Coal Commission*, Sen. Doc. 195, 68th Cong. 2nd sess. (Washington, D.C., 1925), Table 14, p. 1467; U.S. Department of Commerce, Bureau of the Census, *Thirteenth Census of the United States, 1910: Population*, II and III.

Where the traditional political order had relied largely on kinship, personal contacts, and a broad-based party structure, after the turn of the century the level of citizen participation declined, and the average farmer or laborer became isolated from the political process. As early as the 1890s, industrialists such as Stephen B. Elkins in West Virginia and H. Clay Evans in Tennessee had begun to gain control of the political organizations in the mountains and to turn the powers of state and local government toward the expansion of commerce and exploitation of the region's resources.[21] As a result, there emerged in Appalachia a constricted political system based upon an economic hierarchy—those who controlled the jobs also controlled the political system, and those who controlled the political system used their power to exploit the region's natural wealth for their own personal gain. This loss of local political control naturally distressed many mountain people and plunged the region into prolonged industrial violence and social strife.[22]

Behind this transition in political culture lay the integration of the region into the national economy and the subordination of local interests to those of outside corporations. Nowhere was this process more evident than in the concentration of large amounts of mountain land in the hands of absentee owners. Beginning in the 1870s, northern speculators and outside businessmen carved out huge domains in the rich timberlands and mineral regions of Appalachia. By 1910, outlanders controlled not only the best stands of hardwood timber and the thickest seams of coal but a large percentage of the surface land in the region as well. For example, in that portion of western North Carolina which later became the Great Smoky Mountains National Park, over 75 percent of the land came under the control of thirteen corporations, and one timber company alone owned over a third of the total acreage.[23] The situation was even worse in the coal fields. According to the West Virginia State Board

21. See John Alexander Williams, "The New Dominion and the Old: Antebellum and Statehood Politics as the Background of West Virginia's 'Bourbon Democracy,' " *West Virginia History* 33 (July 1972), 322; Gordon Bartlett McKinney, "Mountain Republicanism, 1876–1900" (Ph.D. diss. Northwestern Univ. 1971), 170.

22. See Gordon B. McKinney, "Industrialization and Violence in Appalachia in the 1890's," in Williamson, ed., *An Appalachian Symposium*, 131–144.

23. Map, "North Carolina Portion of the Great Smoky Mountains National Park, Showing Individual Ownership," Western Carolina Univ., University Archives, Hunter Library.

of Agriculture in 1900, outside capitalists owned 90 percent of the coal in Mingo County, 90 percent of the coal in Wayne County, and 60 percent of that in Boone and McDowell counties.[24] Today, absentee corporations control more than half the total land area in the nine southernmost counties of the Mountain State.[25]

The immediate effect of this concentration of landholding was to dislodge a large part of the region's people from their ancestral homes. A few former landowners managed to remain on the land as sharecroppers or tenant farmers, and occasionally a family continued to live temporarily on the old homeplace, paying rent to absentee landlords.[26] But a great number of the displaced mountaineers migrated to the mill villages and mining towns, where they joined the ever-growing ranks of the new industrial working class. In the Cumberland Plateau, less than a third of those employed in 1930 remained in agriculture. The rest had moved to the mines or into service-related jobs.[27] Uprooted from their traditional way of life, some individuals were unable to reestablish permanent community ties, and they became wanderers drifting from mill to mill, from company house to company house, in search of higher pay or better living conditions. Most dreamed initially of returning to the land after a few years of public work, but the rising land values that accompanied industrial development soon pushed land ownership beyond the reach of the average miner or millhand.

Caught up in the social complex of the new industrial communities, many mountaineers found themselves unable to escape their condition of powerlessness and dependency. By coming to a coal mining town, the miner had exchanged the independence and somewhat precarious self-sufficiency of the family farm for subordination to the coal company and dependence upon a wage income. He lived in a company house, he worked in the company mine, and he purchased his groceries and other commodities from the company

24. West Virginia, State Board of Agriculture, *Fifth Biennial Report of the West Virginia State Board of Agriculture for the Years 1899 and 1900* (Charleston, W.Va., 1900), 371.
25. Tom D. Miller, "Absentees Dominate Land Ownership," in *Who Owns West Virginia?*, reprinted from the *Herald Adviser* and the *Herald-Dispatch* (Huntington, W.Va., 1974), 1–3.
26. James Lane Allen, "Mountain Passes of the Cumberlands," *Harper's Magazine* 81 (Sept. 1890), 575; Herbert Francis Sherwood, "Our New Racial Drama: Southern Mountaineers in the Textile Industry," *North American Review* 216 (Oct. 1922), 494; Campbell, *The Southern Highlander*, 87, 314.
27. U.S. Department of Agriculture, *Economic and Social Conditions*, 3.

store. He sent his children to the company school and patronized the company doctor and the company church. The company deducted rent and school, medical, and other fees from his monthly wage, and, under the prevailing system of scrip, he occasionally ended the month without a cash income. He had no voice in community affairs or working conditions, and he was dependent upon the benevolence of the employer to maintain his rate of pay.

Socially, if not physically, the working-class mountaineer was more isolated in his new situation than he had been on the family farm, for industrialization introduced rigid class distinctions into the highland culture.[28] Traditional status distinctions had always existed, but there were few economic differences within the rural population. With the coming of the industrial age, however, the separation between employer and employee became all too apparent. In the company town, the miners lived in small dwellings in the hollow near the tipple, while mine superintendents often built palatial structures high on the hillside overlooking the town.[29] Surrounded by elegant trees and well-kept grounds, these homes clearly defined the operator's social rank. In some communities, the railroad track literally divided the town in two, separating the more substantial residences of the managing class from the miners' shacks. The social gap between the classes increased, moreover, as managers and professional personnel developed lifestyles and formal institutions different from those of the working class.

By 1930, most mountaineers, whether they remained on the farm or migrated to the mill villages, timber towns, or coal camps, had become socially integrated within the new industrial system and economically dependent upon it as well. To say the least, this dependence was not on their own terms—that is to say, it was a product not of mountain culture but of the same political and economic forces that were shaping the rest of the nation and the western world. The rise of industrial capitalism brought to Appalachia a period of rapid

28. See Edward E. Knipe and Helen M. Lewis, "The Impact of Coal Mining on the Traditional Mountain Subculture," in J. Kenneth Moreland, ed., *The Not So Solid South: Anthropological Studies In a Regional Subculture* (Athens, Ga., 1971), 28.

29. Mack H. Gillenwater, "Cultural and Historical Geography of Mining Settlements in the Pocahontas Coal Fields of Southern West Virginia, 1880 to 1930" (Ph.D. diss., Univ. of Tennessee, 1972), 87; R.G. Lyman, "Coal Mining at Holden, West Virginia," *Engineering and Mining Journal* 52 (15 Dec. 1906), 1171.

growth and social change which those who hold to the static image have chosen to ignore. The brief prosperity brought on by the bonanza of modernization broadened the mountaineer's economic horizon. It aroused aspirations, envies, and hopes. But the industrial wonders of the age promised more than they in fact delivered, for the profits taken from the rich natural resources of the region flowed out of the mountains, with little benefit to the mountain people themselves. For a relative handful of owners and managers, the new order yielded riches unimaginable a few decades before; for thousands of mountaineers, it brought a life of struggle, hardship, and despair. Considered from this perspective, the persistent poverty of Appalachia has not resulted from the lack of modernization. Rather, it has come from the particular kind of modernization that unfolded in the years from 1880 to 1930.

Arnold Toynbee blamed the social conditions of Appalachia on the barbaric culture of mountain people, but one native mountaineer found another kind of barbarism at work in the region. Writing in *The Hills Beyond*, Thomas Wolfe lamented the tragic changes that had come over his beloved homeland in the years after Reconstruction. "The great mountain slopes and forests of the section," he wrote,

> had been ruinously detimbered; the farm-soil on the hillsides had eroded and washed down; high up, upon the hills, one saw the raw scars of old mica pits, the dump heaps of deserted mines. . . . It was evident that a huge compulsive greed had been at work: the whole region had been sucked and gutted, milked dry, denuded of its rich primeval treasures; something blind and ruthless had been here, grasped, and gone. The blind scars on the hills, the denuded slopes, the empty mica pits were what was left. . . . Something had come into the wilderness, and left the barren land.[30]

This book attempts to describe the economic and social revolution that swept the mountains at the turn of the century, creating modern Appalachia. It is a study based on the premise that the socioeconomic conditions that have emerged in southern Appalachia are in fact a product of the modernization of American life. As used in this study, "modernization" refers not only to the transition from a traditional to a modern society but to a specific set of changes that have accom-

30. *The Hills Beyond* (New York, 1941), 236–37.

INTRODUCTION

panied that transition in America since the late nineteenth century: the growth of urbanization and industrialization, the rise of corporate capitalism and the bureaucratic state, the development of a national market economy, the concentration of political and economic power, and a weakening of cooperative life and work in local communities and family life. It is within this context of modernization, I believe, that one must turn for an understanding of the paradox of Appalachia—a rich land inhabited by a poor people.

Historians and social scientists have long studied the phenomenon of modernization, but their efforts have generally concentrated on urban industrial centers. Little attention has been focused on the surrounding rural areas or on the impact of modernization on peripheral communities that provide labor and resources to the modernizing core. While the modernization of Appalachia was part and parcel of the modernization of America and was spurred by a small group of indigenous elites, the transformation of Appalachia was brought about by the diffusion of change from the developing industrial centers outside the mountains. Indeed, there is considerable evidence that modernization, as an urban industrial process, begins in core areas and spreads outward, extending employment opportunities into the outlying or peripheral areas but essentially using those areas to the core's advantage. Thus, a peripheral area like Appalachia may experience short-term growth without development and suffer the long-term consequences of dependency, inadequate social services, absentee ownership, and a colonial economy.[31]

It is important to note, moreover, that modernization does not affect all areas of the periphery with equal intensity. In Appalachia, industrialism altered some communities more dramatically than others, and throughout the region many aspects of the traditional or premodern culture remained intact long after they had disappeared in the rest of the country. The coal miner in West Virginia experienced the impact of modernization in a manner quite different from the hillside farmer in North Carolina, and some residents of southwest Virginia witnessed the arrival of the machine age more than thirty years before their neighbors in eastern Kentucky. But by the eve of the Great Depression, all were bound together by their common loss of autonomy and by their common relationship to the new order.

31. See Eugene A. Conti, Jr., "The Cultural Role of Local Elites in the Kentucky Mountains," *Appalachian Journal* 7, no. 1–2 (Autumn-Winter 1979–80), 51–68.

This larger, shared impact of modernization in the mountains is examined in the pages which follow. The communities and experiences I have selected reflect the basic issues confronting the whole region. The focus of this study is the patterns of economic and social change that made miners and millhands out of mountaineers. These patterns are most clear in the coal mining towns and lumber mill camps of the region, but they also underlay the experience of the mica pits, paper mills, and textile towns.[32]

The story of the transformation of Appalachia is more than an historical quest for the roots of poverty and powerlessness in one American subregion, since that quest challenges the very assumptions of progress upon which our contemporary society is built. The failure of modernization in the mountains raises the fundamental questions of our time—questions of power, greed, growth, self-determination, and cultural survival. In the answers to those questions lie our fragile hopes for the future. We in America must be driven to search for those answers for, as the mountaineers have learned, progress may not be inevitable.

32. The migration of thousands of mountaineers to the cotton mill districts of the piedmont South is an important chapter in the modernization of the mountains. But because the cotton mills lay largely outside the mountains and because their story is similar to that of the coal mining towns, it will not be examined in detail here.

# MINERS,
# MILLHANDS,
# AND
# MOUNTAINEERS

# CHAPTER ONE

# ON THE EVE OF
# A REMARKABLE DEVELOPMENT

*Generally speaking, the proportion which the aggregate of the other classes of citizens bears in any state to that of its husbandmen, is the proportion of its unsound to its healthy parts, and is a good enough barometer whereby to measure its degree of corruption. While we have land to labour then, let us never wish to see our citizens occupied at a workbench or twirling a distaff.*

*–Thomas Jefferson, Notes on Virginia*

FEW AREAS of the United States in the late nineteenth century more closely exemplified Thomas Jefferson's vision of a democratic society than did the agricultural communities of the southern Appalachians.[1] Long after the death of Jefferson and long after the nation as a whole had turned down the Hamiltonian path toward industrialism, the southern Appalachian Mountains remained a land of small farms and scattered open-country villages. Although traditional patterns of agricultural life persisted in other parts of the nation—in the rural South, the Midwest, and the more remote sections of the Northeast—nowhere did the self-sufficient family farm so dominate the culture and social system as it did in the Appalachian South. Indeed, by the late 1880s and the 1890s, urban scholars and journalists had come to view the mountains as one of the last great strongholds of rural frontier life. "Appalachian America," wrote William Goodell Frost in 1899, was "one of God's grand divisions," an anachronism

---

1. For the purpose of this study, southern Appalachia is defined as that portion of the Appalachian mountains that lies south of the New River in Virginia and West Virginia. Unless otherwise stated, the region includes 112 counties in southern West Virginia, eastern Kentucky, southwestern Virginia, eastern Tennessee, western North Carolina, and north Georgia. For a history of similar events in northern West Virginia, see John Alexander Williams, *West Virginia and the Captains of Industry* (Morgantown, W.Va., 1976).

of people who seemed "to be living to all intents and purposes in the conditions of the colonial times."[2]

It had been Jefferson's dream that America might remain a society in which land ownership was widely diffused and in which agrarian rather than mercantile or manufacturing interests would be dominant. Even before his death in 1826, however, that dream had begun to fade. Aggressive territorial expansion and the growth of manufacturing, banking, and transportation enterprises were rapidly moving the nation toward a nonagrarian economy. On the eve of the Civil War, over two-fifths of the American population had left agricultural pursuits for employment in the industrial and service sectors of the economy, and in the decades following the war, the growth of industrialization, urbanization, and railroad construction reached unparalleled proportions. By 1880, nonfarm production accounted for almost 75 percent of the gross national product. Within a century after Jefferson's death, the majority of Americans would reside not on the family farm, but in teeming urban centers.[3]

The southern mountain country was relatively untouched by the early phases of American industrialization. Small quantities of coal were mined and marketed in parts of western Virginia as early as the 1790s. Gold, copper, and lead mines were opened after the turn of the century in parts of northern Georgia, western North Carolina, and eastern Tennessee, and in the Great Kanawha Valley a major saline industry had developed by the 1830s. But these and other nonagrarian enterprises had relatively little impact upon the economy and lifestyles of the mountain people. The limitations of terrain, a restrictive transportation network, and the relative absence of slavery served to limit the growth of commercial agriculture in the region and to facilitate the survival of traditional cultural patterns and a family-based economy and social system.

Throughout most of the nineteenth century, there was little in Appalachia to attract capitalist development. The region's natural wealth of timber, coal, and other mineral resources was remote and inaccessible to the mercantile centers of the South and Northeast, and until technological change and industrial growth created a demand for these resources, they were to remain a potential rather than an

2. "Our Contemporary Ancestors," 311. See also Shapiro, *Appalachia On Our Mind*.
3. Harold G. Vatter, *The Drive to Industrial Maturity: The U.S. Economy, 1860 to 1914* (Westport, Conn., 1975), 3, 172.

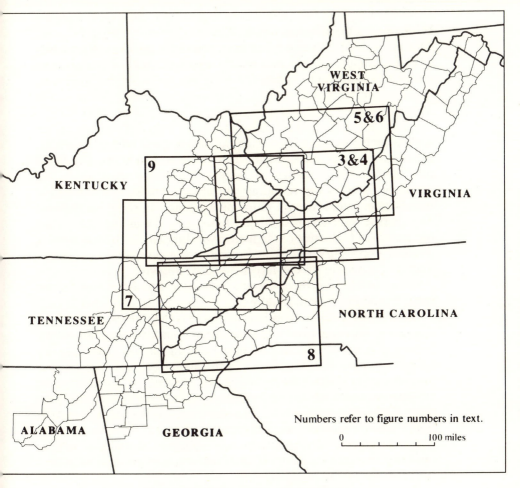

*1. Index Map of the Appalachian South*

actual source of wealth. Only as the national economy entered a new stage of expansion in the years following the Civil War did the natural wealth of Appalachia begin to attract outside capital. The sudden imposition of industrial capitalism at that time brought dramatic changes to this most rural area of American life. By the third decade of the twentieth century, the Jeffersonian dream in Appalachia had become a nightmare of exploitation, corruption, and social tragedy. While the southern mountains remained a predominantly rural area, changes in land ownership, economy, and the political system had left the region's people dependent, impoverished, and powerless within a new and alien social order.

## PREINDUSTRIAL APPALACHIA

Appalachia on the eve of industrialization was a land of scattered, loosely integrated, and self-sufficient island communities. Separated from each other by a sea of ridges, mountain communities had developed since their founding as separate social systems living largely unto themselves. Communication among these settlements was sparse, and except for major upheavals such as the Civil War, interaction with the rest of the nation was limited. Social institutions in the region were still oriented toward local community life rather than the concerns of the larger society, allowing each mountain community to maintain a certain autonomy and inner stability in politics, economy, and social life.

Structurally, if not culturally, mountain communities of the 1880s resembled other relatively remote, open-country American neighborhoods. Isolation, which became a prominent theme in most descriptive accounts of Appalachia in the late nineteenth century, was not unique to the southern mountains. Indeed, it was a feature common to much of rural America, especially the South and Midwest, where the absence of good roads, river, and water transportation made communications difficult.[4] Rutted and muddy highways, widely scattered villages, and homes separated by miles of wilderness characterized the majority of American farm communities until well into the twentieth century.[5]

In Appalachia, the rugged terrain and the insulation of the moun-

4. Abraham Berglund, George T. Starnes, and Frank T. DeVyver, *Labor in the Industrial South: A Survey of Wages and Living Conditions in Three Major Industries of the New Industries of the New Industrial South* (Charlottesville, Va., 1930), 18.

5. Walter A. Terpenning, *Village and Open Country Neighborhoods* (New York, 1931), 45. For a vivid description of an open-country rural farm community in Michigan in the late 1880s that is strikingly similar to descriptions of life in the southern mountains at that time, see pp. 42–108. Cf. Charles Dudley Warner, "On Horseback," *Atlantic Monthly* 56 (July–Oct. 1885), 88–100, 194–207, 388–98, 540–54.

tains themselves made communications especially difficult, but the region was never entirely cut off from contact with the outside world. Trade with nearby valley communities, seasonal work out of the mountains, postal delivery of letters and periodicals (supported by a high rate of literacy), and regular penetration of remote communities by peddlers and politicians kept mountain residents informed of issues and events in the larger society. Such contacts brought new ideas, new technologies, and new items of material culture into the mountains, where they were sifted into the prevailing culture.[6] Significantly, however, outside contacts during the preindustrial period occurred on the highlander's own terms and had only marginal influence on the quality and direction of mountain life. The relative seclusion of mountain neighborhoods from the changes that were sweeping life in urban America provided a sense of security and continuity which sustained a regional culture based upon strong relationships to the land and to family and kinship groups.

Perhaps more than in other rural areas, the land itself shaped the development of culture and social patterns in the mountains. Each community occupied a distinct cove, hollow, or valley and was separated from its neighbors by a rim of mountains or ridges. Land ownership usually terminated at the ridge top, reinforcing the community's identity and independence, but the hillsides were generally considered to be public land open for use by all members of the community. Economic and social activities were largely self-contained within these geographic bowls, with individual households relying upon themselves or their neighbors for both the necessities and pleasures of life. The land was such a dominant factor in mountain culture that neighborhoods often drew their names from the creeks or branches that penetrated the settlement (Spring Creek community, Walker's Branch community, East Fork community) and that further divided the larger community into numerous subcommunities.

Analysis of premodern demographic patterns in the southern mountains indicates that in Appalachia, as in other rural areas, settlement and land-use patterns varied according to terrain, social conditions, and type of economy. The mountain landscape favored the establishment of five forms of settlements—gap, cove, hollow,

6. See Gene Wilhelm, Jr., "Appalachian Isolation: Fact or Fiction?" in J.W. Williamson, ed., *An Appalachian Symposium* (Boone, N.C., 1977), 77–90.

ridge, and meadow communities—but cove and hollow settlements predominated throughout the region.[7] The natural protection, arable soil, good water, and abundant timber of the coves and hollows were ideal for the support of the cultural traditions and simple agricultural technology of the Scotch-Irish and German pioneers who settled the mountains. The earliest pioneers chose the fertile lands near the mouth of the hollow, while their descendants and later arrivals settled farther upstream toward the headwall. In the Cumberland Plateau of eastern Kentucky and the Allegheny Mountains of West Virginia, this type of settlement formed a linear pattern of homesteads strung out along the narrow hollow floor. By the late nineteenth century, population growth and agricultural expansion in these plateau counties had begun to force some hollow families onto the less desirable slopes and ridge lands, where they struggled to eke out a living on arid and rocky soil. Ridge settlements were less common in the Blue Ridge and Smoky Mountain country of North Carolina, Georgia, and eastern Tennessee, where the predominance of larger coves permitted oval patterns of settlement around the foot of the slopes, leaving the interior basin open for cultivation and expansion.[8]

Both cove and hollow settlement types favored the dispersal of farms along the bottomland, but this dispersal did not mean the isolation of mountain homesteads. Appalachian pioneers, like pioneers on other frontiers, generally migrated into the region in family or community groups and settled in small clusters of two or three homesteads separated from each other by as little as one-half mile.[9] These loose clusters of farms allowed mountain settlers to maintain a certain level of independence while retaining social contacts and community life. Later generations added to these clusters, creating kin-related groups, but a concentration of more than a handful of households was rare. Even commercial settlements that developed at the mouths of hollows or gaps remained small, seldom containing more than a store, a mill, a church, and a school. Larger towns, usually county seats, were even more widely scattered and were slow to gain the size and social importance of their counterparts in the low country.

7. Gene Wilhelm, Jr., "Folk Settlements in the Blue Ridge Mountains," *Appalachian Journal* 5, no. 2 (Winter 1978), 207, 240.
8. *Ibid.*, 219–20, 234–35.
9. *Ibid.*

This diffusion of settlement and the land ownership patterns that evolved in the mountains during the nineteenth century served to minimize the establishment of organized communities and formal social institutions. Politics and religion were the two major opportunities for mountain residents to engage in organized community life, but these institutions were themselves organized along kinship lines. Local political factions divided according to kin groups, and local churches developed as communions of extended family units. Both institutions reflected the importance of personal relationships and local autonomy in their operation and structure. Tied by rather tenuous bonds to the larger society (as was evident during the Civil War), the mountain population reflected the values and social patterns characterizing most premodern rural communities.

## SOCIAL STRUCTURE

The absense of highly structured communities and formal social institutions contributed to the evolution of a comparatively open and democratic social order in the mountains. Not until late in the nineteenth century did significant economic differences begin to create conscious class distinctions among mountain residents. Unlike the rest of the South, where the emergence of commercial agriculture spawned a highly stratified social system based on black slavery (and later on tenancy and sharecropping), the self-sufficient, family-based economy of the southern mountains served to inhibit the growth of a rigid social hierarchy.

Most mountaineers owned their own land and occupied and cultivated that land with the manpower provided by their own families. While slavery existed in almost every mountain county before the Civil War and prospered among a few wealthy families in the larger valley communities, the "peculiar institution" never influenced Appalachian culture and society as it did that of the lowland South. In fact, settlements of free blacks thrived in some areas of Appalachia both before and after the war, and their descendants came to have much in common culturally and economically with their white neighbors.[10] Mountain farmers shared a common interest in the land, and its cultivation demanded little technology or capital. The posses-

10. See William Lynwood Montell, *The Saga of Coe Ridge: A Study In Oral History* (Knoxville, 1970); Carter G. Woodson, "Freedom and Slavery in Appalachian America," *Journal of Negro History* 1 (April 1916).

sion of a milk cow, a few wandering hogs, some chickens, and a horse or mule was adequate to meet most of the family's needs. "With the help of kin and neighbors, even the poorest man was able to play his part in the hollow settlement."[11]

Status (rather than class) distinctions, therefore, were the more important social divisions in traditional mountain society. These distinctions were functions not of economics (wealth, land owner-ship, or access to natural resources), but of the value system of the community itself. In remote mountain neighborhoods where eco-nomic differences were minimal, measures of social prestige and privilege were based on personality characteristics or such traits as sex, age, and family group. The rural social order was divided not into upper, middle, and lower classes, but into respectable and nonrespectable groups, and each local community determined its own criteria for respectability. This status system, of course, tended to break down in the villages and county seat towns, where class distinctions (and thus class consciousness) were more noticeable.

In the rural areas of Appalachia, the lack of overt class conscious-ness was reflected in the emergence of strong egalitarian attitudes and beliefs. "The mountain farm family," wrote one observer of rural life, "recognizes no social classes either in the community or out." There were people with whom individuals did not care to associate, she added, "but each family feels itself as good as the best people in the state."[12] Most social events where a large crowd might be present, such as singings and workings, were commonly attended by all who wished to come, regardless of social or moral status.[13] "I'm as good as you are" and "I'm as good as he is" were stock expressions recorded in almost every account of premodern mountain life. As one author romantically phrased it, "A virile sturdy manhood, in the midst of a rugged environment, where the struggle for existence has been so difficult—all these things have fostered within the moun-taineer's breast an intense spirit of freedom and independence, com-mon to the dwellers of all highland regions."[14]

Whether or not the spirit of freedom and independence is charac-teristic of all mountain people, there seems to have emerged in

11. Wilhelm, "Folk Settlements," 239.
12. Nora Miller, *The Girl in the Rural Family* (Chapel Hill, 1935), 24.
13. Campbell, *The Southern Highlander*, 130–31.
14. W.R. Thomas, *Life Among the Hills and Mountains of Kentucky* (Louisville, Ky., 1926), 87.

Appalachia a system of cultural beliefs that preserved what Herbert G. Gutman has called "a vision of Old America—a belief in America as a land of promise and independence" where men could "be their own rulers" and where "no one should or could become their masters."[15] The relative isolation of Appalachian communities from the centralizing forces of the larger society sustained this democratic dream in the mountains long after the passing of the frontier, and the leveling tendencies of the mountain economy made the idea of equality appear to be as much reality as value. Not until the end of the nineteenth century, when industrialization began to bring overt class consciousness to the region, did this democratic ethos begin to conflict with the mountaineer's perceptions of social reality. This conflict between the traditional mountain culture and the industrial social structure created profound and unresolved tensions within the social order.

The dominance of a democratic ethos, however, did not mean the absence of a class structure in nineteenth-century Appalachia. While status consciousness helped to shape the values and beliefs of mountain neighborhoods, especially at the local level, class distinctions did exist in the larger community, county, and region. Like other areas of the upland South, the southern mountain country contained a minority of wealthier, landed families whose economic power and political influence set them off as an elite group. Usually the first to arrive on the land, such families had acquired large land holdings (often as Revolutionary War grants) and by 1830 had emerged as a resident ruling class.[16] More noticeable in the larger valleys and county seat towns, these wealthier families provided the political leadership in the mountains and often controlled local commercial enterprises. Their descendants, having access to resources and educational opportunities in the flatlands, became merchants, teachers, and lawyers, many often specializing in land litigation and speculation.

Although the planter-lawyer-merchant class provided the most visible political leadership, these mountain elites did not acquire the power or influence of their counterparts in the rest of the South. The prevalence of small-scale agriculture limited the number and wealth

15. *Work, Culture, and Society in Industrializing America: Essays in American Working-Class and Social History* (New York, 1977), 50–52.
16. Williams, "The New Dominion and the Old," 383.

II

of mountain elites and placed greater social power in the larger yeoman-farmer class. In matters of state and national politics, small farmers usually deferred to the leadership of the elites, but this leadership was as much a function of the status system as of wealth. Kinship ties, personality characteristics, and oratorical abilities were primary qualifications for leadership in a political system that emphasized oral voting and face-to-face communications. This premodern political culture provided important dialogue between politicians and their public and reserved considerable power over local matters for the yeoman-farmer majority.[17]

Nevertheless, their political influence, access to resources, and contacts with the outside placed mountain elites in a strategic position to benefit from economic change. As intermediaries between the local culture and the larger society, they came to play an important role in the industrialization of the mountains—purchasing land and mineral rights from local people for resale to outsiders, advertising and promoting the development of mountain resources, and encouraging the construction of railroads and other transportation networks. Many, like John Caldwell Calhoun Mayo of eastern Kentucky and George L. Carter of southwest Virginia, acquired large fortunes as a result of their promotional activities, but they also saw their position in the traditional social order displaced as economic change created a new industrial ruling class.

## TRANSPORTATION

If anything distinguished the mountain elite from less prosperous neighbors, it was access to good bottomland and to communication and transportation networks. Travel was always difficult in the mountains, as it was throughout rural America, and proximity to transportation arteries facilitated one's entrance into commerce. Prior to the coming of railroads in the late nineteenth century, travel was either by foot, horse, or boat, and those who lived closest to primary turnpikes and streams had a clear economic advantage over those who lived in more remote areas.

17. Williams, "The New Dominion and the Old," 338; McKinney, "Mountain Republicanism, 1876–1900," 182–83.

The heart of the transportation and communication system in the mountains was a network of trails and dirt roads connecting each community with the larger villages and towns and in turn with the nearest marketing centers of the low country. The earliest white settlers found the mountain landscape already interlaced with big game and Indian trails, and the settlers quickly turned these ancient paths into major and minor roads. Continued use gradually widened the narrow roadways, which usually ran along the banks of creeks and rivers and frequently crossed the watercourse as it wound toward the headwaters of another stream. Such roads were usually steep and often muddy and impassable in the winter and spring, but they served the limited needs of early settlers and provided for the emergence of a mature, self-sufficient mountain economy.[18]

The primitive quality of mountain roads seems not to have set the region off from other areas of the United States until the mid-nineteenth century. Poor roads were a fact of life for most rural, open-country neighborhoods, especially in the South, and Appalachia was no exception. After 1830, the construction of railroads and macadam turnpikes began to bring improved transportation facilities to some American communities, but the transportation revolution did not affect most rural roads until the twentieth century. Antebellum investors, public and private, were reluctant to risk money on transportation improvements in the mountains because of the high cost of construction and the limited potential for commerce. Internal improvement projects before the Civil War, therefore, tended to be concentrated in the nonmountainous portions of the southern states, leaving the mountain counties to make do with traditional transportation patterns.[19] On the eve of the Civil War, only one major railroad (the Virginia and Tennessee Railroad) penetrated Appalachia, and it ran down the valley of southwest Virginia, having only marginal impact upon the interior mountain counties.[20] Thus, while technological change and industrial growth expanded

18. See Wilhelm, "Appalachian Isolation," 78–83.
19. Mary Verhoeff, *The Kentucky Mountains, Transportation and Commerce, 1750–1911: A Study in the Economic History of a Coal Field*, Filson Club Publication No. 26, vol. 1 (Louisville, Ky., 1911), 52–53.
20. See John Ford Stover, *The Railroads of the South, 1865–1900: A Study in Finance and Control* (Chapel Hill, 1955). Northern Appalachia, especially Pennsylvania, western Maryland, and northern West Virginia, was penetrated by several major railroads in the years before the Civil War, the most notable of which was the Baltimore and Ohio Railroad through northern West Virginia.

transportation facilities in other areas of the nation, there matured in Appalachia a traditional transportation network that met the needs primarily of local and regional, rather than national, markets.

The matrix of trails and roads connecting backcountry communities was part of a regional market system that reached full development in the major turnpikes and "stock roads" that ran throughout the region. Major arteries such as the Kanawha Turnpike in southern West Virginia, the Owingsville and Big Sandy Turnpike in eastern Kentucky, the Wilderness Road serving southwest Virginia and southern Kentucky, and the Buncombe Turnpike in western North Carolina provided a fairly constant stream of traffic eastward and westward that sustained a limited regional commerce and kept the mountains in touch with the low country. Each year, drivers herded thousands of head of cattle, sheep, hogs, chickens, and turkeys over these main stock roads, destined for sale on the great tobacco and cotton plantations of the South. Through the small mountain town of Asheville, North Carolina, for example, there passed annually from 140,000 to 160,000 hogs traveling from farms in Tennessee and Kentucky to markets in South Carolina and Georgia.[21]

The heavy traffic on these turnpikes constituted an important market for local mountain farmers. Not only did the farmers sell their surplus livestock to the passing drivers, but they commonly raised corn and produce to feed the animals and human travelers as they passed through. Along the road, local merchants established stockades or "stands" where the animals could be fed and watered and where travelers could find overnight accommodations. These wayside facilities developed into local trade centers where farmers exchanged corn and other products for retail goods. As late as the 1880s, such establishments provided connections for the mail service and for stagecoach lines, as well as serving as the hub of commercial life for surrounding communities.

Many of these retail establishments were located at points where stock roads paralleled or crossed major streams, and after the Civil War their proprietors began increasingly to use water transportation to supplement the land trade. The larger mountain rivers west of the Blue Ridge, such as the Kanawha, Big Sandy, and Cumberland, were navigable for short distances by steamboats and for many miles

21. F.A. Sondley, *A History of Buncombe County, North Carolina* (Asheville, N.C., 1930), 619.

into their headwaters by small flatbottomed boats called "batteaus." The Big Sandy River between eastern Kentucky and southern West Virginia, for example, was navigable by large steamboats for about one hundred miles and by shallow-draft steamboats for an additional hundred miles up the Levisa Fork and about ninety miles up the Tug Fork.[22] In the late nineteenth century, traffic along the river was very heavy, including at least six steamboats that transported goods and people from Catlettsburg on the Ohio River to Pikeville in the interior.[23] From commercial centers such as Pikeville, goods were then shipped overland by wagon or on push boats, which were poled upstream and rafted downstream, going from settlement to settlement. Until the coming of railroads, navigation by batteau and other craft was an important means of commerce for remote mountain communities; provisions such as refined sugar, spices, tools, and arms and ammunition were brought in by boats that took out agricultural products.

Rivers and streams, as well as roads and turnpikes, also provided a means for the movement and migration of mountain people within and out of the Appalachian region. From the earliest settlement, there was considerable movement of some mountain families within the region, from farm to farm and from one hollow to another. Squatters and small landowners often traded farms or cleared new land in the next valley or on the other side of the mountain. The relative ease with which a young highland family moved its few material possessions and the independent, loosely structured nature of mountain communities facilitated such movement as long as there was open land available.[24] "Allured by rumors from the West," large numbers of mountain families joined the great westward migration of the mid-nineteenth century, settling in Kansas, Oklahoma, Texas, Arkansas, and Nebraska. Many of these outmigrants remained in the West, but a few always returned home "from love of the mountains."[25] This process of outmigration and periodic return of relatives

22. Jean Thomas, *Big Sandy* (New York, 1940), 5–6.

23. Ernest Willis Gibson, "The Economic History of Boyd County, Kentucky" (M.A. thesis, Univ. of Kentucky, 1929), 36.

24. Marion Pearsall, "Some Frontier Origins of Southern Appalachian Culture," *Kentucky Folklore Record 8* (1962), 43; Campbell, *The Southern Highlander*, 133; James Lane Allen, "Through Cumberland Gap on Horseback," *Harper's New Monthly Magazine* 73 (June 1886), 58.

25. See Allen, "Through Cumberland Gap," 62; Marion V. Rambo, "The Submerged Tenth Among the Southern Mountaineers," *Methodist Review* 87 (July

served as a further means of communication between the mountains and the outside world.

Most mountain families, therefore, were not isolated in the fullest sense of the word. Traditional patterns of land and water transportation provided opportunities for contact and trade with other communities and with the rest of the nation, but travel was always difficult and usually time-consuming. Mountaineers commonly walked for miles over rugged terrain to a store or mill and then returned the same day. Packing "a lazy man's load" of a bushel of corn on each shoulder to a mill ten to fifteen miles away was a weekly experience for many mountain folk.[26] Such difficulties in transportation naturally limited the participation of mountain farmers in the national market economy and served to reinforce the vitality of the self-sufficient family farm.

## ECONOMY

The backbone of the preindustrial Appalachian economy was the family farm. Each mountain homestead functioned as a nearly self-contained economic unit, depending upon the land and the energy of a single family to provide food, clothing, shelter, and the other necessities of life. Unlike agrarian sections of the Midwest and nonmountain South that had moved steadily toward dependence on a single cash crop, mountain family farms remained essentially diversified and independent, producing primarily for their own use. By 1880, Appalachia contained a greater concentration of noncommercial family farms than any other area of the nation.

The typical mountain farm of the preindustrial period consisted of a disparate mixture of bottomland and rugged mountainside. The average farm in 1880 contained about 187 acres, of which about 25 percent was cultivated, about 20 percent in cleared pasture, and the remainder in virgin forest.[27] Dotted by numerous springs and crossed by at least one creek or branch, the highland farm was blessed with

1905), 556; Williams, "The Southern Mountaineer in Fact and Fiction," 161; Bina Lorina Morris-Orr, "Life of Bina Lorina Morris-Orr," MS No. 111, Emory and Henry College, 1–4; Maristan Chapman, "The Mountain Man," *Century* 117 (Feb. 1929), 511.

26. Horace Kephart, "Journals," vol. 1, University Archives, Hunter Library, Western Carolina Univ.

27. U.S. Department of Interior, Census Office, *The Tenth Census: 1880, Agricultural Statistics*, III.

*Mountain Farm, Hurricane Fork, Washington County, Tennessee. Courtesy of the Archives of Appalachia, East Tennessee State University.*

excellent water, a mild climate, and a long growing season seldom threatened by early frost. Corn was the staple crop, occupying about 50 percent of the acreage under cultivation, but oats and wheat were also harvested, as well as hay, sorghum, rye, potatoes, buckwheat, and other crops. Every farm had its vegetable garden, beehive, and apple orchard, and often a variety of pear, plum, cherry, or other fruit trees. Wild blackberries and huckleberries were abundant, as well as rabbits, squirrels, quail, and other wild game. By the late nineteenth century, large portions of the mountain hillsides had been cleared (usually by burning or girdling the trees) for raising cattle, sheep,

17

mules, and fowl. But the greatest proportion of the farm, including the "public land" that surrounded it, remained in woodland, and it was here that the family hogs grazed throughout much of the year.[28]

Such farms offered full support and sustenance for mountain families, which often numbered from eight to twelve individuals, including children, parents, and occasionally a grandparent or other relative. Large families were an economic necessity as well as a social boon on remote mountain farms, since they lightened the load of farm operation. In the years following the Civil War, Appalachian farms supported one of the highest birth rates of any area of the country—a fact contributing significantly to the steady rise of population in the region.[29] The family work unit, with the aid of a horse or a pair of mules, provided all the labor necessary to sustain a simple and comfortable life. As one observer noted, "An intelligent and industrious family, no matter how isolated, [could] raise most of its 'living.' "[30]

The daily operation of the farm centered on the growing of all of the vegetables that the family used: corn, beans, and potatoes for the table, field corn for fattening the hogs, hay for feeding the livestock, and small grains such as oats and wheat for flour. Planting, cultivating, and harvesting were done by hand, since simple tools and traditional agricultural techniques proved most practical on the mountainous terrain. "All of the wheat, all the heavy grains were cut with a cradle which required the help of a lot of people . . . and most of the grass for hay was cut with a scythe and harvested in that way . . . raked, and stacked."[31]

The kitchen garden was the mainstay of the food supply, and mountain gardens were often quite large. "Usually they were worked by the wife or the women folks in the family with the help of the men

28. For descriptions of preindustrial mountain agriculture, see Raine, *The Land of Saddle-Bags* 230; Allen "Through Cumberland Gap," 50–59; Warner, "On Horseback," 88–100; Judge Watson, "The Economic and Cultural Development of Eastern Kentucky from 1900 to the Present" (Ph.D. diss., Indiana Univ., 1963), 8–9; Bureau of Agricultural and Labor Statistics of the State of Kentucky, *Biennial Reports*, vols. 1–9 (Frankfort, Ky., 1876–1892).
29. Edward Alsworth Ross, "Pocketed Americans," *New Republic* 37 (9 Jan. 1924), 171. See also Hal Seth Baron, "A Case for Appalachian Demographic History," *Appalachian Journal* 4 (Spring-Summer 1977), 211–12.
30. Raine, *The Land of Saddle-Bags*, 230.
31. Dr. C.C. Hatfield, Saltville, Va., n.d., interview, transcript by Jeane Seay (Emory and Henry Oral History Project, File 25, Emory and Henry College, Emory, Va.), 35–36.

for the heavier work such as cultivating with the horse."[32] Plowing was accomplished by use of a single-horse bull tongue or hillside turning plow, and early cultivation consisted of simply plowing between the rows. There was not a wide variety of vegetables in the garden, but there was a large quantity of them, with corn being the most plentiful crop. Over the years, mountain farmers devised unique methods for utilizing limited garden space and for the efficient use of manpower. Green beans, pumpkins, melons, squash, and other vegetables were often planted in with the corn and allowed to grow under or on the cornstalks. Since the corn was worked by hand, "you could very well plant other crops in the corn, especially beans."[33] Thinning and hoeing the garden in late spring was an activity in which the whole family often took part.

Along with the garden crops, the self-sufficient mountain farm also maintained a variety of livestock that provided food, clothing, and other household needs. No farm was without two or three milk cows, a flock of hens, several mules or work oxen, and a drove of shoat pigs. Sheep raised on the rocky hillsides afforded wool that was carded, dyed, spun, and woven into cloth or knit into stockings or carpets for the floor. Geese were kept both to control insects around the house and for their down, which was plucked annually and made into bed ticks and pillows. Even the pack of dogs that commonly "lounged around the cabin door" had its function. More than just pets, dogs were used for hunting as well as for protection and for regulation of rabbits, groundhogs, and other field pests. Before the passage of "progressive" fish and game laws, year-round hunting in the surrounding forests was an important supplement to the family food supply, and a good hunting dog was as vital to the livelihood of the farm as the family milk cow.

The raising of livestock was also the principal commercial enterprise in the mountains before industrialization, and it provided mountain farmers with the means of acquiring the few goods that could not be raised or produced on the farm. According to historian Frank L. Owsley, some of the best grazing land in the South was to be found in the mountains, where the mast from chestnut, oak, and other nut-bearing trees was abundant. "In fact," wrote Owsley, "more cattle,

32. *Ibid.*, 36.
33. *Ibid.*, 36. See also Watson, "Economic and Cultural Development of Eastern Kentucky," 9.

*Sheep Grazing on a High Mountain Pasture in Western North Carolina.*
*Courtesy of the Appalachian Collection, Mars Hill College.*

swine, and sheep per capita were raised in the Appalachians, the
Cumberland Plateau, and the Ozarks than in the bluegrass basins of
Kentucky and Tennessee."[34] Livestock was commonly turned out
into the woodland or driven over the ridge to pastures or high grassy
balds. Split-rail fences enclosed the garden and other field crops,
allowing the livestock to run wild on the hillsides. A traveler in
eastern Kentucky in 1889 reported that the hillsides were "full of
sheep . . . draught mules and beef, milk cattle, and steers." These
were driven in the fall "over the breaks to Virginia and down into the
Bluegrass country, finding ready markets." Large flocks of turkeys
were also collected each autumn, "300 to 500 in a gang," and driven

34. *Plain Folk of the Old South* (Chicago, 1965), 45. See also Lewis Cecil Gray,
*History of Agriculture in the Southern United States to 1860*, II (Gloucester, Mass.,
1958), 876, 884.

to flatland markets where they brought from three to five cents per pound.[35]

While cattle, sheep, and other livestock were grazed in large numbers, hogs were most important to the preindustrial mountain economy, "for the hardwood growth produced immense crops of chestnuts, acorns, walnuts, and hickory nuts, and in the rich, narrow valleys excellent corn could be grown."[36] Hogs were allowed to fatten on the mast in the forest until late fall, when they were brought in and fed on corn for several weeks to harden the flesh. Half a dozen hogs were then slaughtered and placed in the smokehouse for the family's needs, and the rest were traded or sold to passing drovers. The annual production of hogs in the mountain counties of southern West Virginia, eastern Kentucky, southwest Virginia, western North Carolina, eastern Tennessee, and northeast Georgia reached almost one and a quarter million head in 1880, before the sawmills cut the timber and eliminated the woodlands as pasture for hog produc- tions.[37] Prior to the coming of the timber industry and the purchase of woodlands by private corporations, the southern Appalachian Moun- tains were one of the major hog-producing areas of the United States.

In addition to raising hogs and other livestock, mountain farmers supplemented their income by occasionally cutting timber and gathering roots and herbs. Beginning in the late antebellum period, local farmers cut selected trees from the banks of the larger rivers and floated the timber to sawmills downstream. This small-scale logging provided off-season work and an opportunity to trade at the mercan- tile centers, but until late in the century it returned only a meager income to most farmers. Some families with larger numbers of males in the household operated small sawmills for homes and outbuild- ings. Occasionally, an individual specialized in making chairs, split- ting shingles for roofing and siding, or cutting fence posts and traded these items to neighbors for similar goods or services.

For many mountain families, however, a more important activity was the gathering of medicinal herbs and roots, especially ginseng, from the forests. During the late summer, before the crops were harvested, families spent much of their "lay-by" time collecting

35. Goldsmith Bernard West, "A Revolution: Capital Pouring into Eastern Kentucky," *Manufacturers' Record* 16 (10 Aug. 1889), 24.

36. Owsley, *Plain Folk of the Old South*, 46.

37. Based upon analysis of 112 counties. U.S. Department of Interior, Census Office, *The Tenth Census: 1880, Agricultural Statistics*, III.

ginseng, yellow-root, witch hazel, sassafras, galax, golden-seal, and bloodroot. Most local merchants were willing to accept these plant products in exchange for store commodities. After drying and packaging the plants, the merchants then shipped them to redistribution centers in Philadelphia, New York, and Cincinnati. Between 1880 and 1900, the price paid by merchants for a pound of ginseng ranged from two to five dollars.[38] One Logan County, West Virginia, merchant advertised in 1890 that "a pound of seng will get you a good pair of boots or a fine suit of clothes, and the girls can find some of the cheapest dress goods ever sold."[39]

Mountain residents seldom received cash for their surplus livestock, roots and herbs, or other commercial products. Like other parts of rural America in the late nineteenth century, the mountains were lacking in legal tender money, and barter became almost the sole means of exchange. Even after the resumption of specie payments in 1878, the problem of inadequate money supply continued to be felt in the region. The scarcity of banking facilities contributed to the difficulty. Some banks were established in county seat towns before the Civil War, but the war destroyed most of these banks, and they never reopened.[40] Until industrialization brought a boom in bank formation after the turn of the century, the buying and selling of goods was conducted on a product-for-product basis. The center of this barter economy was the local merchant, who exchanged retail commodities for surplus agricultural products and extended credit. Other businesses, including the hundreds of neighborhood mills in the region, operated on a similar basis, providing services in exchange for part of the product itself. This form of commerce reinforced the autonomy of the local market system and provided mountain communities with considerable freedom from the fluctuations of the national cash economy.

38. Ellen Churchill Semple, "The Anglo-Saxons of the Kentucky Mountains: A Study in Anthropogeography," *Bulletin of the American Geographical Society* 42, no. 8 (1910), 580.
39. Logan County *Banner*, 14 Aug. 1890, quoted in Edwin Albert Cubby, "The Transformation of the Tug and Guyandot Valleys: Economic Development and Social Change in West Virginia, 1888–1921" (Ph.D. diss., Syracuse Univ., 1962), 129.
40. See Hugh Asher Howard, "Chapters in the Economic History of Knox County, Kentucky" (M.A. thesis, Univ. of Kentucky, 1937), 116–17; Semple, "The Anglo-Saxons of the Kentucky Mountains," 580–81.

## MATERIAL CULTURE

The independence and self-sufficiency of the mountain homestead was evident not only in the economic system but in the material culture and social life of the region as well. From the earliest settlement, mountain residents relied almost entirely upon abundant timber, stone, and other natural resources for the construction of homes, barns, tools, furniture, and farm implements, and upon the fellowship of neighbors and kin for most social activities. Everything about the mountain homestead reflected a society that had adapted to and harmonized with its surroundings by making effective use of local resources and by altering traditional cultural patterns to fit new physical conditions. Within this environment emerged a regional culture with strong attachments to the land and a profound sense of place. The land, the homestead, one's kin, and one's neighbors formed the matrix for the daily lives of most mountaineers and the context from which they would confront the social patterns of the new industrial age.

Perhaps no other aspect of Appalachian culture reflected this accommodation to environment more than the mountain homestead itself. The hand-hewn log cabin, which with the help of local color writers became the very symbol of traditional mountain life, exemplified utility, simplicity, and permanence. Such cabins were not the only type of housing in the Appalachian region, but, as in most remote rural areas of the eastern United States, the log structure was the predominant building type until late in the nineteenth century. While timber was abundant on every mountain homestead, the long distances to sawmills made the construction of frame structures impractical outside of the villages and valley communities before the 1880s and 1890s. In the most sequestered hollows and coves of the region, log cabins continued to be built well into the twentieth century.

Most Appalachian log cabins were constructed of shaped pine timbers, notched at the ends and carefully mortised. The space between adjoining logs was commonly chinked with split pieces of wood trimmed and driven into the cracks and then daubed with mud or a limestone and rock mixture. Split white oak shingles covered the roof, and the floor consisted of shaved chestnut slabs (puncheons), trimmed smooth on top and fitted together on rough-hewn sills. Windows were absent in most early log homes, although they became popular after the Civil War, as did porches extending along the front and sometimes the back of the cabin, adding "a picturesque effect to the whole" structure.[41] Most chimneys were built of native stone cemented with clay, but the poorer cabins often had "stick chimneys" made of laths daubed with clay and tilted away from the cabin in case of fire. Built entirely by hand with simple tools and natural materials, the mountain log cabin was a plain but usually sturdy and durable structure. "It was the kind of a house," wrote Emma Belle Miles, "that a tornado might roll over and over in one piece and leave about as solid as before."[42]

Most early cabins consisted of one large room, with a loft above and often a "shed room" added to the back for additional space. The single open room served as kitchen, bedroom, and living area for the entire family and occasionally for a traveler or guest. Later, if the family prospered, another room might be built adjacent to the original structure, forming a double or "dog-trot" cabin with a covered entry or porch between. This open-room type of construction limited privacy, but it strengthened family unity and provided for simple and efficient heating in the winter. During the summer months, when the thick-walled cabin could be uncomfortably warm, the family spent most of the daylight hours out-of-doors—in the fields, on the porch, or under the shade of surrounding trees.

Interior design was equally simple. Closets were few, if not totally absent, in mountain cabins, and clothes along with the rest of the family's possessions were hung on pegs in the walls. Initially, furniture was handmade, consisting of tables, chairs, cupboards, and rope beds. But increasingly after the 1840s, iron cook stoves, washtubs, kettles, and other manufactured goods became commonplace. Travelers in the 1880s and 1890s even reported "discovering" pianos, organs, and fine carpets in some mountain cabins miles away from the nearest railroad, and one outlander was astonished to find "live gold fish in a glass tank" at a mountain residence in what he called "the most isolated spot this side of the Rockies."[43] More common, however, were the basic necessities of a self-sufficient life: the small flax wheel, the larger spinning wheel, the hand loom, and their products, the colorful mountain quilts and coverlets which adorned the walls, chairs, and beds.

41. Semple, "The Anglo-Saxons of the Kentucky Mountains," 569.
42. *The Spirit of the Mountains* (New York, 1905), 77.
43. John Fox, Jr., *Blue-Grass and Rhododendron* (New York, 1906), 160–63.

*A Mountain Cabin, Madison County, North Carolina. Courtesy of the Appalachian Collection, Mars Hill College.*

The location of the cabin was as important to the mountain family as the structure itself. Building under a sheltered north slope rather than on the ridge top protected the house from winter winds and facilitated access to water and roads. Good water was a commodity valued by mountain farmers, and the site chosen for the cabin was usually as near as possible to a spring. In open-country mountain settlements, houses were seldom constructed within sight of each other but, instead, were spread out, each in its own separate hollow or cove. Solitude and privacy were such dominant cultural values that they fostered dispersed settlement patterns and the continual penetration of the deeper mountain wilderness long after the passing of the frontier. As one mountain woman recalled, "We who live so far apart that we rarely see more of one another than the blue' smoke of each other's chimneys are never at ease without the feel of the forest on every side—room to breathe, to expand, to develop, as well as to hunt and to wander at will. The nature of the mountaineer demands that he have solitude for the unhampered growth of his personality, wing-room for his eagle heart."[44]

Sequestered as they were, mountain residents nevertheless took considerable pride in the neatness and comfort of the homestead. Far from being dreary or monotonous, the mountain home had its flower garden, daffodils, lilies, dahlias, and sunflowers, and in the spring nature provided a floral mosaic of dogwood, redbud, flag-lilies, larkspur, devil-in-the-bush, and hundreds of other wildflowers. Boxwoods, grown from sprigs carried from England by the earliest pioneers, could be found around every cabin door, and, although the yard was usually bare of grass, it would be "swept smooth and pretty" throughout most of the year. Journalists who traveled through the mountains found a certain charm in this tranquil setting that influenced their romantic descriptions of highland life.[45]

All mountain homes, however, were not cabins, although this fact was generally overlooked by the local-color writers. One- and two-story frame houses began to be constructed in the more established valley communities as early as the 1830s, and they became popular throughout the region after the Civil War. Sometimes built over existing one-room log cabins, frame houses were made increasingly feasible by the construction of neighborhood sawmills. By the 1880s, frame structures were almost as numerous as log cabins in many areas of the mountains.[46]

The larger frame houses were similar to farm dwellings constructed throughout the South during this period, consisting of from four to twelve rooms stacked on two levels, with a stairwell in the

44. Miles, *The Spirit of the Mountains*, 19–20; Campbell, *The Southern Highlander*, 87.

45. See Charles Egbert Craddock (Mary Noailles Murfree), *In the Tennessee Mountains* (Boston, 1892), 17–18; Muriel Earley Sheppard, *Cabins in the Laurel* (Chapel Hill, 1935), 1–2; Semple, "The Anglo-Saxons of the Kentucky Mountains," 517; Campbell, *The Southern Highlander*, 72, 123.

46. Hariette Wood, "The Kentucky Mountaineers: A Study of Four Counties of Southeastern Kentucky" (M.A. thesis, Univ. of North Carolina, 1930), 32; Thomas, *Life Among the Hills*, 1–2; H. Paul Douglass, *Christian Reconstruction in the South* (Boston, 1909), 315.

middle and rock chimneys on either side. Each room had its own fireplace and its own door opening onto long double porches, which ran the length of the house in front and occasionally in back. The exterior of the house was covered with unpainted lapboard siding, and the interior floors were made of finished lumber. The interior walls of these mountain farm houses were usually panelled with milled chestnut, pine, or other boards and decorated with photographs, tintypes, or prints from magazines. Furnishings, even in the wealthier houses, continued to be primarily handmade until after the turn of the century, although in the larger homes the pieces were more lavish and diverse.[47]

Those who could not afford to build the double-frame house, however, increasingly constructed smaller "box houses" consisting of two to four rooms on a single level. Built of undressed planks set up vertically with "weather strips" covering the cracks between the boards, the frame box house was similar in many ways to the traditional log cabin. One or two fireplaces provided the heat for the structure, and a room was usually set off in the back for a kitchen. The ever-present porch extended across the front of the house, giving the dwelling a cabinlike atmosphere. The box house became the prevailing house type in the region near the turn of the century, after the coming of the timber industry made lumber more readily available.[48]

Although they were not the lavish windowed and screened houses that had begun to emerge in urban America in the late nineteenth century, most mountain houses were sturdy, warm, and comfortable. Above all, they fitted the value system of the mountain people themselves. In a region where most living took place out-of-doors, the cabin served primarily as an eating and sleeping place, a place of shelter and security. The close relationship to the land that evolved as a major cultural trait among mountain people was reflected in the construction and environment of the house as it was in no other aspect of their material culture. The cabin helped to shape and strengthen that basic unit of social life—the family. The coming of industrialization, with its introduction of a new material culture and an urban form

47. Semple, "The Anglo-Saxons of the Kentucky Mountains," 571; Wood, "The Kentucky Mountaineers," 32; Leonard W. Brinksman, "Home Manufacturers as an Indication of an Emerging Appalachian Subculture, 1840–1870," *West Georgia College Studies in the Social Sciences* 12 (June 1973), 50–58.
48. Wood, "The Kentucky Mountaineers," 32.

of life in the company towns, brought dramatic changes in the living patterns of many mountaineers and resulted in adaptations and adjustments in the family and the traditional culture.

## FAMILISM

In preindustrial Appalachia, as in most traditional rural societies, the family was the central organizing force of social life. Not only was the family the basic economic unit within the self-sufficient agricultural setting, but kinship set the matrix within which politics and government, as well as organizations for religion, education, and sociability, developed. The influence of the family and kin groups was felt in almost every aspect of mountain life. For the mountaineer, the collective welfare of the family was a primary value, and "individual needs were subordinated to the needs of the family."[49]

The importance of familism in the social order did not mean that the Appalachian family was an extended family unit. Contrary to the popular image of the region, which would have a dominant patriarch "sternly ruling over a large household of adult offspring and their spouses and children," the basic kin group in the mountains was the nuclear family.[50] Like those in other areas of the nation, most Appalachian households consisted of a husband, a wife, and their dependent children. Only occasionally would this nuclear unit include a grandparent, a single aunt, or other relative. What made the mountain family pattern distinctive, however, was the emphasis placed upon maintaining close ties with an extended network of kin. The nuclear family, while functioning as a separate unit, was in fact enmeshed in a larger network of kin relationships that formed the substance of community life.[51]

Next to the basic function of reproduction, the primary responsibil-

49. Harry K. Schwarzweller, "Social Change and the Individual in Rural Appalachia," in John D. Photiadis and Harry K. Schwarzweller, eds., *Change In Rural Appalachia: Implications for Action Programs* (Philadelphia, 1970), 54.

50. George L. Hicks, *Appalachian Valley* (New York, 1976), 35.

51. Hicks, *Appalachian Valley*, 35. See also John B. Stephenson, *Shiloh: A Mountain Community* (Lexington, Ky., 1968), 43–90; Elmora Messer Matthews, *Neighbor and Kin: Life in a Tennessee Ridge Community* (Nashville, 1965), 3–9; Harry K. Schwarzweller, James S. Brown, and J.J. Managalam, *Mountain Families in Transition: A Case Study of Appalachian Migration* (University Park, Pa., 1971), 23–44.

ity of the preindustrial family was economic, the procurement of the means of subsistence for family members. In the southern mountains, the family not only functioned as a self-contained economic unit, but it dominated the economic system itself. The mountain farm was a family enterprise, the family being the proprietor, laborer, and manager; the satisfaction of the needs of the family was the sole objective of running the farm. "The size of the holding, the kind of crops produced, the division of labor, were all dependent for the most part upon the size of the family and its consumption needs; and everything was organized in such a way that the family itself was able to satisfy all its needs in respect to food, beverages, clothing, shelter, and tools by the utilization of its own forces."[52]

As part of a working and consuming unit, therefore, family members were dependent upon each other for their well-being. The heavier work of clearing land and building houses was shared by every able member of the nuclear family and often by neighbors and kin on the basis of mutual aid. In the daily rhythms of farm life, each family member had his or her own well-defined role and responsibilities. Individuals were free to pursue their own needs and interests, but these were not allowed to displace the collective needs of the group. Obligations to the family came first, and this economic condition created intense family loyalties that not only insured the survival of the group, but also provided a strong feeling of security and belonging for individuals.

This close-knit family system also proved to be an effective means of education and socialization in the mountains, especially after Reconstruction, when the organized educational system deteriorated from neglect and discrimination by the state governments. In a society where occupational specialization was low and where social relationships were informal, personal, and spontaneous, the family provided both practical on-the-job training and experience in interpersonal relations. What formal education the mountain youth acquired in the nineteenth century usually occurred in the small community school, which was often taught by an aunt or an uncle and attended primarily by neighbors and kin. Opportunities for higher education were always available outside the mountains (and in some

52. Pitirim A. Sorokin, Carle C. Zimmerman, and Charles J. Galpin, *A Systematic Source Book in Rural Sociology* (Minneapolis, 1931), 124.

cases within), but with few exceptions only the wealthier families could afford such luxuries. For most mountaineers, education took place within the familiar setting of the family and community, and this type of education provided continuity for the culture, reinforcing traditional values and beliefs.[53]

Other social institutions functioned in a similar manner. Religion was organized around family and kinship units, with single families dominating the neighborhood church. These family churches maintained strict independence from mainline denominations and usually drew their ministers from the local congregations. Religious beliefs and practices varied from community to community and from church to church, and differences over doctrine and interpretation of the scriptures led to a proliferation of small churches throughout the region.[54] The mountain church, as an extension of the family, served as an important medium of social control, legitimizing and sustaining the mores of the community. In rural areas where law enforcement was sparse, the family and the family church were responsible for policing the wrongdoing of community members. Transgressions against the social mores left a mark not only upon the individual, but upon the larger family unit; consequently, the kin group functioned to control such transgressions. Thus, social order was maintained not so much through legal institutions and governmental agencies as through kinship and primary group relationships.

Politics, too, bore the influence of the family system, for the basic unit of political organization was the kin group. Family membership rather than economic class determined the voting patterns of mountain communities, and family patriarchs became the brokers of local political power. Office-seekers measured their support by the size of their family, neighbors, and kin, and officeholders considered the interests of family to be their most important political debt. Nepotism became a privilege, if not a right, of election and helped to cement the power of the family group. Such a system led to inefficiency, incompetence, and fragmentation of authority within local government, but it allowed for a high rate of political participation and a feeling of

53. See David H. Looff, *Appalachia's Children: The Challenge of Mental Health* (Lexington, Ky., 1971), 116; Stephenson, *Shiloh*, 54–55; U.S. Bureau of Education, *A Statistical Study of the Public Schools of the Southern Appalachian Mountains*, by Norman Frost, Bulletin No. 11 (Washington, D.C., 1915), 10–22.

54. See Elizabeth R. Hooker, *Religion in the Highlands* (New York, 1933); Earl D.C. Brewer, "Religion and the Churches," in Thomas R. Ford, ed., *The Southern Appalachian Region: A Survey* (Lexington, Ky., 1967), 201–81.

local control.[55] Throughout most of the nineteenth century, moreover, the influence of government on the lives of individuals was marginal and much less overt than the power of the family group itself.

The strength and cohesiveness of the family, as reflected in religion, education, and the political system, was made possible by the interdependence of age and sex roles in the mountains. As in most traditional societies, roles and expectations for each family member were clearly defined, and, although they were beyond the control of the individual, they provided rights and privileges for individuals as well as obligations to the family group. Influence and authority, for example, grew with age for men and women, and older citizens were usually afforded considerable respect and esteem. Youth was a time of comparative freedom, although children were expected to do their share of the farm work and to contribute to the welfare of the family. Maturity, however, brought with it increased responsibilities and hard work, and it was during the mature years that sex roles were most clearly and unequally defined.

Mountain society was most certainly a patriarchal society. Adult white males held the greatest power, privilege, and freedom within the social order. Men controlled the political system, held most of the property, and made most of the final decisions in family matters. They were responsible for the heavy work around the farm—clearing land, plowing, planting, tending the livestock, and general construction—and they were the principal traders and negotiators with the outside world. They were free to travel, and they spent much of their time in the woods, hunting and fishing both for pleasure and necessity. In times of special need, women might assist in activities supposedly alloted to men, but men were expected almost never to do women's work. Interests outside the domestic realm were the primary responsibility of men, and they were trained from an early age to assume the obligations and rewards of the dominant role.

Women's roles were more clearly confined to the home, and this led many urban observers to consider the lives of mountain women to be narrow, dull, and oppressive. Women seldom traveled far from home, except during migrations of the entire family, and during their reproductive years, they were usually burdened with the respon-

55. See Robert M. Ireland, *Little Kingdoms: The Counties of Kentucky, 1850–1891* (Lexington, Ky., 1977).

sibilities of running a large household. In addition to the daily activities of cooking, cleaning, spinning, weaving material for clothes, knitting stockings, and making quilts and blankets, the mountain woman fed and milked the cows, slopped the hogs, fed the chickens, hoed the corn, carried water from the spring, washed clothes in an iron kettle in the side yard, and gathered and chopped wood for the fire and the stove. In her younger years, she often bore a child a year and was primarily responsible for the health and discipline of ten to fifteen children.[56] It is not surprising, therefore, that many mountain women looked prematurely old and that many died at an early age. "The woman," wrote Nora Miller, "lived a life of physical labor and drudgery. Her faith in a reward in the next world for sufferings and work well done on earth is about all the encouragement or incentive which she has for living."[57]

But the life of the mountain woman, though hard, was not without its rewards. In the preindustrial social setting, the woman was the most important figure in the basic social unit, the family. Her role and responsibilities within the domestic realm granted her significant authority over the household, respect in the community, and a strong sense of identity and personal gratification. The "men folk" were often away for weeks at a time working, trading, or hunting, and the women were left to run the family farm. Social gatherings such as church, dances, quilting bees, corn shuckings, and the like provided numerous opportunities for interaction with neighbors and kin and helped to develop a feeling of community and interdependence among the women of the settlement. Ties were strong and enduring, and life was meaningful within the limitations prescribed by the culture. There were few opportunities, however, for self-expression and recognition outside the family and kin group.

For men and women in the southern mountains, kinship defined the fabric of personal behavior and social life. It determined the interactions among people, shaped individual identities, and provided the arena for community affairs. In a region where formal social ties were few, familism served to a marked degree as the essence of the community itself.

56. Semple, "The Anglo-Saxons of the Kentucky Mountains," 568.
57. *The Girl in the Rural Family*, 22.

## COMMUNITY AND SOCIAL LIFE

"There is no such thing as a community of mountaineers," wrote Emma Belle Miles. "They are knit together, man to man, as friends, but not as a body of men. A community, be it settlement or metropolis, must evolve on some kind of axis, and must be held together by a host of intermediate ties coming between the family and the State, and these are not found in the mountains."[58] The dearth of formal relationships and institutions tying mountain residents one to another and to the outside world has led many writers, like Emma Belle Miles, to argue the absence of community altogether in the southern mountains. The rugged terrain and long distances between settlements minimized opportunities for contact outside of the family and kin group and fostered the growth of the much-noted individualism of mountain people. But the scarcity of those types of formal relationships that gave structure to other American neighborhoods does not imply the absence of shared interests, common traditions, or a sense of community in the region. On the contrary, there existed in every mountain cove and hollow an informal network of communications and social activities that operated through the kinship system to provide fellowship, association, and community life.

No part of this informal network had greater influence on the social life of the region than the church. Although services were held infrequently (usually only once or twice a month), church worship, camp meetings, and revivals provided opportunities to visit with neighbors and kin and to share the latest gossip and news. Ministers, when not elected from among the local congregation, were usually circuit riders who served a number of churches and provided an additional avenue for communication among settlements. "Singings" and church services were often all-day affairs that included "dinner on the grounds" following the morning session. Families occasionally traveled up to twenty miles to attend services, and even farther for revivals or special meetings, spending the night with relatives or friends.[59] As one individual recalled, such occasions were cause for much excitement.

58. *The Spirit of the Mountains*, 71.
59. Rebecca Harding Davis, "By-Paths in the Mountains," *Harper's New Monthly Magazine* 61 (Sept. 1880), 533.

*A Store and Merchant's Home, Sodom, North Carolina c 1885. Courtesy of the Appalachian Collection, Mars Hill College.*

When they would have church near our house, I remember as high as thirty or forty people staying and eating and spending the weekend. Mom would take the feather beds off the beds and put them on the floor, and people slept just any place. They were all over the floor. People did a lot of Sunday visiting with the neighbors. I remember almost every Sunday some family ate with us or we went and ate dinner with them. . . .[60]

Weddings, baptisms, reunions, and funerals also brought people together in the common bond of community. Funerals, for example,

60. Panny Hogg Day, Roxana, Ky., interviews by Ricky Day, 1971, Appalachia Oral History Project, Alice Lloyd College, Pippa Passes, Ky., transcript no. 155A, 7.

were great social events throughout the region. Services were often delayed for several months because of the weather or until an itinerate minister was available, but arrangements would be made some time in advance in order to assure a large gathering. In some localities, funeral meetings were scheduled on a regular basis in the fall and spring, and memorial services would be held for all who had died since the last occasion.[61] Families came from miles around to attend the services, staying with relatives or camping on the church grounds. Large funerals often lasted for several days and included the sermonizing of two or more preachers. Naturally, these gatherings were not ones of deep grief to many of those present. They came "in sober wise as the occasion benefited, but something too in the manner of a holiday when neighbor may visit with neighbor seldom seen and learn the news of the intervening years."[62]

Other opportunities for social intercourse occurred throughout the year, as the rhythms of farm life generated times of celebration and common work. As in most premodern communities, mountain families often gathered to share the heavier work of planting, harvesting, clearing "new ground," or raising cabins and barns. Community "workings" provided an occasion for companionship as well as a way of getting the work done, and they usually turned into major social events.

They sent out word in the neighborhood and everybody would come. They'd pitch in, and cleared up maybe two or three acres of ground for planting crops in one day. It was called "new ground" . . . and everybody pitched in and cut down the trees. They called it "grubbing." It was a lot easier and nicer to work with a group and get it done than to just linger along by yourself trying to clear three or four acres of ground. . . . All the family would come. The women did the cooking, and I'm telling you it was really cooking.[63]

The harvesting of corn in the fall was an opportunity for a corn shuck or a dance, and the first frost brought the men and older boys together for a hunting party. Women gathered periodically for quilting bees and to assist each other in times of birth, illness, and death. Prior to the establishment of formal institutions of social welfare, the com-

61. Wood, "The Kentucky Mountaineers," 48.
62. Campbell, *The Southern Highlander*, 149.
63. Panny Hogg Day interview, 8–9.

munity worked together to help those with special needs, whether they were the sick, the aged, or the poor. "Helping out" was seen to be an integral responsibility of community life.

The shared responsibilities for work extended into the public as well as the private realm in the preindustrial community. The construction of schoolhouses and other public buildings were often community endeavors, with neighbors providing both labor and materials. Following an old colonial custom, public highways were maintained by the free labor of residents along the way. By law, every male between the ages of sixteen and fifty, "except ministers and the physically handicapped," was required to work the roads each year under an overseer appointed by the county. Each male worked from three to ten days a year, depending on the needs of the county, and was expected to provide his own tools. Failure to comply or to hire a substitute could result in a court fine. The custom proved to be "neither satisfactory nor efficient in the building or maintenance of roads" and was abandoned with the coming of industrialization, but for early mountain neighborhoods, it fostered a greater sense of community and provided another opportunity for social life.[64]

Community spirit and social interaction reached its height, however, in the fevered gatherings of court and election days. The circuit court met in county seat towns two or three times a year, usually in the spring, summer and fall, depending upon the state constitution, and attending court sessions was a major form of entertainment. Families from surrounding areas poured into the county seat towns to listen to the trials, to shop at local stores, to bargain with numerous pack peddlers, and to renew old acquaintances. Wagons often lined the streets into and out of town, and large crowds congregated on the courthouse steps. "During the session, the whole county is practically in town, men, women, and children. They camp there; they attend the trials; they take sides. . . ."[65] In the course of murder trials or other controversial cases, heated discussions occasionally broke out among the listeners, disrupting the trial and spilling the debate over into the town. Arguments between the kin of litigants sometimes ended in violence, assuring a docket for the next court session.

This holiday spirit continued on election days, when large crowds

64. Henry P. Scalf, *Kentucky's Last Frontier* (Pikeville, Ky., 1972), 366; Jim Byrd, Valle Crucis, N.C., interview, Laurel Shackelford and Bill Weinberg, eds., *Our Appalachia: An Oral History* (New York, 1977), 25.
65. Warner, "On Horseback," 99.

gathered to vote or to listen to campaigning politicians. Mountain elections commonly had a high rate of participation, with entire families turning out at the polls. Until the turn of the century, voting was done by voice rather than by secret ballot, and this practice encouraged people to linger at the polls observing the outcome of an election. Local politicians were always available, shaking hands, talking with family leaders, and providing entertainment for those present. This predominantly oral means of communication created a political network in which the transmission of ideas and information was a two-way process. "Unlike those on the receiving end of modern mass communications, listeners at the court day hustings and political entertainments could talk back."[66] Although deference preserved the political hegemony of local notables, it was a personal deference given to individuals who had long been part of the daily life of the community.

Campaign speeches, therefore, were judged primarily for their entertainment value. The ability to call constituents by name and to refer to their life experiences, to play the banjo or fiddle, and to harangue on favorite local issues were important assets on the political stump, and they helped to make election day festivities a prominent feature of community social life. Occasionally, issues were ignored altogether at the hustings, and campaigns degenerated into little more than name-calling and character assassination. But truly vital issues almost never arose in local politics, and national issues seldom attracted major concern.[67] Like other aspects of the mountain social system, politics was simple, informal, and personal. The expenditure of large amounts of money and the detailed explanation of issues were avoided in favor of face-to-face contacts, strong family ties, and long-established membership in the community itself.

By 1880, there had developed in Appalachia political, economic, and social patterns that combined societal traits common to most preindustrial rural communities with distinct cultural characteristics shaped by the long interaction of mountain people with their environment. Mountain culture and society had evolved in an atmosphere that encouraged self-sufficiency, traditionalism, and a certain independence from the larger society. Like other rural American com-

66. Williams, "The New Dominion and the Old," 338.
67. McKinney, "Mountain Republicanism, 1876–1900" 165. See also Williams, "The New Dominion and the Old," 390.

munities in the nineteenth century, mountain neighborhoods were slow to be affected by the centralizing forces of modernization. During the period from 1830 to 1880, when urban growth, commercial expansion, and improved transportation networks began increasingly to move the nation down the road toward a more unified, industrial state, Appalachia remained a peripheral area tied to a conventional way of life.

Two factors, land and family, were interwoven as the basic threads sustaining that fabric of life. For mountain residents, land held a special meaning that combined the diverse concepts of utility and stewardship. While land was something to be used and developed to meet one's needs, it was also the foundation of daily existence, giving form to personal identity, material culture, and economic life. As such, it defined the "place" in which one found security and self-worth. Family, on the other hand, as the central organizing unit of social life, brought substance and order to that sense of place. Strong family ties influenced almost every aspect of the social system, from the primary emphasis upon informal personal relationships to the pervasive egalitarian spirit of local affairs. Familism, rather than the accumulation of material wealth, was the predominant cultural value in the region, and it sustained a lifestyle that was simple, methodical, and tranquil.

This traditional mountain social system became increasingly anachronistic in the rapidly industrializing society of the late nineteenth century. As the forces of industrial capitalism reached out into the peripheral areas of American society, the natural wealth of Appalachia grew more and more attractive. And after 1880, the effort to tap these resources brought about dramatic changes in the mountain social order.

CHAPTER TWO

# A MAGNIFICENT FIELD
# FOR CAPITALISTS

IN THE SUMMER of 1888, Charles Dudley Warner, a New York journalist and coauthor with Mark Twain of *The Gilded Age*, made a journey along the Wilderness Road from Pineville to Cumberland Gap in eastern Kentucky. As was the fashion with northern journalists who ventured into the southern backcountry in the late nineteenth century, Warner published an account of his travels the following spring in *Harper's New Monthly Magazine*.[1] This was not Warner's first trip to the mountains, nor was this his first effort to describe the region which Will Wallace Harvey had labeled "A Strange Land and Peculiar People."[2] Four years earlier, after riding through the Blue Ridge country of southwest Virginia, east Tennessee, and western North Carolina, Warner had written a major travelogue entitled "On Horseback."[3] The latter had established its author as one of the leading figures in the new literary "discovery" of Appalachia. His journey into eastern Kentucky in 1888 promised to provide more of the same local-color material that had interested his urban middle-class readers.[4]

Leaving the railroad near Pineville, Warner and his party traveled the thirteen miles to Cumberland Gap by wagon and then, crossing into Virginia, rode horseback up the Powell River Valley to Big Stone Gap. The scenery along the way was much the same as that which Warner had found in the Blue Ridge. "The road had every variety of badness conceivable—loose stones, ledges of rock, boulders, sloughs, holes, mud, sand, deep fords." Settlements were few—only "occasional poor shanties" and "rugged little farms"—

1. "Comments on Kentucky," *Harper's* 78 (Dec. 1888–May 1889), 255–71.
2. *Lippincott's Magazine* 12 (Oct. 1873), 429–38.
3. *Atlantic Monthly* (July–Oct. 1885).
4. The best description and analysis of the literary discovery of Appalachia is to be found in Shapiro, *Appalachia On Our Mind*, 1–58.

39

but the landscape was spectacular with "the great trees . . . frequent sparkling streams, and lovely mountain views." The ineffable beauty of this virgin land, however, hid a "primitive and to a considerable extent illiterate" population that had long been isolated from the moving world. Amid the splendors of the great forests and swift streams were depressing scenes of poverty, ignorance, and lawlessness. Warner was appalled by the reported lawlessness of this area, which he attributed not only to conditions in the mountains during "the war" but to the "abominable cookery of the region" as well. "The race of American mountaineers occupying the country from western North Carolina to eastern Kentucky," he concluded, "is an interesting study. Their origin is in doubt. They have developed their peculiarities in isolation."[5]

Yet, in contrast to his adventure in the Blue Ridge, Warner found much in eastern Kentucky to inspire hope for the region's future. The picturesque hills, which had so long secluded the natural beauty of the region and had isolated the mountaineers from the currents of modern life, had also guarded the treasures of the mountains—the rich stores of coal, timber, and iron ore. The Civil War had removed major obstacles to the exploitation of this vast supply of natural wealth, and recent "scientific investigation [had] made the mountain district . . . the object of the eager competition of both domestic and foreign capital."[6] The entire country from the Breaks of the Big Sandy River to Big Creek Gap in the Cumberland Mountain was "on the eve of an astonishing development—one that will revolutionize eastern Kentucky, and powerfully affect the iron and coal markets of the country." This region of "clear, rapid streams, stuffed with coals, streaked with iron, abounding in limestone, and covered with superb forests . . . [appealed] as well to the imagination of the traveller as to the capitalist." As Warner observed; "I saw enough to comprehend why eager purchasers are buying the forests and the mining rights, why great companies, American and English, are planting themselves there and laying the foundations of cities, and why the gigantic railway corporations are straining every nerve to penetrate the mineral and forest heart of the region. . . It is a race for the prize."[7]

5. Warner, "Comments on Kentucky," 266–70.
6. *Ibid.*, 258.
7. *Ibid.*, 263.

And what of the mountaineers? The arrival of the "commercial spirit," Warner believed, would transform this benighted society. Other writers had found the mountain people to be a "worthless, good-for-nothing, irreclaimable" lot, but Warner was not so despondent about their future. "Railroads, trade, the sight of enterprise and industry, will do much with this material." Business and enterprise would bring law and order, sobriety, education, health care, and the other fruits of the modern age. Now that an industrializing America had need for the abundance of fuel that had been so long stored in the mountains, a new day was dawning for the mountaineers. Because of the vast developments about to occur in the Cumberlands, this land had become "one of the most important and interesting regions in the Union."[8]

Warner was not alone in his optimism about the potential industrialization of the Appalachians. As early as the 1870s, politicians, businessmen, and journalists had begun to promote the wealth of the mountains in newspapers and boardrooms throughout the United States and Europe. The untapped treasures of the hill country, these individuals believed, offered innumerable possibilities for the accumulation of personal wealth. Nowhere in the eastern United States could one find the vital industrial elements of coal, iron ore, timber, and water in such vast quantities and so close to one another. Among many promoters in the South, the natural resources of the Appalachians offered not only the opportunity for the accumulation of great personal wealth but for the revitalization of southern society as well. Lying in the very heartland of the South, the mountains harbored the materials necessary for building a "new civilization"—a New South constructed from the ashes of the old, but patterned in a more modern industrial mold. In the years from 1870 to 1900, therefore, for both personal and social reasons, advertising the mountains became an important component of the New South creed.

Yet the promotion of industrial development of the Appalachians reflected more than just opportunism or the romantic visions of a defeated South. The coming of what Warner called "the commercial spirit" to the mountains was part of a larger drama taking place in the

8. *Ibid.*, 271, 263. For an excellent comparison of Warner's essay with twentieth-century hopes for Appalachia, see John B. Stephenson, "Appalachia and the Third Century in America: On the Eve of an Astonishing Development—Again," *Appalachian Journal* 4 (Autumn 1976), 34–38.

nation as a whole. Throughout most of the nineteenth century, the forces of modernization had largely bypassed the mountains while fundamentally restructuring the fabric of American life. In the years following the Civil War, those forces were rapidly moving the nation down the road toward urban-industrial maturity, and the abundant resources of Appalachia provided vital fuel for that final industrial drive. As technological developments increased the productive capacities of urban centers in the Northeast, South, and Midwest, capitalists began to turn to surrounding rural areas for the human and natural resources to undergird expansion. The exploitation of peripheral rural areas for the benefit of industrializing urban centers became a requisite of industrial growth, resulting in unequal economic development and prolonged social tension between urban and rural communities. Appalachia, being one of the most rural areas of eastern America and rich in natural resources, provided a stage upon which much of this great social drama was played out. In a rapidly industrializing society, the wealth of the Appalachians became a passkey to affluence and power. Indeed, "it was a race for the prize."

Journalists like Charles Dudley Warner themselves played an unwitting role in this drama. The popularity of local-color literature in the 1870s and 1880s was in part due to the new monthly magazines that emerged in the years immediately following the war. Magazines such as *Harper's*, *Atlantic*, *Lippincott's*, and *Cosmopolitan* appealed widely to urban middle-class readers whose ranks were multiplying as a result of the industrial revolution. The new-found affluence and leisure time of the middle class supported a growing literary industry that thrived on tales of romance, travel, and adventure in strange and exotic corners of the nation and the world. Because of its proximity to the urban Northeast, the hyper-rural quality of its society, and the very fact of its southernness (albeit part of the "other South"), Appalachia was ideally suited to be a source for local-color literature. Not only was the mountain landscape romantic and picturesque, but the mountain social system seemed to contrast markedly with the "new civilization" emerging in the northern cities.

Attracted to the mountains by the local-color literature, ever-growing numbers of urban visitors flocked to the Appalachians after 1880 for a respite from city life. These newly rich tourists and traveling journalists supported a seasonal tourist industry in the region, but they developed only marginal contacts with the local mountain people. More often than not, they ended by viewing "the natives," as they called the mountaineers, as quaint and primitive, if not degenerate, and they usually returned to the North with accounts of a beautiful and fabulously rich landscape inhabited by a race who lacked an appreciation of its potential. Unable to reconcile the disparity between mountain life and their own affluent urban life, northern visitors identified the mountain people with other "backward peoples" whom the leading industrial nations at that time were seeking to "develop," and to whom the term "natives" was commonly applied.[9] As a result of tourism and the local-color literature, the mountaineers would subsequently become "hillbillies" and "poor whites," the subjects of a massive missionary movement to the region which over the next half-century would seek to bring these "our contemporary ancestors" into the mainstream of American life.[10] During the twentieth century, "hillbilly culture" would become the standard means of rationalizing the poverty of an exploited region. In the late nineteenth century, it became a major justification for the swift acquisition of mountain land and resources by outsiders.

During the same years, therefore, that American and European capitalists were beginning to discover the vast natural wealth of the Appalachians, American intellectuals were themselves discovering the mountains and the mountain people. As capitalists worked to bring the resources of the land into the industrial age, intellectuals increasingly strove to "uplift" and "Americanize" the mountaineers. The two groups occasionally differed over tactics for changing the region—businessmen emphasizing the need for economic development while most missionaries spoke of cultural change, education, and human concern—but ultimately both were components of the larger modernizing process. "Profit motive and missionary motive," Vann Woodward has observed, "have often gone hand-in-hand in the development of 'backward people.' "[11] Appalachia was no exception.

The emergence of economic and intellectual interest in the Appalachians in the late nineteenth century marked the beginning of the decline of the stable, traditional society that had evolved in the mountains. Although major aspects of modernization were not to be

9. Comer Vann Woodward, *Origins of the New South, 1877–1913* (Baton Rouge, 1951), 109.
10. See Shapiro, *Appalachia On Our Mind*, 32–84.
11. *Origins of the New South*, 114.

felt in the region until after the turn of the century (and even later in some remote areas), the years from 1880 to 1900 were among the most critical decades in the region's history. The penetration of the region during these years by outside speculators, land developers, and industrialists launched a revolution in land use and ownership that drastically altered the mountaineer's relationship to the land. As ownership and control of the land were transferred from the mountaineers to the spokesmen of the new industrial order, the fate of the region became irretrievably tied to that of the larger society. The selling of the mountains and the subsequent arrival of the railroads were, as Warner noted, the first stage in the remaking of mountain life.

## THE SELLING OF THE MOUNTAINS

By the year in which Charles Dudley Warner made his journey into eastern Kentucky, the mineral and timber wealth of the Appalachians was already well known to American capitalists. As early as the 1740s, the journals of explorers and land surveyors had documented the rich coal and iron deposits of the mountains. Early speculators in frontier lands like Thomas Jefferson, Robert Morris, and Thomas Walker were all aware of the great coal seams of the "western country," but it was not until the post–Civil War years that interest in the potential of these resources quickened.[12] Throughout most of the antebellum period, the difficulties of transportation, the absence of any real market, and the deep agrarian biases of southern leaders had prevented the large-scale development of the mountain reserves. In the years immediately following the war, however, a sudden rush of activity in commerce, investment, and new technology focused increasing attention on the mountains as a source of materials to fuel the industrial revolution. Among a new generation of southern leaders, moreover, the road to wealth seemed no longer to lead to the plantation but rather to the coal and iron fields of the Appalachians.

The rise of the industrial spirit in the South after Reconstruction did not substantially alter the basic structure of southern society. The South remained primarily an agricultural region until well into the twentieth century. Yet, changes in the character and outlook of

12. Jerry Bruce Thomas, "Coal Country: The Rise of the Southern Smokeless Coal Industry and Its Effect On Area Development, 1872–1910" (Ph.D. diss., Univ. of North Carolina at Chapel Hill, 1971), 23–26.

southern leadership did take place in these years, opening large areas of the South, especially the Appalachians, to exploitation by absentee investors. Whether or not southern leaders themselves benefited economically from the new commercial enterprises (and many did), their receptive attitude toward industrial development eased the way for the penetration of southern regions by northern capital. To that outspoken band of southerners who believed that the future of their region lay in commercial and industrial growth, the abundant resources of the Appalachians provided a major incentive for capital investment. Beginning in the 1870s and growing in intensity in the 1880s and 1890s, advocates of the New South creed ardently promoted the industrialization of the South and the development of the timber and mineral reserves of the southern mountains. If the South was to fulfil its destiny as a leading center of industry, they argued, it must exploit the "exhaustless treasures" of its mountains.[13]

The New South creed was part of a national booster spirit that emerged in the late nineteenth century, and, like its larger counterpart, was predominantly an urban phenomenon. Its loudest proponents were members of the new middle class that had begun to rise in major southern cities.[14] Proselytes of the creed could be found in most towns and many villages throughout the postwar South, but the industrial faith burned brightest in three cities of the Southeast: Atlanta, Louisville, and Richmond. Each had evolved as an important railroad center, had developed a large manufacturing base, and supported a powerful business community. Moreover, each was home to a leading newspaper whose pages became fliers for the dissemination of the faith.

The Richmond *Whig*, under the control of conservative politician and railroad president William Mahone, was without equal in its promotion of railroads, mining, timber, and iron manufacturing in the Virginias. General Mahone had acquired extensive railroad interests in southwest Virginia, and his newspaper became a major advocate of "new ways for the Old Dominion." Across the mountains in Louisville, the *Courier-Journal* and its fiery editor Henry Watterson—sometimes spokesman for the Louisville and Nashville Railroad—called for the industrial development of Kentucky and the attraction of "Eastern Capital" to that state's coal fields. But the most

13. Henry W. Grady, the Atlanta *Constitution*, quoted in Woodward, *Origins of the New South*, 166.
14. Woodward, *Origins of the New South*, 150–53.

outspoken apostle of the new order was Henry Grady of the Atlanta *Constitution*. In his years with the *Constitution*, Grady developed a national reputation as the leading disciple of the New South creed. As orator and editor, he advertised the opportunities for investment in the South and encouraged southern businessmen to exploit the industrial potential of their region.

These three metropolitan newspapers combined to spread the gospel of industrialism throughout the South and much of the nation. A line drawn through the urban headquarters of each of these presses would form a triangle completely enclosing the heartland of the Appalachian South. It was only natural, therefore, that as these centers of modernization sought to expand their industrial bases, they turned to their own "internal periphery" and to the natural resources of the mountains.[15] In the years after 1870, these and other New South papers brought increasing pressure to bear upon politicians and state officials to publicize this backcountry wealth.

Convincing southern state leaders of the need for publicity was relatively easy during the initial postwar years. In this era of social and economic depression, politicians from all parties were interested in improving business conditions. During the 1870s and 1880s, campaigns were launched in every southern Appalachian state aimed at attracting foreign immigration and commercial investment. State authorities established immigration bureaus and dispatched agents to New York and Europe to spread the word of southern opportunities. Exhibitions of state resources were creatively displayed at commercial conventions throughout America and Europe, and by the turn of the century geological surveys were being commissioned to detail the extent of the states' mineral wealth for the benefit of potential buyers.

West Virginia, for example, started early to alert settlers and investors to its untapped wealth. In 1864 the legislature created a special position, commissioner of immigration, to promote the "boundless natural resources" of the Mountain State. John H. Diss Debar, the first incumbent, produced some 19,000 items of promotional literature during his term in office, culminating in 1870 with *The West Virginia Handbook and Immigrant's Guide*. Debar's handbook touted the scenic splendor, rich farmland, "varied treasures of the forest and the mine," and even the healing waters of the

15. For an analysis of the internal periphery concept, see Walls, "Internal Colony or Internal Periphery? A Critique," 319–49.

state, describing West Virginia as the "Switzerland of America."[16] West Virginia politicians themselves took an active role in advertising their state's resources. According to a report to the *Manufacturers' Record* in 1906, West Virginia had been noted for many years for the fact that

> the entire machinery of State government has been used to attract capital to the State to develop its railroads, its coal, and its timber interests. A succession of four or five Governors—Fleming, Atkinson, White, and MacCorkle—were widely known . . . in the financial circles of the East, not for their political activity, but for their activity in telling the Eastern people and the Eastern press about the undeveloped wealth and unbounded opportunity for investment in West Virginia.

In Congress, the report added, the same conditions had prevailed, especially among men like Senators Henry Gassaway Davis and Stephen B. Elkins, who had concentrated their energies not only on building their own railroad and coal-mining empire in the northeastern part of the state but in "making known to every financial friend the possibilities of West Virginia. In this respect West Virginia holds a unique position not duplicated by the governmental machinery of any other State in the South."[17]

To varying degrees, other Appalachian states followed the pattern established by West Virginia. In his annual message to the legislature in 1869, Governor Stevenson of Kentucky called for the establishment of aggressive policies to recruit foreign labor and capital. "For a sufficient supply [of labor]," he wrote, "we must look to foreign immigration. But our need does not stop there. We must look to Europe also for capital . . . if we desire to increase our population and develop our industrial and mineral wealth."[18] To accomplish this end, the governor recommended several propaganda vehicles that might acquaint the northeastern capitalist and "the iron master of Europe" with Kentucky's resources. Two years later, the legislature of Kentucky acted on one recommendation and established its own

16. Williams, *West Virginia and the Captains of Industry*, 166. Joseph H. Diss Debar, *The West Virginia Handbook and Immigrant's Guide* (Parkersburg, W. Va., 1870).
17. Albert Phenis, "The Coal Resources of Eastern Kentucky," *Manufacturers' Record* 50 (18 Oct. 1906), 338.
18. "Governor's Message," *Kentucky House Journal, 1869–70*, quoted in Alan J. Banks, "The Emergence of a Capitalistic Labor Market in Eastern Kentucky, 1870–1915" (unpublished paper, 1978), 13.

Bureau of Immigration.[19] Tennessee had established an immigration board in 1867, and by 1900 North Carolina, Virginia, and Georgia had each created similar boards.[20]

Despite the enthusiasm of politicians and state development agencies, however, the effectiveness of state advertisement campaigns was limited by small appropriations. Conservative or "Redeemer" governments of the New South were willing to encourage immigration to their states and to grant tax exemptions, liberal charters, and other special privileges to promote industrial growth, but they were reluctant to burden state treasuries with large publicity budgets.[21] As a result, the bulk of promotional work was carried on by private associations, and by individuals and corporations. Especially active were railroad companies, who widely distributed their own materials as well as state and local propaganda literature. Major railroad lines such as the Louisville and Nashville, the Western North Carolina, the Chesapeake and Ohio, and the Norfolk and Western played important roles in attracting investors to the lands along their mountain extensions.

Notwithstanding the efforts of organized groups, the promotional activity that was most influential in the development of the mountains was that carried on by private speculators. Riding into the mountains in the years following the Civil War, these men surveyed iron and coal deposits, purchased land or mineral rights from local residents, and attempted to entice railroads and industrialists to the area. Many of these "mineral men"—or "mineral hunters," as mountain people called them—were ex-military officers who had served in the region during the Civil War and had become familiar with the untapped wealth of the land. Others were the paid agents of northern capitalists who sought to invest in the lucrative resource potential of the South. Together with a zealous band of local promoters, they prepared the way for the invasion of the larger corporations.

Among the earliest and most ardent promoters of coal and iron

19. Banks, "The Emergence of a Capitalist Labor Market," 15.
20. Constantine G. Belissary, "The Rise of Industry and the Industrial Spirit in Tennessee, 1865–85," *Journal of Southern History* 19 (1953), 207; Woodward, *Origins of the New South*, 297.
21. For examples of privileges granted to the Chesapeake and Ohio Railroad by West Virginia in the 1870s, see Ronald D Eller, "Mountain Road: A Study of the Construction of the Chesapeake and Ohio Railroad in Southern West Virginia, 1867–1873" (M.A. thesis, Univ. of North Carolina at Chapel Hill, 1973), 67–68.

development in the southern mountains were two former Confederate officers, General John Daniel Imboden and Major Jedidiah Hotchkiss. As early as 1872, General Imboden was urging legislators and prominent citizens of Virginia to exploit the forgotten coal and iron fields of the Appalachians. "Within this imperial domain of Virginia," he told a Richmond gathering, "lie almost unknown to the outer world, and not fully appreciated by their owners," greater mineral deposits than could be found in all of England and which, if tapped, would "attract hither millions of money, and enterprising thousands of people to aid in the restoration of the 'Old Dominion' to a foremost rank amongst the States of the Union." Such developments, he argued, would make Richmond the southern rival of Pittsburgh and Philadelphia.[22]

Imboden himself had invested heavily in coal lands at Hawk's Nest, West Virginia, along the line of the nearly completed Chesapeake and Ohio Railroad (C & O). He hoped to transfer that land to other capitalists, and shortly after his speech in Richmond, he succeeded in attracting a group of English investors to his Hawk's Nest properties.[23] The general spent most of the following decade promoting land development along the C & O and in Wise County, Virginia. In 1880, he bought 47,000 acres of mineral land in Wise County, and he and his son purchased one-sixth interest in an additional 100,000 acres. Later, as agent for certain "gentlemen of large means" who were officials of the Baltimore and Ohio Railroad, Imboden acquired over 21,000 acres for approximately 35 cents an acre.[24] During the 1880s, he worked to build a railroad into his coal properties and lobbied in southern capitals for coal interests. Following a lobbying expedition to North Carolina, he commented on the elegant people he had met in Raleigh. He reported that he had told them about Wise County and "how nice it was . . . and interested them so much that when our road is built they are coming out to see for themselves. They think it must be delightful to see and mingle with primitive people."[25]

22. John Daniel Imboden, *The Coal and Iron Resources of Virginia: Their Extent, Commercial Value, and Early Development Considered* (Richmond, 1872), 1–3, quoted in Thomas, "Coal Country," 40.
23. Thomas, "Coal Country," 41.
24. Helen Lewis, "Fatalism or the Coal Industry," *Mountain Life and Work* 45 (Dec. 1970), 11.
25. Quoted in *ibid.*, 11–12.

The work of General Imboden, however, was surpassed by that of his friend, Major Jedidiah Hotchkiss, who might fairly be called the father of coal development in parts of southwest Virginia and southern West Virginia. Long before the coming of the railroad, Hotchkiss was promoting the mineral wealth of the Flat Top Mountain region along the headwaters of the Bluestone, Elkhorn, Big Sandy, and Guyandotte rivers. He was primarily responsible for attracting the Philadelphia capital that constructed the Norfolk and Western Railroad (N & W) and transformed the Flat Top area into one of the most productive coal fields in the world. Born and educated in New York, Hotchkiss came to the South in the 1840s and accepted a job as tutor for a wealthy family near Staunton, Virginia. During the Civil War, he espoused the southern cause and became a leading cartographer for the Confederate Army. Familiar with the Pennsylvania and Virginia countryside, Major Hotchkiss drew hundreds of maps and battle plans for the Army of Northern Virginia, including those for General Lee's ill-fated Gettysburg campaign. After the war, Hotchkiss accepted a position as head of the topographical department at Washington College, where Robert E. Lee was president, but following Lee's death in 1870 he resigned in order to pursue his interests in engineering and land promotion.[26]

While serving as General Lee's topographical engineer in the western Virginia campaign of 1861, Hotchkiss had observed large outcroppings of coal along the eastern base of Flat Top Mountain. He was convinced that the outcroppings were part of a huge coal seam of unusual quality, and after resigning from Washington College, he sought to persuade northern and English investors of the value of these coal deposits. Unfortunately, the Flat Top Mountain area was rugged, little known, and remote from transportation facilities, and many prominent geologists refused to believe that substantial coal deposits could be found in the vicinity. Greater attention, moreover, was drawn to the New River coal fields currently being opened by the C & O Railroad, and Major Hotchkiss experienced years of frustration trying to convince capitalists to develop this hidden wealth.[27]

In 1873, the owners of the Wilson Cary Nicholas grant, a Revolutionary War grant of 500,000 acres around Flat Top Mountain, hired

26. Frederick E. Saward, "The Pocahontas Coal Field: Recent Developments from Major Hotchkiss' Survey of Thirty Years Ago," *Manufacturers' Record* 42 (24 July 1902), 7; Thomas, "Coal Country," 43-44.
27. Thomas, "Coal Country," 46–47.

Hotchkiss to make a survey and evaluation of their holdings. Hotchkiss in turn hired Captain Isaiah Welch, a fellow Confederate officer and noted geologist, to make a detailed examination of the property and report on timber and mineral deposits. Welch entered the tract along Laurel Creek in Tazewell County, Virginia, and quickly discovered a seam of coal thirteen feet thick, which was then being used to fuel a local blacksmith shop. Since this seam was "about twice the height of the highest seams then known," he continued to follow the outcroppings north into Mercer, McDowell, and Wyoming counties in West Virginia before returning home.[28] Welch's report thoroughly confirmed the presence of valuable coal deposits in the Flat Top district and generated a flurry of interest in developing the area. Major Hotchkiss subsequently persuaded a group of Philadelphia capitalists headed by Thomas Graham to purchase "some of the best land in the territory" and to begin construction of a narrow-gauge railroad, but the business depression of the 1870s prevented the realization of these plans.[29]

Throughout the depression, Hotchkiss continued to promote the industrial potential of the mountains, traveling to England and to northern financial centers to talk with possible investors. Early in 1880, just as the economy was showing signs of recovery, he launched a major effort to reach a broad range of capitalists by beginning publication at Staunton of *The Virginias: A Mining, Scientific, and Industrial Journal Devoted to the Development of Virginia and West Virginia*. The purpose of the journal was to "collect and publish full and reliable information concerning the mineral deposits of these States . . . and how they may be made profitable."[30] *The Virginias* served as a medium for disseminating information about industrial activity in the mountains and for introducing the editor's theories to leading American and European capitalists. As a result of this publication and Hotchkiss's persistent promotional work, in 1881 the Philadelphia backers of the newly created N & W Railroad became interested in the Flat Top coal fields. Following a personal inspection of the area by Vice-President Frederick J. Kimball, the N&W began development of the area. With

28. "The Pocahontas--Flat Top Coal Field," *Manufacturers' Record* 52 (25 July 1907), 33; "Pocahontas No. 1 Retires," *Norfolk and Western Magazine* 33 (1955), 521; Thomas, "Coal Country," 47–51.
29. Thomas, "Coal Country," 47–51.
30. *The Virginias* 1 (Jan. 1880), 1.

some Staunton associates (Echols, Bell, and Catlett), Hotchkiss organized a land company and began purchasing large tracts of land in the new coal field. Much of this land was later sold to Norfolk and Western interests.[31]

Speculators such as Imboden and Hotchkiss had their counterparts in other areas of the southern mountains, but none were so active in the 1870s and 1880s as the Virginia promoters. Their efforts, however, served to draw attention to industrial developments throughout the region. Events in the Flat Top and New River coal fields, for example, led to a rise of interest in coal lands in other areas of southern West Virginia. In the late 1880s, a stream of speculators poured into remote sections of Mingo, Logan, Raleigh, and McDowell counties, starting a minor land boom years before the arrival of any railroad. Typical of these early developers were men like Colonel Alexander McClintock of Lexington, Kentucky; Stuart Wood of Philadelphia; Dr. James O'Keeffe of Tazewell Court House, Virginia; and Henry C. King of New York. Many of these men sought to take advantage of the obscure land titles characteristic of the mountains by resurrecting old titles that often conflicted with newer ones granted by the state of West Virginia. "Consequently," argues the historian of this section, "a long series of legal battles arose threatening the security of many persons who had actually settled the lands of the counties. . . ."[32]

A similar rush of interest in land speculation swept the mountains of Tennessee and North Carolina in these years, although the prize was primarily the virgin timber and purported iron deposits of the territory. Expectations for the development of iron in the mountains failed to mature, partly because of the low quality of the ore, but speculators in the late nineteenth century were convinced of the region's potential for iron production.[33] Great iron centers had evolved to the north of the mountains in Pittsburgh and on the region's southern fringe in Birmingham. It seemed logical that East Tennessee, with its proximity to the new coal fields and its purported deposits of iron ore, would become one of the leading industrial centers of the South. As one developer maintained in 1889,

31. Joseph T. Lambie, *From Mine to Market: The History of Coal Transportation on the Norfolk and Western Railway* (New York, 1954), 35.

32. Cubby, "The Transformation of the Tug and Guyandot Valleys," 180.

33. See "The False Lure of Virginian Iron," in Thomas, "Coal Country," 93–123.

What we need to make East Tennessee the most prosperous and desirable section of the South is capital. That would be a panacea for our financial ills and would disarm poverty of its terrors. It would put us on the high road to wealth. . . . We need hundreds of blazing furnaces distributed over this region, along the foothills of our mountains, lighting up their gorges and developing and utilizing the iron embedded in their bowels. . . . What a magnificent field for capitalists![34]

Spurred by the rise of the industrial spirit, two cities in East Tennessee, Knoxville and Chattanooga, became centers for speculative activity in the surrounding mountains. After the revival of the economy in 1880, northern financiers sent an army of agents into these urban centers to survey the possibilities for investment. One of the leading examples of this northern invasion was H.B. Wetzell, a native of Pennsylvania and former Michigan businessman who came to live in Knoxville in the early 1880s to investigate "the natural resources of the southern Appalachian region from West Virginia to Alabama." Finding that the region was "A Country of Infinite Wealth-Creating Possibilities," Wetzell stayed on for over a decade, traveling on foot and horseback throughout the mountains and buying timber and mineral properties for northern investors.[35]

In eastern Kentucky, the pioneer coal prospector of these years was Richard M. Broas of New York City. An engineer and former captain in the Union Army, Broas had spent the postwar years searching for oil in Pennsylvania and for gold and silver in the Sierras. In 1881, he came to the Big Sandy Valley between West Virginia and Kentucky to examine coal lands for the "Walbridge interests" of Toledo, Ohio. Failing to discover coal at the mouth of the Tug and Levisa forks of Big Sandy, Broas was hired by Nathanial Stone Simkins of Massachusetts to push on up the river and examine lands in the Miller's Creek section of Pike County. There, and later in the valley of the Elkhorn, he found seams of coal with immense possibilities and began a ten-year effort to promote the development of the mineral lands of the Elkhorn district.[36] Like Hotchkiss in

34. C.W. Charlton, "Mineral Wealth of East Tennessee," *Manufacturers' Record* 14 (12 Jan. 1889), 13–14.

35. H.B. Wetzell, "The Southern Appalachian Region: A Rare Combination of Advantages, A Country of Infinite Wealth-Creating Possibilities," *Manufacturers' Record* 25 (20 July 1894), 404–6.

36. Charles E. Beachley, *History of the Consolidated Coal Company, 1864–1934* (New York, 1934), 59; Scalf, *Kentucky's Last Frontier*, 332.

southwest Virginia, Broas met with repeated rebuffs, but this did not prevent his acquiring options on large tracts of land and mineral rights in the area. Between 1887 and 1891, Broas purchased or leased thousands of acres of mineral property in Pike and Letcher counties.[37] At the height of his buying venture, he employed about twenty surveyors and a number of title attorneys. Most of his mineral leases were purchased at one dollar per acre in tracts of from 100 to 400 acres, generally from poor, often illiterate farmers.[38] After the turn of the century, the Broas lands were eventually sold to the Consolidation Coal Company, and it was estimated by the company's geological and mining experts that the seams contained approximately 12,000 tons of coal per acre.[39]

The first timber and mineral buyers who rode into the mountains were commonly greeted hospitably by local residents. Strangers were few in the remote hollows, and a traveler offered the opportunity for conversation and a change from the rhythms of daily life. The land agent's routine was simple. Riding horseback into the countryside, he would search the coves and creek banks for valuable timber stands or coal outcroppings, and, having found his objective, he would approach the cabin of the unsuspecting farmer. As one mineral man recalled, "there was always a cordial welcome for the stranger and many a time the head of the house [would call] from the door of a cabin 'get off your horse and come in and warm up—you know pore folks have pore ways but we're glad to see you.' "[40] This greeting was usually followed by an invitation to share the family's meal and simple accommodations for the night. After dinner, while entertaining the family with news of the outside world, the traveler would casually produce a bag of coins and offer to purchase a tract of "unused ridgeland" which he had noticed while journeying through the area.[41] Such an offer was hard to refuse in most rural areas, where hard money was scarce, life was difficult, and opportunities were few.

37. Scalf, *Kentucky's Last Frontier*, 332–33; Randall Lawrence, "The Mineral Rights Buyer In Pre-Industrial Appalachia: A Study of Richard M. Broas" (unpublished paper, Mountain Collection, Hutchins Library, Berea College, 1975).

38. Warren Wright, "The Big Steal," in Helen Lewis, *et al.*, eds., *Colonialism in Modern America: The Appalachian Case* (Boone, N.C., 1978), 163–65.

39. Beachley, *History of the Consolidated Coal Company*, 61.

40. Neil Robinson, "The Mineral Man," *President's Address to the West Virginia Coal Mining Institute* (Charleston, W.Va., 1913), 2.

41. *Ibid.*, 2–4; Harry M. Caudill, *Night Comes to the Cumberlands: A Biography of a Depressed Area* (Boston, 1963), 73.

*Timber and Mineral Buyers at a Mountain Cabin in the 1880s. Courtesy of the Appalachian Photographic Archives, Alice Lloyd College.*

Some buyers, moreover, like Richard M. Broas, offered to purchase only the minerals under the land, leaving the surface to the ownership and use (and tax liability) of the farmer. The land would be disturbed at some future date, but it was difficult for the mountaineer to envision the scale and impact of industrial change. These "broad form deeds," as they were known in eastern Kentucky, effectively transferred to the land agents all of the mineral wealth and the right to remove it by whatever means necessary, while leaving the farmer and his descendants with the semblance of land ownership. It was not until the railroads penetrated the district that those who had concluded such deals realized their mistake. Not only had they lost all rights to the minerals below the land, but they had also relinquished such other rights to the surface of the land as to limit its use for residential or agricultural purposes.[42]

In this way, millions of acres of land and even greater quantities of timber and mineral rights passed out of the hands of mountain residents and into the control of absentee owners. Most mountain families sold their land voluntarily, but the negotiations were hardly between equals. The mountaineer had little knowledge of the value his natural resources had to distant industrial centers, nor was he able to comprehend the changes that would come to the mountains as a result of efforts to tap those resources. Despite its importance to mountain life and culture, land was often taken for granted by the mountaineers, for it had always been plentiful and ownership had never been a deterrent to common use. The prices paid by land agents during these early years varied greatly from state to state and according to the potential wealth of the property, but amounts generally ranged from twenty-five cents to three dollars per acre. Some mountaineers were reported to have sold entire mountains rich in coal and timber for a mule, a saddle horse, or a hog rifle.[43]

A few residents, however, were reluctant to sell their land at any price, and aggressive land buyers occasionally turned to illicit methods. Obscure land titles, lost deeds, and poor records were common in most mountain counties, and speculators were quick to turn this to their advantage. The land buyer usually had greater understanding of litigation procedures and access to the courts, and the result was that some families who had resided on the land for generations lost the ownership of their property. A common practice, for example, of the American Assocation, Ltd., of London, England—a major developer in Bell County, Kentucky, and Claiborne and Campbell counties, Tennessee, in the late nineteenth century—was

42. Frank Duff, "Government in an Eastern Kentucky Coal Field County" (M.A. thesis, Univ. of Kentucky, 1950), 14–15; Caudill, *Night Comes to the Cumberlands*, 74.
43. Based upon analysis of "Abstracts of Titles of the Burt and Brabb Lumber Company's East Kentucky Lands" and "Records of Land Grants and Warrants," Box 7, folder 4, Burt and Brabb Lumber Company Papers, Special Collections, King Library, Univ. of Kentucky; also John Gaventa, "Power and Powerlessness: Quiescence and Rebellion in an Appalachian Valley" (Ph.D. diss., Oxford Univ., 1975), 72.

to acquire rights of a single heir to a piece of property left to several family heirs. When the other heirs would refuse to sell, the company would go to court and ask for a judgment of whether the property could be "fairly and impartially partitioned" and whether "said property is of such a nature so that its sale could be of manifest interest to all parties." Invariably, the court would rule that it could not be divided, and that it should be sold at a "public auction" to the highest bidder—also invariably, the American Association. At one such sale in 1889, 2,000 acres of land granted to its original settlers in 1839 were bought at auction for 200 dollars.[44]

These and other methods of deceit in land acquisition soon angered local residents, and resistance began to develop toward the "mineral hunters." By the turn of the century, travelers into the mountains were increasingly greeted with hostility.[45] By 1900, the land agent was as likely to be met with a rifle as a "halloo," and he would seldom be invited inside the cabin. "When land values began to rise," lamented an official of the Virginia Coal and Iron Company, local people "believed the company was trying to deal unfairly with them and many assumed a hostile attitude toward the company and its employees."[46] By the time this hostility developed, however, the transition to absentee control was already well under way in the region.

Despite the crucial role played by outside agents in the selling of the mountains, that played by local speculators was almost equally important. Especially after many residents began to question the integrity of outside interests, native middle-class entrepreneurs served as effective brokers for absentee investors and as energetic missionaries of the new industrial faith. Particularly in the larger villages and towns, the relatively small mountain middle class and landed elite actively promoted the development of Appalachia's natural resources as a panacea for their own as well as the region's financial ills. Local merchants and lawyers speculated widely in timber and mineral lands and advertised the potential of mountain

---

44. Gaventa, "Power and Powerlessness," 73–74.
45. For examples of this hostility see Julian Ralph, "Our Appalachian Americans," *Harper's Magazine* 107 (1903), 33; Fox, *Blue-Grass and Rhododendron*, 217; Elizabeth Skaggs Bowman, *Land of High Horizons* (Kingsport, Tenn., 1938), 22.
46. E.J. Prescott, *The Story of the Virginia Coal and Iron Company* (Big Stone Gap, Va.: Virginia Coal and Iron, 1946), 43.

property in the leading business journals and newspapers. Often serving as agents of northern capitalists, such individuals quietly bought up land from their neighbors at nominal prices.

By 1900, the emergence of new urban centers within the region had brought about the concentration of many resident speculators and promoters in towns such as Charleston, Bluefield, Ashland, Paintsville, Bristol, and Asheville. These development centers (called "growth centers" by modern planners) served as convenient extensions of the eastern industrial core into the Appalachian heartland. In many ways, they functioned in the same exploitative relationship to their surrounding rural counties as did the larger metropolises of the South and Northeast to the region as a whole. Promoters of industrialization increasingly used these centers as bases of operation from which to launch their invasions of the outlying rural districts.

The mountains had always contained a small ruling class whose economic power and political influence were derived from long-standing ownership of large tracts of land. Having evolved over the years into a planter-lawyer-merchant class, these mountain elites had much in common with the wealthier planters of the lowland South. Many had remained loyal to the Confederacy and the Democratic party. After Reconstruction, they joined with other "Redeemer" or "Bourbon" Democrats in writing new state constitutions and enacting a new series of land laws. While these laws further confused the system of land registry in the mountains, they benefited many of the same lawyer-politicians, who specialized in litigation of disputed land titles. When outside capitalists sought to acquire land in the mountains in the 1870s and 1880s, resident lawyers grew rich on corporation retainers and through ownership of valuable real estate. During the next three decades, the new laws passed by "conservative" politicians not only contributed to the wealth of the mountain elite but facilitated, with the help of that elite, "the eventual transfer of titles and mineral rights from small proprietors to mining and lumber corporations."[47]

Resident land developers could be found in almost every mountain county at the turn of the century, but a handful were especially notable for their success. Typical of these were two southwest Vir-

47. Williams, "The New Dominion and the Old," 391–407; Williams, *West Virginia and the Captains of Industry*, 7–8.

ginia men, Rufus A. Ayers and George L. Carter, who amassed
considerable power and wealth between 1880 and 1920 promoting
railroad, coal, and iron developments. Ayers, for instance, began to
promote the coal lands of southwest Virginia in the early 1880s,
helping to draw the attention of northern capitalists to the area. The
son of a prominent Virginia planter who had settled in Bristol before
the Civil War, Ayers in 1872 had moved to Estillville in Scott
County, where he commenced to practice law. During the next three
decades, he became active in industrial speculation and organized the
Appalachia Steel and Iron Company at Big Stone Gap, operated a
large tannery, managed the Wise Terminal Railway and the Big
Creek branch of the N&W Railway, and helped to found the Virginia, Tennessee and Carolina Steel and Iron Company. The latter
firm was capitalized at over two million dollars and controlled coal
lands in Wise, Dickenson, and Buchanan counties, Virginia, and iron
deposits in Tennessee and North Carolina. In 1898, Ayers acquired
approximately 10,000 acres of coal lands in Tazewell and Buchanan
counties and with a Michigan businessman organized the Stone Gap
Colliery at Glamorgan. Like a number of other southwest Virginia
industrialists, Ayers was a Bourbon Democrat and served for a time
as the attorney general of the state of Virginia. His many investments
allowed him eventually to retire to a 2,500-acre estate, Holston
Springs, on the banks of the Holston River.[48]

Ayers's younger contemporary, George L. Carter, achieved even
greater success. Born in 1858, Carter was the son of a Confederate
captain who owned a farm of "several hundred acres" near Hillsville,
Virginia. In the 1880s young Carter acquired an interest in iron
production and eventually became general manager of the Dora
Furnace at Pulaski. Purchasing a number of small coal mines to
provide coke for his furnace, he later organized the Tom's Creek
Coal Company and became one of the leading coal operators of
southwest Virginia. In the 1890s, he consolidated his holdings into
the Carter Coal and Iron Company and built or purchased iron
furnaces in Roanoke, Johnson City, Bristol, Big Stone Gap, Buena
Vista, and Middlesboro. After acquiring 300,000 acres of coal lands
in Dickenson, Russell, and Wise counties, Virginia, he organized
the Clinchfield Coal Company and began to construct a series of

48. Luther F. Addington, *The Story of Wise County, Virginia* (Wise County,
1956), 213–18.

railroads into these properties. Finally, in 1908, with heavy backing from northern capitalists, these railroads were reorganized as part of the Clinchfield Railroad with Carter as its head.[49] After 1910, his interests extended from Elkhorn City in Kentucky through southwest Virginia and western North Carolina to Spartanburg, South Carolina, making Carter one of the most powerful men in the mountains.

While Ayers and Carter were amassing fortunes in southwest Virginia, other mountaineers were planning to benefit from the industrial development in eastern Kentucky. Early in the 1870s, local men such as the Honorable Charles B. Faris, Judge Granville Pearl, and General Jarvis Jackson were actively promoting the development of coal and timber lands in Rockcastle, Laurel, Knox, Bell, and Whitley counties, Kentucky. They advertised the resources of these counties, where they were large landholders, in the newspapers of Louisville and Chicago, and they encouraged outside capitalists to visit the Cumberland Plateau. Later, the *Mountain Echo*, a newspaper at London, Kentucky, was created to help with this promotional work.[50]

When interest in eastern Kentucky lands began to mature after 1890, many local leaders became mineral buyers, representing either themselves or outside corporations. Even Corporal Fess Whitaker, for example, a local hero from Letcher County, worked for several years as a land buyer on Rockhouse Creek and Caudill's Branch for the Kentucky River Coal Corporation, a major land company in the Hazard Coal Field.[51] Yet, no local developer benefited more from the land boom in eastern Kentucky than John Caldwell Calhoun Mayo, a quiet schoolteacher and land speculator from Johnson County. Between 1892 and 1907, Mayo acquired over half a million acres of coal land, making him Kentucky's largest landholder and one of its wealthiest citizens.

John C. Calhoun Mayo was born in 1864 in Pike County, Kentucky, the son of Thomas Jefferson Mayo, a prominent schoolteacher, and Elizabeth Leslie Mayo, a member of the "famous Leslie

49. *Ibid.*, 223–27.
50. Howard, "Chapters in the Economic History of Knox County, Kentucky," 80–81.
51. Fess Whitaker, *History of Corporal Fess Whitaker* (Louisville, Ky., 1918), 70.

family" of Virginia. He spent his early years in Paintsville, Johnson County, and was educated at Kentucky Wesleyan College, graduating in 1883. Following graduation, he taught mathematics for a time at the college. It was here that he developed an interest in geology and learned the importance of the coal deposits in eastern Kentucky.[52] Mayo then returned home to Paintsville, where he studied law and was admitted to the bar. In 1886, he began teaching school in Johnson and Pike counties, but he spent his weekends and vacation months riding through the Big Sandy Valley in search of coal lands. His training as a lawyer had acquainted Mayo with the confusion surrounding land grants and deeds in the mountains, and he used this knowledge to persuade local farmers to sell options on coal lands for small fees. By 1890, he had acquired options on thousands of acres of eastern Kentucky mineral lands, usually paying between fifty cents and a dollar per acre.[53]

In that year Mayo began looking for outside capital in order to purchase mineral options on a larger scale. Within three years he had sold 10,000 acres of his holdings to E. T. and A. R. Merritt of Minnesota, owners of the Mesabi iron ore beds. The Merritt brothers further offered to pay $16 per acre for any other acreages he could buy.[54] Mayo immediately reinvested his profits in more coal lands—again at the same low prices to local settlers. The Merritt brothers' interests collapsed in the Panic of 1893, but four years later Mayo induced Peter L. Kimberly of Chicago to finance land purchases in Pike, Floyd, and Letcher counties. In 1901, Mayo, Kimberly, and several other Pennsylvania and Illinois capitalists formed the Northern Coal and Coke Company to exploit the 400,000 acres of coal lands that Mayo had acquired along the headwaters of the Big Sandy—including much of the same property Richard M. Broas had prospected in the 1880s. This company and large tracts of Mayo's

52. John E. Buckingham, "John C. Calhoun Mayo," 1, unpublished MS in folder marked "Broad Form Deed Controversy," Mountain Collection, Hutchins Library, Berea College; "John Caldwell Calhoun Mayo," *National Cyclopedia of American Biography* 45: 172.
53. Buckingham, "Mayo," 3. Ownership of land in the mountains was uncertain because of the confusion of grants originally issued by Virginia and taken over by Kentucky. Many of the grants had been issued for service during the Revolutionary War, but the grantees had not taken up the land. As a result, the lands were later transferred to other settlers or taken up by squatters.
54. Scalf, *Kentucky's Last Frontier*, 527, n. 5.

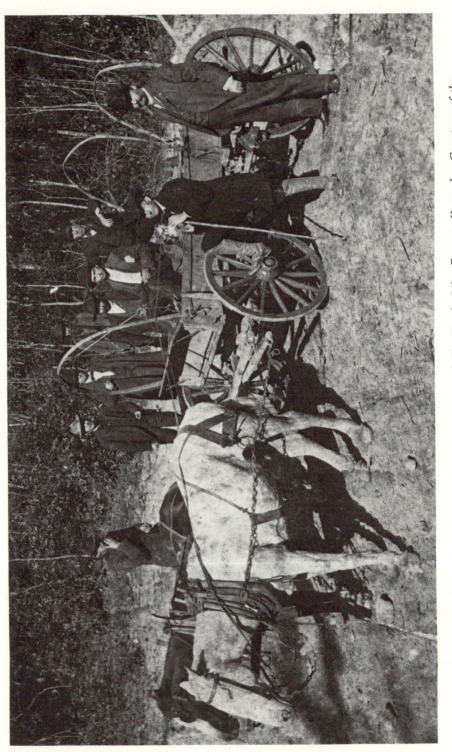

*A John C.C. Mayo Exploration and Inspection Party, Shelby Creek, Pike County, Kentucky. Courtesy of the Appalachian Photographic Archives, Alice Lloyd College.*

land were subsequently sold to Consolidation Coal Company, which began major operations in the Elkhorn district in 1902.[55]

Throughout this period, Mayo continued to purchase land in northeastern Kentucky and to arrange overland trips into the coal fields for railroad men, financiers, and coal operators.[56] By 1907, he controlled or owned outright 700,000 acres of mountain land, held principal interest in several banks and coal companies in Kentucky and southwest Virginia, and was a chief stockholder in Consolidation Coal. Politically a Democrat, Mayo frequently used his wealth and influence to support favored candidates and legislation, and in 1906 he was instrumental in the passage of new state land and tax laws that recognized the titles of the settlers of the coal lands upon which his mineral options were based.[57] At the time of his death, Mayo's fortune was reported to be worth over twenty million dollars.[58]

Men like Ayers, Carter, and Mayo played an important part in the industrialization of the mountains, easing the way for the entrance of absentee capital. By purchasing land and mineral resources from local residents for minimal amounts and transferring them to outside corporations at a profit, they accumulated great personal wealth, but they handed over the region's economy and its future to absentee control. Using their wealth and political influence to promote development, they helped to spread the gospel of "progress through industrial growth" into most of the hamlets and villages of the region. Indeed, during the last two decades of the nineteenth century, faith in the industrial potential of the Appalachians was as strong among mountain leaders as it was among the outside businessmen and speculators who sought to exploit the region. "The people," wrote a dissenting mind in the 1880s, "have been educated to believe that our immediate development must be obtained at any cost and regardless of sacrifices; the public mind has become saturated with an idea that progress means one railroad where there is no railroad, and two railroads where there is only one." Things had evolved to such a point, he lamented, that anyone who would raise a voice against this

55. Buckingham, "Mayo," 3–5; *National Cyclopedia of American Biography* 45: 172; Scalf, *Kentucky's Last Frontier*, 528; *Manufacturers' Record* 44 (12 Sept. 1903), 135.

56. Buckingham, "Mayo," 6–7.

57. *Ibid.*, 7; *National Cyclopedia of American Biography* 45: 172; Mary Lucille Chapman, "The Influence of Coal in the Big Sandy Valley" (Ph.D. diss., Univ. of Kentucky, 1945), 207.

58. Watson, Economic and Cultural Development of Eastern Kentucky," 44.

"reckless and . . . foolish sacrifice of our local wealth" was not only ostracized from politics but from all other avenues to the public ear.[59]

One of the few stands taken by a public agency in opposition to the selling of mountain land was made by the West Virginia Tax Commission in 1884. Its remarkable report warned the state's citizens that nonresidents were rapidly carrying off the most valuable resources of the state, threatening to leave West Virginia in the near future "despoiled of her wealth and her resident population poor, helpless, and despondent." In recent years, the report argued, the home population had lost more than one-half of the property it owned at the end of the Civil War and the transfer of property to nonresidents was rapidly accelerating. The measure of a state's prosperity, the commissioners added, was the amount of wealth and property being accumulated by her citizens. The state whose property was "rapidly passing from her present population or home people into the hands of non-residents" was "going backwards" and was doomed to ruin. "The question," they concluded, "is whether this vast wealth shall belong to persons who live here and who are permanently identified with the future of West Virginia, or whether it shall pass into the hands of persons who do not live here and who care nothing for our State except to pocket the treasures which lie buried in our hills."[60]

The warning of the tax commission went unheeded. According to the *Manufacturers' Record* in 1892, more than a million dollars a month was going into the coal hands of southwest Virginia and West Virginia, and capitalists were rapidly penetrating other areas of the Appalachian South.[61] By 1892, large, primarily nonresident interests owned over 80 percent of the mineral lands of Bell County, Kentucky. More than 60 percent of the land in Harlan, Leslie, Letcher, and Rowan counties, Kentucky, was owned by nonresident taxpayers.[62] With the transition in land ownership, the power to shape the future of the mountains was transferred to the boardrooms and office chambers of New York, Philadelphia, and Richmond. With a zeal fired by greed and ambition, the "developers" descended on the mountains to tap their newly acquired wealth.

59. James Murray Mason, in West Virginia Tax Commission, *Second Report, State Development* (Wheeling, W. Va., 1884), 3.
60. West Virginia Tax Commission, *Second Report, State Development* (Wheeling, W. Va., 1884), 1–3.
61. 19 (7 March 1891), 12.
62. Banks, "The Emergence of a Capitalistic Labor Market in Eastern Kentucky," 23–24.

## EARLY INDUSTRIAL DEVELOPMENTS, 1870—1900

To urban middle-class Americans of the late nineteenth century, nothing symbolized the progress of American civilization quite as much as the railroad. Not only had the great surge in railroad construction after the Civil War helped to create a modern market economy, but the iron horse itself seemed to embody the energy, force, and technology of the new order. In fact, the fanning out of railroads from urban centers was an integral part of the modernizing process, tying the natural and human resources of rural areas to the industrializing core. If the mountains were to fuel the advance of industrial capitalism, they too would have to be breeched by the iron horse. "Capitalists and speculators," wrote a western North Carolinian in 1889, "have but very little wish to visit and examine counties without a railroad."[63] Those resident mountain speculators who were most successful in their efforts, therefore, were those who were able to attract the interest of railroad men.

The coming of railroads to the Appalachian South was almost as dramatic as the selling of the land itself. In 1870, only one railroad line penetrated the region, and it ran down the valleys of southwest Virginia and eastern Tennessee, connecting Norfolk with Knoxville. This valley line had little impact on the surrounding mountain communities.[64] By 1900, however, four major railroads had extended branch lines into the heart of the region: the Chesapeake and Ohio (C&O) into southern West Virginia, the Norfolk and Western (N&W) into southwest Virginia, the Louisville and Nashville (L&N) into eastern Kentucky and eastern Tennessee, and the Southern into western North Carolina. Three decades later, a complex network of branch lines, narrow-gauge railroads, and other private lines had been laid across the mountains to open up the region's natural resources. On the eve of the Great Depression, only a few mountain counties were without access to a railroad of some kind.[65]

Ironically, the first railroad to make its way into the southern mountains after the Civil War was not constructed primarily to tap the

63. Thomas P. Williams, "The Mineral Wealth of North Carolina," *Manufacturers' Record* 15 (23 Feb. 1889), 13.
64. The Baltimore and Ohio Railroad had been constructed across northern West Virginia, but that area lies outside of southern Appalachia as defined for this study.
65. U.S. Department of Agriculture, *Economic and Social Conditions*, maps, 76–77.

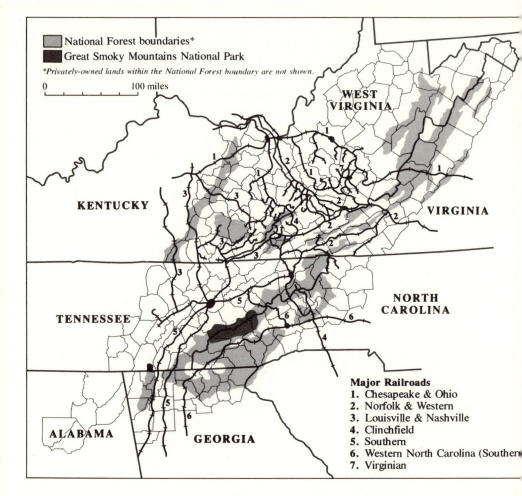

*2. Major Railroads of the Appalachian South*

region's mineral and timber wealth. The C&O Railroad was part of Collis Potter Huntington's dream for a transcontinental trunk line that would stretch from San Francisco to Newport News, Virginia. Shortly after opening the Southern Pacific Railroad in California, Huntington and a group of New York bankers and businessmen

66

purchased a controlling interest in the C&O, a struggling Virginia line extending from Richmond to Clifton Forge on the West Virginia border. Huntington hoped that the C&O would provide the critical eastern link in his coast-to-coast railroad, and he immediately undertook to complete the new line across West Virginia to the Ohio River. The route of the "mountain extension" of the C&O took it across some of the most rugged country in the eastern United States and required almost three years of construction, using primarily black labor imported from eastern Virginia. At one point during the construction of the Big Bend tunnel in Summers County, one of the ex-slaves raced a newly acquired steam drill and, defeating the machine, gave rise to the legend of John Henry.[66]

The C&O reached the new town of Huntington on the banks of the Ohio River in January 1873, opening up much of central and southern West Virginia to development. Along the New and Kanawha rivers in Raleigh, Fayette, and Kanawha counties, the arrival of the railroad started a major land and construction boom that saw the establishment of a number of towns, sawmills, and coal mines. By 1876, over two dozen collieries had opened along the new line, and sawmills were under construction at St. Albans, Hinton, and Huntington. Within a decade after the railroad's completion, the population of the counties along the line increased by almost 60 percent.[67]

As with later mountain railroads, absentee capitalists were quick to buy up valuable timber and mineral land along the route of the C&O. President Huntington and several of the company's New York directors formed the Central Land Company of West Virginia and acquired thousands of acres of land, including the 6,000 acres upon which the town of Huntington was built. Other speculators such as George Bartholomew and Samuel Coit of Hartford, Connecticut, John H. Hambleton of Baltimore, Henry Whitcomb of Richmond, and William Henry Aspinwall and Abiel Abbot Low of New York invested heavily in coal lands in Raleigh and Fayette counties. Abram S. Hewitt, both before and after he became the reform mayor of New York City, acquired substantial tracts of coal lands near

66. Ronald D Eller, "Mountain Road," 32–57. For the legend of John Henry, see Louis Watson Chappell, *John Henry: A Folk Study* (Jena, Germany, 1933); Guy Benton Johnson, *John Henry: Tracking Down a Negro Legend* (Chapel Hill, 1929).
67. Eller, "Mountain Road," 58–81; Thomas, "Coal Country," 67.

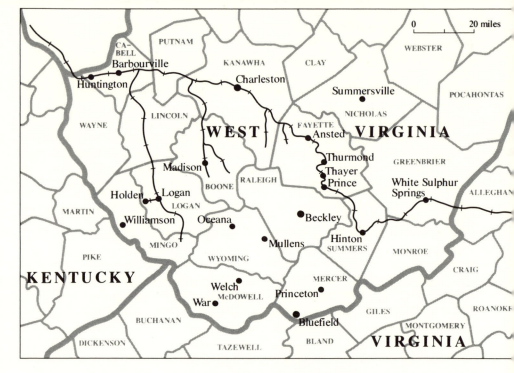

*3. Chesapeake and Ohio Railroad*

Ansted and on Loup Creek in Kanawha County.[68] Despite these investments, however, the development of the New River and Kanawha coal fields was slow, partly because of the depression of the 1870s but primarily because of the failure of President Huntington to recognize the industrial potential of Appalachian coal.

Throughout the 1870s and 1880s, Huntington continued to manage the C&O according to his larger transcontinental strategy. Arguing that railroads could not compete profitably with water haulage on coal traffic, he concentrated his efforts on extending the line's termini rather than developing its local possibilities. As a result, important

68. Eller, "Mountain Road," 70–75; Thomas, "Coal Country," 79–80; *Manufacturers' Record* 29 (6 March 1896), 93; *ibid.* 30 (11 Dec. 1896), 330; Allan Nevins, *Abram S. Hewitt, With Some Account of Peter Cooper* (New York, 1935), 592.

spurs were not constructed to potential coal veins, and track and rolling stock were allowed to deteriorate, while funds were diverted to lavish facilities at Huntington and Newport News.[69] In 1873, the railroad defaulted on its bonded debt, but in 1878 it was reorganized by Huntington at considerable profit to himself and his northern associates. By 1884, Huntington had acquired or constructed lines from New Orleans to Louisville, across Kentucky to the C&O terminus at Huntington, and from there to the Virginia coast. The creation of this eastern chain of railroads was achieved at considerable cost to the maintenance and development of the C&O, and, because of its circuitous route, it still did not provide Huntington with a competitive transcontinental line. Finally, in 1888, Huntington abandoned his dream and sold the C&O to the Drexel-Morgan-Vanderbilt interests of Philadelphia and New York. Under the management of the new president, Melville E. Ingalls, the C&O began a rebuilding and expansion program which would eventually make it one of the leading coal carriers on the East Coast. Between 1890 and 1910, the C&O extended branch lines into the rapidly developing coal fields to the south of the New River in West Virginia and up the Big Sandy Valley in eastern Kentucky.[70] With this conscious effort to increase the railroad's coal trade, the development of the New River and Kanawha coal fields began in earnest.

By the time the C&O realized the opportunities that the company might derive from coal mining, other northern capitalists had begun to develop the Pocahontas (Smokeless) coal fields to the south of New River. In 1881, Jedidiah Hotchkiss had interested Frederick J. Kimball, the president of the new N&W Railway, in the coal lands of the Flat Top Mountain region. Kimball believed that the rich coal deposits of this district would not only provide cheap fuel for his growing railroad but would also allow the N&W to compete with the C&O in the profitable eastern coal trade.[71] With the support of E.W.

---

69. Eller, "Mountain Road," 62, 78–83; Paul R. Coppock, "Huntington's Pacific-to-Atlantic Rails Through Memphis," *West Tennessee Historical Society Papers* 9 (1955), 9–11; Cerinda W. Evans, *Collis Potter Huntington* (Newport News, Va., 1954), 533–34.

70. Charles Wilson Turner, *Chessie's Road* (Richmond, 1956), 95; James Poyntz Nelson, *The History of the Chesapeake and Ohio Railway Company: Its Antecedents and Subsidiaries* (Richmond, 1927), 30–31.

71. Lambie, *From Mine to Market: The History of Coal Transportation on the Norfolk and Western Railway* (New York, 1954); 26–36; Thomas, "Coal Country," 73.

Clark and Company of Philadelphia, the owners of the N&W, Kimball began construction of the New River Division into the heart of the Flat Top area. The completion of this branch line to the new mining town of Pocahontas in Tazewell County in 1883 opened for exploitation one of the largest coal fields in the United States and set in motion events that would drastically transform life in this corner of the mountains.

From the outset, therefore, the N&W Railroad branched into the mountains for the primary purpose of tapping and developing the vast natural wealth of the region. Where Collis P. Huntington had viewed the construction of the C&O as little more than a necessary link in a larger transcontinental chain, Kimball considered the expansion of the N&W into the mountains and the promotion of coal mining to be vital to the livelihood of the line itself. "From the very start," observed the *Manufacturers' Record* in 1890,

> the policy of the company has been the extension of its system into the heart of the great mineral regions, the development of the natural resources of the State, and the encouragement of new industrial enterprises of every character. In short, it has been the very apparent aim of the directors of the affairs of this company not to encourage speculation, but to promote the growth of the territory tributary to its system.[72]

The N&W was the product of the consolidation of several railroads in southwest Virginia. The trunk of the system was the old Atlantic, Mississippi and Ohio Railroad, purchased at auction by the Clark banking firm early in 1881. The line originally functioned as a freight carrier between Norfolk and Bristol, on the Virginia-Tennessee border, but after Kimball turned the system toward the mountains, the line carried primarily coal traffic. During the early 1880s, the company constructed extensive piers and coal warehouses at Lambert's Point in Norfolk and moved its head offices closer to the coal fields. Almost overnight, the quiet valley town of Big Lick became the booming industrial town of Roanoke, as the N&W planners used that community as the headquarters for their assault on the nearby mountains. Within a decade, the population of Roanoke exploded from fewer than 400 to more than 25,000 people.[73]

72. "A Mother of Industry: Grand Work of a Railroad Company in Virginia," *Manufacturers' Record* 18 (6 Sept. 1890), 7.
73. *Manufacturers' Record* 13 (14 July 1888), 13; *ibid.*, 18 (Sept. 1890), 7.

To profit more directly from the wealth they had uncovered and to assure a steady flow of traffic on their railroad, the directors of the N&W took an active role in the development of the Flat Top coal and timber lands. Shortly after the decision to build the New River branch, Edward W. Clark, senior partner of E.W. Clark and Associates, moved to acquire ownership of the best lands in the Flat Top region. Another group of Philadelphia capitalists owned railroad right-of-way and options on approximately 100,000 acres of land in the New River district of Tazewell County, and after purchasing control of those interests, Clark and others formed the Southwest Virginia Improvement Company to open coal mines and build a mining town at the terminus of the new line.[74] In the fall of 1881, construction began on a town to be called Pocahontas. By the time the railroad arrived in 1883, Pocahontas was a thriving boom town of fifty houses, a company store, a butcher shop, a dressmaking and millinery establishment, a newspaper, and two saloons, with one hundred coke ovens and a pile of 40,000 tons of coal on the ground.[75]

Meanwhile, speculators unconnected with the N&W, who had learned of the railroad's plans to build into the Flat Top–Pocahontas region, had acquired most of the valuable coal property in West Virginia adjacent to the lands of the Southwest Virginia Improvement Company. One of these speculators was Jedidiah Hotchkiss, who with his associates Echols, Bell, and Catlett of Staunton, Virginia, had purchased large tracts of land in the Flat Top field. Aware that the N&W people would like to monopolize control over all the lands in the Flat Top region, Hotchkiss threatened to sell his lands to the C&O. This move frightened E.W. Clark into negotiating a deal to acquire the lands owned by Hotchkiss and his associates, as well as other properties in Mercer, McDowell, Wyoming, Boone, Raleigh, and Logan counties in West Virginia. In 1888, Clark consolidated these lands into the Flat Top Coal Land Association.[76]

Although the originator and financial head of this land monopoly was E.W. Clark, a good part of the capital was supplied by the

---

74. "The Pocahontas–Flat Top Coal Field," *Manufacturers' Record* 52 (25 July 1907), 33; Lambie, *From Mine to Market*, 31–33.

75. "Pocahontas No. 1 'Retires,'" *Norfolk and Western Magazine* 33 (1955), 523; Thomas, "Coal Country," 75.

76. David Emmons Johnston, *A History of Middle New River Settlements and Contiguous Territory* (Huntington, W. Va., 1906), 352–53; Lambie, *From Mine to Market*, 37–38; Thomas, "Coal Country," 77–78.

banking firms of Drexel and Company of Philadelphia and Vivian, Gray and Company of England, and by T.W. Powell of London.[77] The purpose of the Flat Top Coal Land Association, as outlined in its charter, included not only the acquisition of mineral and other lands in the states of Virginia, West Virginia, and North Carolina, but also the "development, improvement . . . and the leasing thereof" for the purposes of logging, coal mining, iron manufacture, or any other purposes.[78] By 1890, the association owned almost the entire Pocahontas–Flat Top region, including 10,000 acres in Tazewell County, Virginia; 45,000 acres in Mercer County, West Virginia; 55,000 acres in McDowell County, West Virginia; and over 90,000 acres in Wyoming and Raleigh counties, West Virginia.[79] The only other major landowner was Samuel A. Crozer, an Upland, Pennsylvania, cotton manufacturer who had purchased 12,000 acres on the lower Elkhorn Creek from Hotchkiss in 1884 and who was leasing land to several operating companies.[80]

The practice of concentrating land ownership in the hands of huge land companies was to become characteristic of the development of much of the Appalachian coal field.[81] Unlike other coal areas, where independent operators owned the land upon which they mined, the concentration of landholdings in the mountains contributed significantly to the gluttonous exploitation of the region's coal deposits and to the overdevelopment of the industry itself. Not only were leases on coal lands easy to obtain, but also the land companies actively encouraged the establishment of as many coal operations on their properties as the narrow mountain valleys could accommodate. This practice was extremely profitable to the land companies, who had generally acquired the property at nominal fees. The land in the Pocahontas–Flat Top field, for example, was purchased at $1.50 to $2.00 an acre, and five years later was worth over $100 an acre.[82] Typically, this land, when leased to a mining company, would bring

77. Lambie, *From Mine to Market*, 38.
78. Johnston, *A History of Middle New River Settlements*, 353.
79. "A Mother of Industry," *Manufacturers' Record* 18 (6 Sept. 1890), 7; *ibid.* 14 (12 Jan. 1889), 13.
80. Lambie, *From Mine to Market*, 39.
81. U.S. Census Office, *Fourteenth Census of the United States: Mines and Quarries* XI (1920), 284. In 1920 in West Virginia, Virginia, and Kentucky, more than twice as many mines operated on land held under lease as on land owned by the operating company.
82. Lambie, *From Mine to Market*, 39.

a royalty of ten cents per gross ton of coal mined or a payment of $7.50 per acre minimum royalty, whether the coal was mined or not. The leasee, moreover, agreed to pay all the taxes and not to remove standing timber over ten inches in diameter.[83]

In some cases, the owners of the land companies profited in other ways from the development of the coal deposits. For example, E.W. Clark and Company, the chief stockholders in the Flat Top Land Association, also controlled the N&W Railway, which transported the coal, and the Southwest Virginia Improvement Company, which became the largest producer of coal in the Flat Top field. Later, Clark and his associates organized the Pocahontas Coal Company, through which all of the coal on the N&W was sold.[84] By 1896, the Clark interests had collected over $800 per acre from the lands that were leased to mining companies, and they were transporting and selling over 3 million tons of coal per year.[85] Another Philadelphia banking firm, Drexel and Company, which held stock in the N&W companies and in the C&O, also acquired some 47,000 acres of coal land in the Winding Gulf field of Raleigh County, leasing the land under the name of the Beaver Coal Company.[86] The Flat Top Coal Land Association, the Crozer Land Company, and the Beaver Coal Company were the principal land companies in southern West Virginia, and together they controlled coal production in that area of the mountains.[87]

After the completion of the New River Division from Radford to Pocahontas, Virginia, in 1883, the development of the Flat Top coal field escalated rapidly. In 1888, the line of the N&W was extended into McDowell County, West Virginia, by tunneling 3,100 feet through Flat Top Mountain. The opening of the coal beds of McDowell County suddenly transformed that remote and sparsely settled county into the leading coal-producing county in the state. Between 1880 and 1900, the population of the county increased by over 600 percent, and coal production reached over 4 million tons per

83. William Purviance Tams, Jr., *The Smokeless Coal Fields of West Virginia: A Brief History* (Morgantown, W.Va., 1963), 31. See also George Wolfe to Justus Collins, 23 Sept. 1916, Justus Collins Papers, West Virginia Collection, West Virginia Univ.

84. *Manufacturers' Record* 18 (6 Sept. 1890), 7.

85. Thomas, "Coal Country, 81; *Manufacturers' Record* 45 (14 April 1905), 275.

86. Tams, *The Smokeless Coal Fields*, 30.

87. *Ibid.*, 29.

*4. Norfolk and Western Railroad*

year. By 1905, McDowell mines produced more coal in a year than had the entire state of West Virginia in 1890.[88]

The year following the completion of the tunnel into McDowell County, President Kimball began the N&W's Ohio extension in order to connect with the growing industrial markets of the Midwest. The new line extended for over 190 miles from the headwaters of the Elkhorn Creek in McDowell County, west through neighboring Mingo County, and on to Kenova on the Ohio River.[89] Completed in the fall of 1892, the Ohio extension not only gave the N&W access to

88. U.S. Census Office, *Twelfth Census of the United States*, 1900, vol. I. Pt. 1 (Washington, D.C., 1901); *Manufacturers' Record* 39 (28 March 1901), 180; Cubby, "The Transformation of the Tug and Guyandot Valleys," 265.
89. Lambie, *From Mine to Market*, 128–31.

Chicago and the Great Lakes ports, but it opened up another coal field in southern West Virginia, the Logan coal field in Mingo and Logan counties. As was the case in the Flat Top and Winding Gulf coal fields, E.W. Clark and his New York, English, and Pennsylvania associates gained control of a majority of land in the Logan coal field before the tracks of the N&W reached the area. Under the name of the Guyandot Coal Land Association, these capitalists held for lease about 200,000 acres of valuable coal and timber lands.[90] The development of the new Logan coal field, however, was slow, following the depression of 1893, and the expansion of coal mining activity in the district did not revive until after the turn of the century.

The last major extension of the N&W during these feverish days of the railroad's growth was an extension into the Clinch Valley of southwest Virginia, where rich coal deposits had been discovered in Wise County along the Kentucky border. Construction of the Clinch Valley Branch began in 1887 on a line running from Bluefield, on the New River Division, to Norton, near the Kentucky state line, a distance of 103 miles.[91] The tracks of the N&W reached Norton in 1891, along with those of the L&N Railroad, which had constructed a branch up the Powell River Valley from Cumberland Gap. About this time another line, the Virginia and Southwestern—originally backed by Massachusetts interests—was completed from Bristol to Appalachia, Virginia, just below Norton.[92] The completion of these three lines opened up markets for Wise County coal in the Southeast, the West, and the eastern seaboard, and the rapid economic development that followed quickly turned Wise County into the leading coal-producing county in the state. In 1902, the coal production for Wise County totaled more than 2.4 million tons, three times that of any other county in Virginia.[93]

The two largest developers of the Wise County fields were the Virginia Coal and Iron Company, a Pennsylvania firm, and the Virginia Iron, Coal and Coke Company, financed by New York capital. Together, these two companies controlled a majority of the coal and coke produced in the county. The older of the two firms was

90. *Manufacturers' Record* 24 (1 Sept. 1893), 82; Lambie, *From Mine to Market*, 124.
91. *Manufacturers' Record* 18 (6 Sept. 1890), 7.
92. *Ibid.*, 14 (13 Oct. 1888), 13; John Leggett Pultz, "The Big Stone Gap Coal-Field of Virginia and Kentucky," *Engineering Magazine* 27 (Oct. 1904), 71.
93. Pultz, "The Big Stone Gap Coal-Field," 72.

the Virginia Coal and Iron Company, founded in 1882 by Edward K. Hyndman, Judge John Leisenring, and others of the Connellsville, Pennsylvania, coal region. These men had been attracted to Wise County by General J.D. Imboden, who had convinced them of the potential wealth of Virginia coal. With Imboden serving as their attorney and land agent, the Connellsville syndicate had purchased about 67,000 acres of coal lands on the headwaters of the Powell River, paying as little as 35 cents an acre for some tracts.[94] In the late 1880s, other companies began to acquire land in the area, and a new town sprang up at Big Stone Gap, near the Virginia Coal and Iron Company properties. Shortly thereafter, the company hired Rufus A. Ayers to manage its development, and in 1890 the first coal openings were made and the first coke was produced at Stonega, near Big Stone Gap. Progress was slow until railroads reached the area, but by 1896 the company was producing over 7,000 tons of coal a month and operating more than five hundred coking ovens.[95]

While most of the coke from the Virginia Coal and Iron Company ovens went into the furnaces of steel companies in Illinois, Wisconsin, and Alabama, the coke from the Virginia Iron, Coal and Coke Company fired that company's own furnaces in nearby valley towns.[96] This company was the product of the promotional activity of George L. Carter, who sold his coal properties on Tom's Creek in upper Wise County to New York capitalists interested in developing iron furnaces in southwest Virginia. Carter later became the guiding spirit in another large operation in the area, the Crane's Nest Coal and Coke Company, which acquired 150,000 acres of coal lands in Wise and Dickenson counties.[97] After the N&W extended into the Clinch Valley, the Tom's Creek properties became the major supplier of coal and coke for Virginia Iron, Coal, and Coke Company rolling mills and pipe works at Middlesboro, Johnson City, Embreeville, Pulaski, Bedford, and Max Meadows. By the turn of the century, the

94. *Manufacturers' Record* 30 (25 Dec. 1896), 367; E.J. Prescott, *The Story of the Virginia Coal and Iron Company, 1882–1945* (Big Stone Gap, Va., 1946), 19–23.
95. Prescott, *The Virginia Coal and Iron Company*, 54–67.
96. *Manufacturers' Record* 30 (25 Dec. 1896), 367; *Manufacturers' Record* 41 (27 March 1902), 165.
97. *Manufacturers' Record* 41 (27 March 1902), 165; *ibid.*, 45 (16 June 1904), 489.

company owned thirty-six iron mines, operated two big coal mines, and worked 2,500 coke ovens.[98]

The intense activity around Big Stone Gap in the 1890s attracted the attention of scores of small coal operators, merchants, lawyers, and land speculators who flocked to the area with hopes of cashing in on the big boom. One of these speculators subsequently became the Gap's best-known citizen, John Fox, Jr. Fox came to Wise County in 1888 with his two older brothers, James and Horace, who had owned a coal-mining business at Jellico, Tennessee. Originally from Paris, Kentucky, James and Horace had moved to Jellico in the early 1880s to participate in the opening of mineral lands near Cumberland Gap. John had visited his brothers at Jellico and Cumberland Gap during summer vacations from Harvard, and it was during these visits that he first became fascinated with the people and culture of the southern mountains. Later, when Horace and James followed the coal industry into Virginia, John abandoned his newspaper career in New York and joined his brothers in land speculation and mineral development at Big Stone Gap.[99]

As the boom in Wise County lands burgeoned in the early 1890s, John Fox, Jr., made effective use of the contacts he had made while at Harvard and as a newspaperman in New York. Several of his wealthy northern acquaintances helped the Fox brothers with loans and independent investments in mineral property.[100] During his trips into the surrounding Virginia and Kentucky mountains to prospect for new coal lands, John continued to nourish his fascination with the mountain people and soon relinquished his interests in real estate to concentrate on writing. His excursions into the mountains and his experiences in pioneering the development of the Gap provided him with the subjects and themes that he would exploit in his fictional sketches.[101]

While the Fox real estate business continued to thrive—later moving its base of operations to New York City—John Fox achieved

98. *Ibid.*, 45 (16 June 1904), 489.

99. Warren I. Titus, *John Fox, Jr.* (New York, 1971), 23–37; "John Fox, Jr.: Personal and Family Letters and Papers" John Fox, Jr. Collection, King Library, Univ. of Kentucky, (unpublished MS compiled by Elizabeth Fox Moore for the Univ. of Kentucky Library Associates, 1955), 41–42.

100. Titus, *John Fox., Jr.*, 37–38.

101. *Ibid.*, 38–39.

international success as a writer and interpreter of southern mountain life.[102] His two most popular novels, *The Trail of the Lonesome Pine* and *The Little Shepherd of Kingdom Come*, helped to confirm America's growing conception of Appalachia as a "strange land and a peculiar people." Like many of his associates at Big Stone Gap, Fox believed that the mountain people were inherently inferior and must inevitably give way to the onrush of the new industrial order.[103] More than any other writer of his day, John Fox, Jr., symbolized the struggle between the economic and intellectual forces of modernization and the traditional patterns of Appalachian life.

It was in Fox's own Kentucky that this struggle often took its most dramatic form, and events of the 1890s were fast moving eastern Kentucky onto the industrial stage. Coal had been mined in the Cumberland Plateau as early as the 1840s, but the lack of markets and adequate transportation had kept production to a minimum. The most successful of the early coal mines were those in the upper Big Sandy Valley in Lawrence and Johnson counties. In 1881, the Ohio and Big Sandy Railroad was completed to Peach Orchard in Lawrence County, where an abandoned mine had recently been reopened. In 1893, the mine employed about five hundred men and produced more than two million tons of coal, but thereafter competition from the larger coal fields of southern West Virginia caused production to decline steadily. The mine was closed again in 1909.[104] Nearby in northern Johnson County, two other companies opened mines on leases at Whitehouse. The Whitehouse Cannel Coal Company and the Sandy River Coal Company began operations in 1887, when the railroad reached their coal lands, but production in this field remained small until the C&O purchased the Ohio and Big Sandy and in 1905 extended its line from Whitehouse to the head of the valley at Elkhorn City.[105]

The most imposing developments in the late nineteenth century in eastern Kentucky, however, were played out at the other end of the

102. *Ibid.*

103. See Shapiro, *Appalachia On Our Mind*, 70–77; Donald Askins, "John Fox., Jr.: A Re-appraisal; or, With Friends Like That, Who Needs Enemies," in Helen Lewis, *et al.*, eds., *Colonialism in Modern America: The Appalachian Case* (Boone, N.C., 1978), 251–57.

104. Chapman, "The Influence of Coal in the Big Sandy Valley," 31–55; Gibson, "The Economic History of Boyd County, Kentucky," 43–47.

105. Chapman, "The Influence of Coal in the Big Sandy Valley," 75–96; Scalf, *Kentucky's Last Frontier*, 28–29.

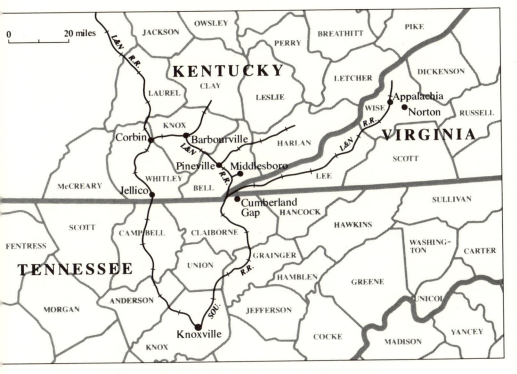

*5. Knoxville Extension, Louisville/Nashville Railroad*

Cumberland Plateau, in Whitley and Bell counties, Kentucky, and in neighboring Campbell and Claiborne counties, Tennessee. Encouraged by the success of the C&O and the N&W in the coal fields of Virginia and West Virginia, the L&N began to build toward the Cumberland Mountains in the 1880s, stimulating a rash of speculation along its projected route. The Knoxville Division of the L&N was extended south from Winchester, near Lexington, reaching Corbin in 1882 and Jellico on the Tennessee border in 1883.[106] At Jellico, the L&N provided a northern outlet for coal being mined in the infant Jellico coal field, which extended from Whitley County, Kentucky, into Campbell, Anderson and Scott counties, Tennessee.

106. Henry Harvey Fuson, *History of Bell County, Kentucky*, II (New York, 1947), 361–62.

By the end of the decade there were five large coal mines operating in the Jellico district.[107]

Following the completion of the Knoxville extension, the L&N then turned east toward the rich coal and timber lands of Pine Mountain in Bell County. Leaving the Knoxville branch at Corbin, the Cumberland Valley Division reached Barbourville, Knox County, in 1887 and Pineville, Bell County, in 1888. Two years later, the line was completed to Norton, Virginia, where it connected with the Clinch Valley Branch of the N&W.[108] The extension of the L&N to Pineville transformed Bell County into a hotbed of industrial activity. Pineville suddenly became a boom town with a modern hotel, macadamized streets, new brick and stone businesses, lumber and planing mills, and elegant residences. A month after the arrival of the railroad, the *Manufacturers' Record* boasted that the town was destined to become the "future mining and manufacturing city of the Appalachian Range."[109]

Much of the promotional activity that surrounded the "new Pineville" was the work of a group of Louisville businessmen and attorneys who had invested heavily in property in the Pineville area. Organized as the Pine Mountain Iron and Coal Company, the Louisville speculators began purchasing tracts of land near the old town limits in the summer of 1887, eventually controlling about 20,000 acres.[110] The Commercial Club of Louisville, which was active in promoting the coal fields of southeastern Kentucky, was engaged to help advertise the area to capitalists, and in 1888 it published a free booklet on the natural resources of the Pineville district.[111] When the railroad reached the city, the Pine Mountain Iron and Coal Company not only owned practically all the land included in the new city limits but many of the new buildings and businesses as well. In 1896, the company was sold and reorganized as the National Coal and Iron Company, under the control of Theodore Harris, president of the Louisville National Banking Company. Under Harris's manage-

107. Goldsmith Bernard West, "Jellico Coal Regions," *Manufacturers' Record* 16 (7 Sept. 1889), 13.
108. Fuson, *History of Bell County*, 362; Howard, "Chapters in the Economic History of Knox County, Kentucky," 52.
109. *Manufacturers' Record* 13 (12 May 1888), 14. See also Allen, "Mountain Passes," 564–66.
110. Allen, "Mountain Passes," 566.
111. *Manufacturers' Record* 13 (12 May 1888), 15.

ment, the firm opened a number of mines on nearby Straight Creek.[112]

Despite the intensity of growth in the Pineville area, industrial speculation in the county reached its height in the birth of the "Magic City" of Middlesborough at Cumberland Gap. In 1886, only sixty families resided in the quiet Yellow Creek Valley at the foot of the Gap, but, as a result of the work of one man, Alexander Alan Arthur, three years later the valley was the site of a burgeoning industrial town of more than 5,000 people.[113] Acclaimed by its promoters as the future location of great iron and steel industries, Middlesborough attracted investors from throughout the United States and Europe, including over twenty million dollars of British capital.[114] At a time when boom towns were common in the Appalachian South, Middlesborough was one of the most far-reaching projects of its kind.

Alexander A. Arthur first came to the area around Cumberland Gap in 1884, to investigate the region for a projected railroad line from East Tennessee. Riding horseback through Yellow Creek and the headwaters of the Cumberland River, he, like others before him, noticed the large quantities of coal, iron ore, and hardwood timber that lay untapped in these remote valleys. An ambitious man who had come to the United States from Scotland and had worked as an agent for a Boston steel firm, Arthur was determined to develop this unexploited wealth. In the summer of 1886, he returned to the Gap with a party of wealthy associates who were vacationing in Asheville, North Carolina. After exploring the area, the group formed the Gap Associates and began buying options on mineral land from the local residents. Not one to do things in a small way, Arthur then embarked for England, where he hoped to induce British steel and banking interests to support the project. He returned the next year, accompanied by a group of eminent British geologists, who examined the Yellow Creek properties and urged their English employers immediately to buy out the Gap Associates, acquire additional land in the area, and organize a new American development

112. J.C. Tipton, *The Cumberland Coal Field and Its Creators* (Middlesborough, Ky., 1905), n.p.

113. *Ibid.*, n.p.; Fuson, *History of Bell County*, 371.

114. *Manufacturers' Record* 16 (14 Sept. 1889), 33–35; Gaventa, "Power and Powerlessness," 63.

company. These recommendations were carried out in 1887, with the formation of the American Association, Ltd., of London.[115]

The American Association, Ltd., was composed of "some of the foremost men of the industrial and financial world of Great Britain." The American investors in the Gap Associates became minor shareholders in the new enterprise; the majority of stock was controlled by British capitalists such as Edmund A. Pontifex, owner of international copper and tin mining companies; Thomas Gair Ashton, the largest cotton spinner in Manchester and the wealthiest commoner in England; and Charles Edward Barnett, a member of the banking firm of Lloyds, Ltd.[116] Shortly after the American Association was organized, the directors hired Alexander Arthur to manage the property and to make plans for its development. Within months, Arthur had acquired almost 100,000 acres of additional land, had laid out sites on 5,500 acres of the Yellow Creek Valley for a new town, and had enticed a number of iron works, planing mills, brick factories, and other industries to the project. Anticipating the growth of iron and steel manufacturers in the city, the town was named Middlesborough after the English iron city of the same name near the mouth of the Tees, in Yorkshire. A Middlesborough Town Company was formed to advertise and sell lots in the town, and another auxiliary company, the Cumberland Gap Construction Company, began erecting buildings and laying railroad spur lines.[117]

By the end of 1889, Middlesborough boasted seven churches, a number of fine hotels, six banks, several residential areas, a library, an opera house, a golf course, and many lavish drinking halls. A tunnel almost a mile long was driven through the mountain under Cumberland Gap to provide access to several railroads straining to reach the "Magic City," and coal tipples sprang up on nearby creeks in anticipation of future demand. Scores of enterpreneurs poured into the city, each with his own grandiose plans for development. Edgar and Frank Watts, of England's prestigious Watts Steel and Iron

115. James McCague, *The Cumberland* (New York, 1973), 194–97; E.B. Wilson, "Middlesborough: The Magic City," in *The Bell County Story, 1867–1967* (Pineville, Ky., 1967), n.p.; *Manufacturers' Record* 16 (14 Sept. 1889), 33.

116. For a list of officers and stockholders in the American Association, Ltd., see *Manufacturers' Record* 16 (14 Sept. 1889), 35.

117. Wilson, "Middlesborough," n.p.; *Manufacturers' Record* 13 (11 Feb. 1888), 28; 14 (25 Aug. 1888), 11; 16 (14 Sept. 1889), 33; 16 (14 Dec. 1889), 45; Allen, "Mountain Passes, 567.

Company, planned to build two great blast furnaces at Middlesborough, and perhaps more later. Others began work on tanneries, lumber mills, mines, and machine shops.[118]

Caught up in the boom town spirit and backed by the seemingly limitless capital of his British directors, Arthur equipped a string of railroad coaches with maps, plats, and pamphlets, and he sent it out across the South and Midwest as a rolling exhibition, spreading the message of the opportunities to be found at Middlesborough.[119] Among those who believed Arthur's propoganda and acquired stock in the Middlesborough Town Company was the beautiful actress Mrs. Lily Langtry, who promised to visit the city as soon as she could "escape the cruel clutches of the double demon—Gout and Rheumatism."[120] Everything about the enterprise seemed to ring of grandeur and success. A bit of magic was being performed in the mountains. The sudden appearance of Middlesborough, wrote the *Manufacturers' Record* in 1889, marked "the beginning of a new era of civilization in the mountain country of Kentucky. This wonderful section, so abundantly blessed by nature with a charming health-giving climate, will, under the influence of a second Birmingham, in Middlesborough be reclaimed from its present wilderness."[121] No mention was made of the mountain families who had lived in the "wilderness" before the arrival of Scottish magician, Alexander Arthur.

Middlesborough continued to grow for the next three years. A fast-spreading fire destroyed much of the downtown area in 1890, but the investors recouped and built again on an even grander scale.[122] A new town, Harrogate, was laid out over the mountain in Tennessee, and a plush, 700-room hotel called the Four Seasons and an adjoining sanitarium were constructed to accommodate the wealthy visitors who flocked to the town. Alexander Arthur erected a palatial home in Harrogate and acquired the baronial title "Duke of the Cumberlands." The American Association continued to acquire land in the area, eventually owning most of the land for miles around Middlesborough and as much as 80 percent of the land in neighboring

118. Gaventa, "Power and Powerlessless," 75–76; *Manufacturers' Record* 16 (14 Sept. 1889), 34–35.
119. McCague, *The Cumberland*, 201.
120. *Manufacturers' Record* 16 (7 Sept. 1889), 31.
121. *Ibid*.
122. Wilson, "Middlesborough," n.p.

Claiborne County.[123] Scores of coal and timber companies leased tracts of land from the association, and company towns shot up on almost every creek to house the thousands of miners who poured into the district.[124]

By 1893, however, ill winds had begun to blow in the international financial markets, eventually bringing an end to the developments at Middlesborough. The first sign of weakness had come in 1890, when the banking firm of Baring Brothers in London closed its doors. Much of the British capital that had financed Middlesborough had flowed through Baring Brothers, and the collapse of that firm sent the value of American Association stock plummeting. Angry, frustrated shareholders in London increasingly criticized Arthur for his extravagance and mismanagement, and eventually he was released from his duties at Middlesborough. When the Watts Brothers fired their first blast furnaces, they discovered to their chagrin that the iron ore of the Cumberlands was of far lower quality than they had been led to believe. Though the flow of money from England dried up, many American investors continued to cling to their faith in the Magic City. Then, in 1893, financial panic hit Wall Street, and America was shaken by an epidemic of corporate failures.[125]

The collapse of American banking brought an end to the boom at Middlesborough. The city's banks failed, and many of its businesses were liquidated. Town lots were sold at a sheriff's sale, and finally the Four Seasons Hotel was torn down and its ornate finishings removed to Chicago. On 27 October 1893, the American Association, Ltd., declared bankruptcy. The following year a new company, the American Association, Inc., was formed, with essentially the same British backers as the old. But Middlesborough would never become the great iron and steel center which its original promoters had envisioned.[126] After the turn of the century the town slowly began to revive. As a symbol of its new life, its English suffix was dropped, and the town became simply Middlesboro. Far from being a great industrial voice in the New South, however, Middlesboro turned its interests inward and concentrated its efforts on the de-

123. Colman McCarthy, "Going Home to Appalachia," Cleveland *Plain Dealer*, 9 Oct. 1975.

124. See Tipton, *The Cumberland Coal Field*.

125. Gaventa, "Power and Powerlessness," 105–7; McCague, *The Cumberland*, 202–3.

126. McCague, *The Cumberland*, 202–3.

velopment of the coal and timber resources of the surrounding mountains. In the twentieth century it became one of the leading coal mining centers of the Cumberland Plateau.

Although the great international financial and industrial schemes at Middlesborough failed, events from 1886 to 1893 did succeed in opening up eastern Kentucky to outside exploitation. The collapse of Middlesborough was hardly noticed by most mountaineers, but the events that the enterprise had set in motion touched the lives of every family living in the area. In the years after 1900, railroads extended their lines deep into the heart of the Cumberland Plateau, tapping the Harlan, the Hazard, the Elkhorn, and other coal fields. At the height of the reign of King Coal, large northern companies opened shafts and constructed mining camps on almost every creek and hollow in the plateau, but the pattern for these developments had been established in the last decades of the nineteenth century. It was during these years that the future of the mountains had received its most crippling blow.

Riding from Pineville to Middlesborough and Big Stone Gap in 1889, Charles Dudley Warner had stumbled upon the revolution that was transforming the mountains. Everywhere about him industrialists, speculators, railroad men, and coal barons were busy remaking the civilization and structure of mountain life. "It is my belief," he wrote, "that this central and hitherto neglected portion of the United States will soon become the theatre of vast and controlling industries." The "remarkable progress" that was taking place in the mountains, he added, would inevitably provide for this region a "prosperous" and "great future."[127]

Unfortunately for Appalachia, only Warner's first prediction was correct. By the turn of the century, the Appalachian South had become the economic colony of the urban Northeast, and Warner's "vast and controlling industries" had begun to sap the region of its mineral and timber wealth. As the resources of the mountains flowed wantonly out of the region, so did any hope for the independence and prosperity of the mountain people. The selling of the mountains, therefore, was only the first stage in the eventual modernization of Appalachia, but it marked the beginning of the process that would make miners and millhands out of the southern mountaineers.

127. Warner, "Comments on Kentucky," 271.

# CHAPTER THREE

# THE LAST GREAT TREES

THE ANCIENT FORESTS of Appalachia had always played an important role in the daily lives of the mountaineers, but with the coming of the railroads, the great trees took on a new importance. Since the earliest settlement, mountain farmers had cut some timber to clear fields and to construct buildings, fence lines, furniture, and farm implements. For generations, hogs and sometimes cattle had been turned out into the forests to graze on the mast of the huge chestnuts, oaks, and hickories. After the Civil War, many farm families had begun to engage in occasional cutting of timber for sale to local sawmills. Almost every mountain county during these years had at least one sawmill, which usually was combined with a gristmill and located along the banks of a stream. North Carolina mountain counties were typical of the region. Jackson County, for example, had seven of these mills in 1883, Haywood County had thirteen, and Ashe County had nineteen.[1] Prior to the 1890s, however, the market for sawed lumber had been localized; the technology employed was simple, and the amount of timber cut made only a slight impact upon the region's vast forest reserves.

As late as 1900, over 75 percent of the southern Appalachian region remained in woodland. Although some of the largest walnut, cherry, and other figured hardwoods had been culled, most of the commercial timber was as yet untouched. Almost 10 percent remained in virgin condition.[2] Travelers through the region in the late nineteenth century commonly reported finding large stands of poplar, oak, spruce, hemlock, and chestnut, in which trees reached from 4 to

1. J.H. Chataigne, *Chataigne's North Carolina State Directory and Gazetteer, 1883–1884* (Raleigh, 1883).
2. U.S. Department of Interior, U.S. Geological Survey, *The Southern Appalachian Forests,* by H.B. Ayers and W.W. Ashe, Professional Paper No. 37 (Washington, D.C., 1905), 15; Horace Kephart Journal, vol. 1, 57, Horace Kephart Papers, Western Carolina Univ.

8 feet in diameter and more than 150 feet in height. "These are the heaviest and most beautiful hardwood forests of the continent," wrote Secretary of Agriculture James Wilson to President William McKinley in 1901. "In them species from east and west, north and south, mingle in a growth of unparalleled richness and variety. They contain many species of the first commercial value and furnish important supplies which cannot be obtained from any other region."[3]

Such a storehouse of virgin timber could not long remain untapped in a nation moving rapidly toward industrialization. Following upon the heels of the promoters, the railroad builders, and the mineral men were agents representing northern lumber barons who had begun to cast covetous eyes on Appalachian timberlands. By the late 1880s, the timber resources of the Northeast and Great Lakes had begun to diminish as a result of industrialization and population growth, and northern lumber producers began to search other areas of North America for their timber supplies. Some looked to the virgin woodlands of Canada; others to the pine and cypress forests of the lower Mississippi and the Gulf Coast; but it was to the coves and ridges of the southern mountains that many of the timber interests turned for their future source of hardwoods.[4] At first, they were content to acquire only the superior trees, but between 1890 and 1920 the lumber barons purchased and cut over huge tracts of mountain timberland, devastating the region's forests in one of the most frenzied timber booms in American history. For thousands of mountaineers, the coming of the timber industry not only meant the loss of valuable woodland, but it meant the introduction of the first major form of nonagricultural work as well. In many areas of Appalachia—especially the noncoal regions—the arrival of the lumbermen heralded the beginning of the new age.

## EARLY LOGGING

Logging in the southern mountains passed through two distinct phases. The first, which began about 1880, was characterized by

3. Quoted in Kephart Journal, vol. 1, 57.
4. *Manufacturers' Record* 13 (18 Feb. 1888), 14. See also Robert S. Lambert, "Logging the Great Smokies, 1880–1930," *Tennessee Historical Quarterly* 21 (Dec. 1961), 350–63; Jarner W. Silver, "Hardwood Producers Come of Age," *Journal of Southern History*, 23 (1957), 427–53; Caudill, *Night Comes to the Cumberlands*, 61–69.

*A Great Yellow Poplar in Southwest Virginia. Courtesy of the Archives of Appalachia, East Tennessee State University.*

selective cutting of choice trees in areas along the more accessible rivers and streams. Long before they established their first sawmills in the region, the northern lumber barons began to send scouts into the mountains to search out and purchase the best hardwood trees. Riding into the hollows on horseback, these scouts located, acquired, and branded the largest black walnut, yellow poplar, and ash trees —wood that had begun to disappear in northern forests. This timber was then felled and transported to portable sawmills or floated down the river to large mills and distribution centers in flatland towns. In this manner, trees of exceptional quality were removed before major operations began. Fifty cents a foot across the stump was the average price paid to local farmers for such trees—a four-foot tree bringing two dollars.[5]

This period of selective cutting did not substantially alter the economy or lifestyles of the mountaineers. The outside timber companies were not yet prepared to buy large tracts of land or stumpage, or to build expensive sawmills in the mountains. This would come later, when the more accessible forests had been expended and the demand for lumber was at its peak. During the early period of logging operations, the companies relied primarily on water transportation and on the seasonal labor of mountain farmers. Only a few large mills were constructed within the region, and these were located along the trunk lines of major railroads. One of the larger mills was built at St. Albans in Kanawha County, West Virginia, and received logs that were floated down the Coal and the Kanawha rivers.[6] Another was established at Waynesville, North Carolina, along the line of the Western North Carolina Railroad in Haywood County. It received quantities of walnut, cherry, and oak supplied by local residents.[7]

Most of the timber cut in the mountains during the 1880s and 1890s was felled by farm families during the slack season in agriculture and transported to big mills at cities such as Nashville, Frankfort, and Cincinnati. Logging became an important source of supplementary income to farm families living along the headwaters of the Tennessee, Kentucky, Big Sandy, and Cumberland rivers, or to anyone who was willing to transport logs over the rugged mountain roads by

5. Stanley F. Horn, *This Fascinating Lumber Business* (New York, 1943), 108.
6. Roy B. Clarkson, *Tumult on the Mountain: Lumbering in West Virginia, 1770–1920* (Parsons, W.Va., 1964), 49.
7. Lambert, "Logging the Great Smokies," 353–54.

wagon. The early timber buyers usually purchased their trees "on the stump" and made arrangements with the seller to deliver the logs to the sawmill. This was generally accomplished in one of two ways. The farmer and his sons could "snake" the huge logs out of the mountains with a team of oxen and carry them to portable sawmills installed for that purpose, or he could drag the logs to the head of a creek and let the spring rains carry his product to market.

The latter method proved to be the most popular and resulted in the construction of a number of "splash dams" along tributaries of the larger creeks. A splash dam was an earthen dam built across a stream above the area being logged. A large gate made of straight poles was constructed in the middle of the dam, and after the logs were dumped into the creek below, the poles were pulled out, allowing the water to carry the logs out into the main waterway.[8] Occasionally, several splash dams would be built on the tributaries of the same creek and would be opened in such a way that all of the logs converged on the main stream at one time, forming a great mass of rocks, water, and timber that roared down the hollow, stripping the creek banks of everything in its path. "They'd let that water open," remembered one mountaineer, "and we lived upon the creek and . . . it just look[ed] like a big thunder cloud a comin'. As it come it raised them logs right off of that water and took 'em right on down the river."[9]

Unfortunately, the splash dam technique not only destroyed the creek bank, it also resulted in considerable loss of logs along the way. Families who lived close to the larger streams, therefore, often chose to tie their logs together into long rafts that were ridden with the spring "tides" down the slow-moving rivers to sawmills in the bluegrass. The average raft would carry about 70 logs, but giant rafts of 100 to 150 logs were not uncommon. Small shelters were sometimes built on the rafts, and oars 20 to 50 feet long were placed on the ends to permit steering.[10] On a clouded and rainy morning in March or April, the mountain men would set off with their rafts on the long

8. Gibson P. Vance, "Logging and Lumbering in Washington County, Virginia," unpublished MS, 1965, vertical files, Emory and Henry Oral History Project, Emory and Henry College, 11.

9. American Jarrell, Bandytown, W. Va., interview by Gary Miller, 26 Feb. 1973, Appalachian Oral History Project, Special Collections, James E. Morrow Library, Marshall University, 9.

10. Clarkson, *Tumult on the Mountain*, 48–49; Gibson, "The Economic History of Boyd County, Kentucky," 34.

journey to the sawmill towns. After trading in the valley communities, they would walk back to their mountain farms to put in another crop and fell more trees to be rafted downstream again the following spring.[11] By the 1890s, logs or rafts were being floated out of all of the mountain counties of Kentucky and many of the counties in West Virginia, Virginia, Tennessee, and North Carolina.[12] Rafting was so popular in parts of Kentucky that at times the mouths of the Cumberland and Big Sandy rivers were blocked for miles by solid lines of rafts. In the spring of 1903, before the arrival of the coal industry in northeast Kentucky, more than one thousand Big Sandy rafts were reported to have touched at Catlettsburg on their way to Cincinnati.[13]

Early logging operations of this kind provided mountain farmers with additional income, but they did not change the agricultural rhythms of daily life. Mountain men had always engaged in seasonal work in the woods—hunting, clearing fields, cutting fence posts, and the like. Now they received added cash income for their efforts. Work continued to be done, moreover, on a family basis, rather than by logging crews. Neither did selective cutting threaten the overall character of mountain timber or destroy the chance for its reproduction. Many of the lower creeks were stripped of their choicest trees, but the high ridges and remote coves were left untouched. Unlike conditions left by later logging operations, no large areas were completely denuded of timber, and fires directly attributable to logging were rare.[14]

From the perspective of outside lumber producers, however, such logging practices were economically inefficient. The percentage of logs lost between the mountains and the sawmills was high. Some were damaged by floods or the accidental breaking of splash dams, while others took years to work their way downstream, arriving at the mill waterlogged and worthless. But the greatest problem for the

11. For an interesting description of logging and rafting practices in eastern Kentucky, see John Fox, Jr., *Blue-Grass and Rhododendron*, 59–61.

12. Clarkson, *Tumult on the Mountain*, 49; Lambert, "Logging the Great Smokies," 352–53; Steven A. Schulman, "The Lumber Industry of the Upper Cumberland River Valley," *Tennessee Historical Quarterly* 32 (Fall 1973), 260–62.

13. Schulman, "The Lumber Industry," 262; Gibson, "The Economic History of Boyd County, Kentucky" 34; Chapman, "The Influence of Coal in the Big Sandy Valley," 23.

14. Lambert, "Logging the Great Smokies," 333.

producers was the uncertainty of supply, which kept many mills shut down during the dry seasons of the year.[15] As the demand for hardwood timber burgeoned, therefore, many of the lumber companies began to supplement their existing operations by acquiring tracts of timberlands in unexploited areas of the mountains. After hiring a logging crew, opening a sawmill, and constructing a timber camp, the company was ready to engage in the sustained production of lumber. These initial companies were subsequently joined by other larger companies, preparing the stage for the second phase of logging in the mountains—the systematic cutting of the remaining timber by large, well-integrated operations.

The purchase of timberland by the companies and the removal of the mills to the site of logging operations were made possible by the opening up of the region by the major railroads. After 1890, most of the railroads had continued to build branch lines deeper into the mountains, enabling the lumber companies to establish their mills close to the source of the timber supply. By adding their own logging railroads to the branch lines, the lumbermen were able to reach the most remote hollows and coves. The money behind this new expansion, like that which had backed the earlier phase of the timber industry's development, was primarily from the North. The outside lumber interests were willing to commit the capital for land acquisition, railroad construction, and labor costs, but they expected high rates of production that could not be achieved by selective cutting. Over the next three decades, the production methods used by these companies resulted in rapid removal of almost all of the region's valuable timber and left the land scarred, burned over, and eroded beyond any level attained with the limited logging practices of the local population.

With the decline of selective cutting, moreover, the production of timber in the mountains was no longer just a seasonal extension of agriculture. As logging shifted from a family enterprise to a highly integrated industrial operation, mountain men spent more and more time away from the farm living in the timber camps and logging towns. By 1906, when large-scale operations were in full swing, there were over 10,000 men employed full time in logging in eastern

15. See *Manufacturers' Record* 68 (9 Sept. 1915), 43. According to the editors of this magazine, "Possibly no other line of endeavor is so wholly dependent upon volume for profits as lumber. . . . Therefore, the ability to operate an efficient plant full time during dull periods is essential to the success of a sawmilling enterprise."

Kentucky alone.[16] The new form the industry took after 1890 was to have a greater impact upon the land and people of southern Appalachia than any of the mountain residents had envisioned.

## THE TIMBER BOOM: 1890–1920

The great timber boom in the mountains had its origins in the last years of the nineteenth century, as northern lumbermen began to acquire land and standing timber in the region. For the most part, the owners of the small, semiportable sawmills were obliged to purchase their timber on the stump from other landowners, while the larger companies preferred to cut from their own extensive tracts.[17] As early as 1885, land and timber companies were being organized to purchase tracts of from 30,000 to 300,000 acres; within a decade, competition for the best timberlands became intense.

In eastern Kentucky, northern companies began to buy timber property in the Big Sandy Valley as early as 1888. In that year, the Thomas Lumber Company and the Chicago Lumber Company acquired tracts in Floyd County and began to cut logs for the Cincinnati market.[18] Three years later, in 1891, the Yellow Poplar Lumber Company of Ironton, Ohio, came to the area and began to purchase large amounts of land along the headwaters of the Big Sandy River. The largest lumber company to operate in the Big Sandy Basin, the Yellow Poplar Lumber Company, owned land not only in eastern Kentucky but also in Dickenson County, Virginia, and Logan and Mingo counties, West Virginia, as well. At its Dickenson County property, the company constructed a huge concrete splash dam near the mouth of Bartlick Creek on Russell Fork, and during the first nine months of its operation loggers put into the Big Sandy River about forty million board feet of choice poplar logs. The dam remained in use until the company ceased operations in 1917.[19]

The completion of the Kentucky Union Railroad from Lexington to Breathitt County in 1891 opened the timberlands of much of the

16. The Lexington *Herald*, 16 Dec. 1906, quoted in Watson, "Economic and Cultural Development of Eastern Kentucky," 132.
17. Kenneth B. Pomeroy and James G. Yoho, *North Carolina Lands: Ownership, Use, and Management of Forest and Related Lands* (Washington, D.C., 1964), 21.
18. Scalf, *Kentucky's Last Frontier*, 214–15.
19. *Ibid.*, 216–18; Cubby, "The Transformation of the Tug and Guyandot Valleys," 136.

central portion of eastern Kentucky to lumbermen. The owners of the Kentucky Union Railroad, one of whom was F.D. Carley of the Standard Oil Company, controlled about 300,000 acres of hardwood forests along the line of the new road.[20] After the turn of the century, these properties became the site of extensive logging operations. Jackson, the largest town in Breathitt County, increased its population fivefold in the decade after the coming of the railroad and became the location of a number of large sawmills, a flooring mill, and a planing mill. Nearby, a Canadian firm built the short-lived timber town of Royalton on the Breathitt-Magoffin County line, and a Cincinnati company, Mowbray and Robinson, developed about 60,000 acres of forest in Leslie and Clay counties.[21]

Similar developments followed the extension of the Cumberland Valley branch of the L&N Railroad into southeastern Kentucky. The events around Middlesborough in the 1890s stimulated the growth of large developments in Whitley, Knox, and Bell counties. Although the American Association, Ltd., owned much of the best timberland, many smaller companies leased land from the association for the production of crossties, lumber, shingles, tanbark, and other materials.[22] By 1910, neighboring Knox County had thirty sawmills in full operation, including those of the Southern Pump Company, the Indian Lumber Company, the Pine Mountain Coal and Lumber Company, and the Bauer Cooperage Company.[23]

One of the largest and most successful of the lumber companies that operated in southeast Kentucky was founded in 1890 by Thomas Jefferson Asher of Clay County. The T.J. Asher and Sons Lumber Company operated a large bandmill near Pineville in Bell County and eventually acquired thousands of acres of timberland in surrounding counties. In 1896, the Asher interests were bought out by the Burt and Brabb Lumber Company, owned by Michigan capitalists. The latter firm had been purchasing mineral and timber properties in Leslie and Harlan counties for several years, acquiring some tracts for as little as twenty cents an acre.[24] After selling his lumber

20. *Manufacturers' Record* 14 (3 Nov. 1888), 13.
21. Watson, "Economic and Cultural Development of Eastern Kentucky," 134–35; *Manufacturers' Record* 70 (9 Nov. 1916), 59.
22. Howard, "Chapters in the Economic History of Knox County, Kentucky," 23.
23. *Ibid.*, 7, 27.
24. James Henry Jeffries to Mrs. Charles W. Burt, 7 Dec. 1937, Correspondence, and "Abstracts of Titles of the Burt and Brabb Lumber Company's Eastern

company to the Michigan group, T.J. Asher invested in about 50,000 acres of coal lands in Bell and Harlan counties and established the Asher Coal Company, which operated mines at Colmar, Varilla, Tejay (named after Asher), Coxton, Wood, and Chevrolet. Elected judge in Bell County for several terms, Asher made a considerable fortune from his coal and lumber properties. According to the historian of Bell County, he was "by far the leading industrialist . . . and one of the greatest businessmen southeastern Kentucky ever produced."[25]

The practice of combining coal and lumber interests became common in eastern Kentucky after 1900, as land companies sought to exploit both the mineral and timber wealth of their properties. In 1912, for instance, bankers from New York and Toronto, Canada, created the Kentucky Coal and Timber Development Company to develop 90,000 acres of land they had acquired in Breathitt and Knott counties. In Bell County, the Pine Mountain Coal and Lumber Company was organized to engage in both mining and logging activities.[26] Perhaps the best known example of this practice, however, was the Stearns Coal and Lumber Company of Ludington, Michigan, which came to eastern Kentucky in 1903 to develop 113,000 acres of coal and timberlands. Founded by Justus S. Stearns, a wealthy lumber baron, the Stearns Coal and Lumber Company built the big company mining and timber town of Stearns in McCreary County and operated mines and logging camps in Whitley and Wayne counties, Kentucky, and Fentress and Scott counties, Tennessee. The company erected a giant lumber mill at Stearns and maintained a private railroad that stretched for almost thirty miles, connecting the company's vast interests.[27]

Other areas of the southern Appalachian coal fields also experienced significant timber booms before the arrival of the coal industry. Most of the counties contiguous with the lines of the C&O and N&W in southern West Virginia began to market lumber shortly after the arrival of the railroads. The major absentee land companies of that

Kentucky Lands," Burt and Brabb Lumber Company Papers, Univ. of Kentucky, Box 7, no. 73W4.

25. Fuson, *History of Bell County,* 370.

26. *Manufacturers' Record* 62 (1 Aug. 1912), 71; Howard, "Chapters in the Economic History of Knox County, Kentucky," 27.

27. *Manufacturers' Record* 43 (18 June 1903), 439; *ibid.,* 58 (27 Oct. 1910), *ibid* 78 (11 Nov. 1920), 117.

section—the Flat Top Coal Land Association, the Beaver Coal Company, and the Guyandot Coal Land Association—leased land not only for coal mining but for timber production as well. The land that was not purchased by the railroads or the coal men was quickly bought up in the 1890s by commercial timbermen. According to the West Virginia State Board of Agriculture in 1900, "alien owners" controlled 75 percent of the saleable timber in Wyoming County, 66 percent of that in Logan County, 60 percent in Mingo County, and 40 percent in McDowell County.[28]

The most extensive logging operations in West Virginia were established north of the New River in Tucker, Pocahontas, and other counties, but large lumber companies also operated throughout southern West Virginia.[29] In the Tug and Guyandot valleys, three companies controlled most of the lumber production: the Little Kanawha Lumber Company, a Maine corporation; the Yellow Poplar Lumber Company; and C. Crane and Company of Cincinnati.[30] The W.M. Ritter Lumber Company, owned by William McClellan Ritter of Pennsylvania, held large tracts of timberland in Mingo, McDowell, Wyoming, and Mercer counties, West Virginia, as well as land in nearby Pike County, Kentucky, and Buchanan County, Virginia. Ritter constructed his first sawmill in 1890 at Oakvale in Mercer County and later built one of the only company-owned timber towns in southern West Virginia at Maben in Wyoming County.[31] Before the end of the great timber boom, the Ritter Lumber Company became one of the largest hardwood producers in the country and the owner of timberlands in almost every state of the Appalachian South.[32]

In southwest Virginia, the evolution of the timber industry followed a pattern similar to that in Kentucky and West Virginia, rising in the 1890s and reaching a peak shortly after the turn of the century. About the time that W.M. Ritter was opening his first sawmills in

28. State Board of Agriculture of West Virginia, *Fifth Biennial Report, 1899–1900*, quoted in Cubby, "The Transformatoin of the Tug and Guyandot Valleys," 139.

29. See Clarkson, *Tumult on the Mountain*, for the history of the timber industry in northern West Virginia.

30. Cubby, "The Transformation of the Tug and Guyandot Valleys," 135–36; Walter R. Thurmond, *The Logan Coal Field of West Virginia: A Brief History* (Morgantown, W.Va., 1964), 18.

31. Clarkson, *Tumult on the Mountain*, 96–97.

32. William M. Ritter Lumber Company, *The Romance of Appalachian Hardwood Lumber* (Columbus, Ohio, 1940), 13–15, 30–33.

*Millhands at a Small Sawmill in Southwest Virginia. Courtesy of George Stephenson, Emory, Virginia.*

Mercer County, West Virginia, a syndicate of Wisconsin timber operators began to produce lumber from about 26,000 acres of timber property in neighboring Giles County, Virginia.[33] Subsidiaries of the N&W Railroad leased timberland to a number of small operators along its line, and later the Clinchfield Timber Corporation, an affiliate of the Clinchfield Railroad, developed almost 25,000 acres of forest in Scott and Wise counties.[34] Much of the lumber produced in the coal counties of Virginia was utilized in the construction of railroads, company towns, tipples, and other needs of the expanding coal industry, but in the noncoal counties of Smyth, Grayson, and Washington to the south, commercial timber production became an important part of the local economy.

During the last decades of the nineteenth century, practically all of the timberland in these counties passed into the hands of outside interests, which after 1900 began rapidly to develop the properties. One of the largest landholders was the Douglass Land Company of New York, controlled by the heirs of George Douglass. The company was founded in 1893 to develop 113,000 acres of land in southwest Virginia, and it subsequently began to lease land to northern lumbermen.[35] Pennsylvania interests acquired some of the best of the Douglass lands on White Top Mountain, Mount Rogers, and the upper valley of the Laurel Fork of the Holston River, and established lumber companies at both ends of the property. The Laurel River Lumber Company operated out of Damascus, and the United States Spruce Lumber Company worked out of Marion.[36]

Other Pennsylvania lumbermen established the Damascus Lumber Company in 1904 and the Hassinger Lumber Company east of Damascus in 1905. The latter company built a sawmill and company town at Konnarock, and the Grayson Lumber Company built similar facilities at nearby Fairwood.[37] Logging operations became so intense in the Mount Rogers area after 1900 that a logging railroad was constructed from Abingdon in Washington County to West Jefferson in Ashe County, North Carolina, to provide an outlet

33. *Manufacturers' Record* 26 (21 Sept. 1894), 118.
34. *Ibid.* 64 (4 Dec. 1913), 64.
35. Gibson P. Vance, "Lumbering in Washington County," 4–5.
36. *Manufacturers' Record* 60 (7 Dec. 1911), 68.
37. Vance, "Lumbering in Washington County," 20–22; J. Richard Campbell, interview by Cynthia Legard, 27 Aug. 1973, Emory and Henry Oral History Project, Transcript no. 86, Emory and Henry College, 3–4.

for finished lumber. The Virginia-Carolina Railroad—or the Virginia Creeper, as the little railroad was called—further opened up the forests along the Virginia–North Carolina border, transforming the local economy into a bustling lumber products center.[38]

These activities in the Blue Ridge counties of southwest Virginia were the precursor of the great logging operations that descended on the mountains of Tennessee, North Carolina, and Georgia after the turn of the century. As the timber industry completed its work in the Cumberland Plateau, it increasingly turned its attention to the magnificent forests of the Great Smoky Mountains and southern Blue Ridge, leaving behind only the ravaged hillsides and occasional scrub oaks to be used for mining props by the emergent coal industry. The lumbermen had launched the new era in the coal fields, but their impact was soon subsumed by the mining of coal. In fact, the Appalachian timber boom reached its peak not in the coal fields, but rather in the logging operations of the Smokies, and there it would have its greatest effect upon the lives of mountain people.

The mountain farmers of the Blue Ridge, like their counterparts in West Virginia and Kentucky, had long engaged in selective logging, but it was not until the coming of the railroads that developments began to stir on a large scale. The major event in the history of western North Carolina in the late nineteenth century, for example, was the arrival of the Western North Carolina Railroad in Asheville on 3 October 1880. The railroad had been twenty-five years in the making, and its construction had been marred by tragedy, war, political intrigue, and considerable human sacrifice.[39] Many in Asheville believed that, with the coming of the iron horse, their region would at last "get into step with other sections of the country that were going forward in the march of progress."[40]

The railroad was soon extended west of Asheville in two directions. The northern branch reached Paint Rock on the Tennessee line in 1882, providing connections with the East Tennessee, Vir-

---

38. Gibson P. Vance, "An Unique Little Railroad: The Virginia Creeper," unpublished paper, Emory and Henry Oral History Project, Emory and Henry College, n.d., 1–4.

39. Willaim Donaldson Cotton, "Appalachian North Carolina: A Political Study 1860–1889" (Ph.D. diss., Univ. of North Carolina, 1954), 37–38; Ina Woestemeyer Van Noppen and John J. Van Noppen, *Western North Carolina Since the Civil War* (Boone, N.C., 1973), 256–61.

40. Quoted in Dudley W. Crawford, "The Coming of the Railroad to Asheville 70 Years Ago," *Asheville Citizen*, 29 Oct. 1950.

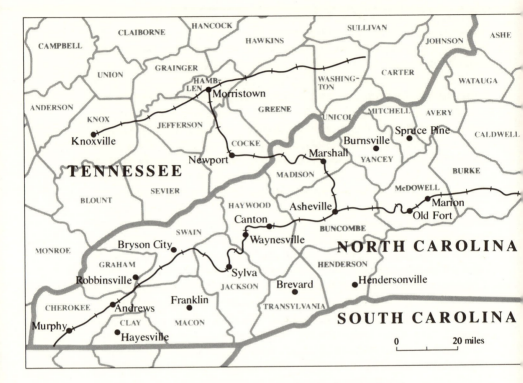

*6. The Western North Carolina Railroad*

ginia, and Georgia Railroad to Knoxville, and the southern branch was constructed to Waynesville in 1884 and to Murphy on the Georgia border in 1890, where it connected with the L&N.[41] The completion of these two branch lines opened up the timberlands of western North Carolina and north Georgia to exploitation. Anticipating the arrival of the railroad, for instance, a group of Minnesota capitalists organized the North Georgia Land Company and began acquiring tracts of land in Pickens, Fannin, Gilmer, and Murray counties, Georgia.[42] Similar speculations occurred in western North

41. Cotton, "Appalachian North Carolina," 38–39.
42. *Manufacturer's Record* 13 (17 March 1888), 30.

Carolina, especially after the reorganization of the railroad as the Southern Railway Company in 1894.[43]

The most dramatic developments, however, occurred in the little mountain town of Asheville. Shortly after the coming of the Western North Carolina Railroad, another line was completed from Spartan-burg, South Carolina, to Asheville, turning that and nearby com-munities such as Tryon, Hendersonville, and Brevard into major tourist centers. Asheville, with a population of only 2,000 in 1880, experienced phenomenal growth, becoming a city of 10,000 by 1890.[44] Soon, tourists by the thousands were pouring into the city for the purported health benefits of its mountain air, water, and climate. As Asheville grew into a major health resort, it also became an important stop for speculators and lumbermen interested in mountain lands. During the next decade, the growth of land sales and logging operations in western North Carolina was staggering.

One of the first outsiders to establish logging operations in western North Carolina was C.F. Buffum, a lumberman from Maine. Buf-fum had operated sawmills on the Penobscot River in Maine, but the dwindling supply of timber in that area led him to western North Carolina, where in 1888 he set up a bandmill on the Tuckaseigee River in Jackson County. His mill was the first of many bandmills in the area.[45] Later that same year, another company, the Linville Land, Manufacturing, and Mining Company of Wilmington, North Carolina, laid out the town of Linville in present Avery County and began to cut timber from the surrounding forests. By 1890, the Una-ka Timber Company of Knoxville had bought up tracts of timber-land in Yancey, Mitchell, Buncombe, and Madison counties, and a Glasgow firm, the Scottish Carolina Timber and Land Company, purchased 120,000 acres of land in Haywood and Madison coun-ties to supply its mill and log boom in Newport, Tennessee.[46] In 1892, the Crosby Lumber Company of Greenville, Michigan, purchased 47,000 acres of land in Graham County, and two

43. Van Noppen, *Western North Carolina*, 258.

44. *Ibid.*, 262; U.S. Department of Interior, Bureau of the Census, *Compendium of the Eleventh Census, 1890* (Washington, D.C., 1892), 296.

45. John Parris, "When Buffum's Band Mill Came to Dillsboro," Asheville *Citizen*, 29 July 1978.

46. Cotton, "Appalachian North Carolina," 57; Lambert, "Logging the Great Smokies," 332.

years later, the Foreign Hardwood Log Company, a New York syndicate, and the Dickson-Mason Lumber Company of Illinois acquired tracts of 78,000 and 34,000 acres, respectively, in Swain County.[47] Another New York firm, the Tuckaseigee Timber Company, operated on 75,000 acres of land in Swain, Jackson, and Macon counties.[48]

The sudden growth of tourism around Asheville in the 1890s directly enhanced the growth of the timber industry in Buncombe and Transylvania counties. In 1895, Joseph H. Silverstein visited the Lake Toxaway area, and, after recognizing the economic potential of the region, "he and a group of associates built the Toxaway Tanning Company, organized the Gloucester Lumber Company, leased a boundary of several thousand acres of valuable timberlands, and built a large band sawmill."[49] Millionaire J.F. Haynes, who came to Transylvania County because of poor health, founded the Brevard Tanning Company at Pisgah Forest to manufacture tannic acid from chestnut bark.[50] Other northern tourists were so impressed with the natural wealth they found in the area that they invested heavily in timber properties. A group of capitalists from Williamsport, Pennsylvania, purchased 50,000 acres of timberland in Buncombe County in 1895 and began development of the property the following year.[51] Later, the Asheville Lumber and Manufacturing Company was organized by a group of Ohio promoters, while investors from Michigan formed a similar firm, the Asheville French Broad Lumber Company.[52]

The most notable tourist and subsequent land developer, however, was George Washington Vanderbilt, grandson of Commodore Cornelius Vanderbilt. The young aristrocrat came to Asheville for his health in the spring of 1888 and was so impressed by the countryside that he decided to purchase land and build a summer estate. Over the next several years, Vanderbilt secretly acquired some 120,000 acres

47. *Manufacturers' Record* 21 (8 April 1892), 41; *ibid.* 26 (17 Aug. 1894), 42; *ibid.* 26 (7 Dec. 1894), 286.
48. Cotton, "Appalachian North Carolina," 57nn.; *Manufacturers' Record* 26 (28 Sept. 1894), 134.
49. Van Noppen, *Western North Carolina*, 262.
50. *Ibid.*
51. *Manufacturers' Record* 29 (21 Feb. 1896), 57.
52. Cotton, "Appalachian North Carolina," 57–58.

of land, including fifty small farms and ten "country places."[53] He then hired the renowned New York architect Richard Morris Hunt and the premier landscape architect Frederick Law Olmsted to design and construct a French Renaissance-style castle unequaled anywhere in the United States. Biltmore House, as Vanderbilt called his 250-room castle, was filled with rare paintings, tapestries, porcelain, and antiques from Europe and surrounded by elegant gardens, greenhouses, and a conservatory. At Olmsted's suggestion, a "model village" was built near the entrance to the estate, housing a hospital, stores, and a church, and a system of forest management was instituted in the Biltmore Forest.[54]

Vanderbilt employed a young Pennsylvania forester named Gifford Pinchot to oversee the development of his forest and to demonstrate the economic value of managed forestry. Determined to show a profit from his forests, Vanderbilt purchased a "private game preserve" of 100,000 acres of virgin timber in Buncombe, Transylvania, Henderson, and Haywood counties, renaming it the Pisgah Forest. Under Pinchot's direction, logging operations were begun at the foot of Mount Pisgah in 1893, but the Pennsylvanian was succeeded two years later by a German forester, Carl Alwin Schenck. Schenck in turn oversaw the construction of a small railroad line into the property, the removal of thousands of board feet of virgin yellow poplar, the planting of seedling trees, and the establishment of the first forestry school in the United States. Schenck, like Pinchot, emphasized not preservation but forest management practices that would assure the continued production of saleable timber. During Schenck's years at Biltmore, the Vanderbilt properties were among the leading producers of hardwood timber in the region.[55]

By 1900, the timber industry had become a major part of the economy of western North Carolina. In addition to the hundreds of small steam mills set up throughout the region, large bandmills with a capacity of more than 50,000 board feet a day were operating at Lenoir, Pinola, and Nantahala, and major tanneries had been erected

53. Carl Alwin Schenck, *The Birth of Forestry in America: The Biltmore Forest School, 1898–1913* (Boone, N.C. 1974), 25.
54. See Van Noppen, *Western North Carolina*, 298–301.
55. Schenck, *The Birth of Forestry*, 27–54; Van Noppen, *Western North Carolina*, 301–7; Harold K. Steen, *The U.S. Forest Service: A History* (Seattle, 1976), 48, 64.

at Morganton, Brevard, Lenoir, Asheville, Marion, Hazelwood, Waynesville, Andrews, and Murphy.[56] The manufacture of lumber and timber products had become the second leading industry in North Carolina, with 1,770 establishments employing some 11,751 workers—and most of these were in the western part of the state.[57] In 1900, the southern Appalachian region as a whole contributed some 30 percent of the total amount of hardwood timber cut in the United States.[58] Yet the advance guard of the timber industry had been able to reach only a fraction of the vast timber reserves, and great sections of remote woodland remained untouched. During the next decade, production continued to expand at an even faster pace, reaching a peak cut of almost 4 million board feet in 1909 (nearly 40 percent of the national production).[59] At the height of the timber boom in the Smokies, many of the pioneer companies were replaced by larger corporations that often operated on a multistate basis. These corporations brought greater amounts of capital and new technologies to the exploitation of the region's natural resources, constructing railroad lines deep into the timberlands and building temporary company towns to house the thousands of families employed by their operations.

One such firm was the William M. Ritter Lumber Company. Organized, as we have seen, in 1890 in West Virginia by a Pennsylvania lumberman, the company became the largest timber company operating in the southern Appalachians, and Ritter himself became known as "the dean of the Hardwood Lumbermen of America." In addition to extensive holdings of timber property in West Virginia, Virginia, Kentucky, and Tennessee, Ritter acquired almost 200,000 acres of timberland in western North Carolina, including a 70,000-acre tract in Macon and Clay counties, 70,000 acres in Swain County, and a large tract in Mitchell County. Under the name of the Wilson Creek Lumber Company, Ritter also purchased properties in Caldwell and Burke counties.[60] In 1909, another Ritter firm, the

56. U.S. Geological Survey, *The Southern Appalachian Forests*, 19.
57. U.S. Department of Interior, U.S. Census Office, *Twelfth Census of the United States, 1900: Manufacturers*, III.
58. U.S. Department of Agriculture, *Economic and Social Conditions*, 35.
59. U.S. Department of Agriculture, Forest Service, *Timber Growing and Logging Practice in the Southern Appalachian Region*, by E.H. Frothingham, Technical Bulletin No. 250 (Washington, D.C., 1931), 10.
60. Ritter Lumber Company, Romance of Appalachian Hardwood Lumber, 31.

*Logging Camp Housing of the W.M. Ritter Lumber Company, Big Branch, Dickenson County, Virginia. Courtesy of the Archives of Appalachia, East Tennessee State University.*

Hazel Creek Lumber Company, began operating a large bandmill at Procter in Swain County and the following year ran a railroad spur, the Smoky Mountain Railroad, up the Hazel Creek watershed.[61] By 1913, Ritter's enterprises had acquired over two billion board feet of hardwood timber in the Appalachian region.[62]

Other companies were dwarfed by Ritter's vast holdings, but they nevertheless had a major impact upon the region's forests. In the

61. *Ibid.*, 14, 30; John Parris, "They Felled the Giants of the Woodland," Asheville *Citizen*, 27 March 1977.

62. *Appalachian Trade Journal* 10 (Jan. 1913), 20; Ritter Lumber Company, *Romance of Appalachian Hardwood*, 15.

same year that Ritter opened his bandmill on Hazel Creek, another West Virginia firm, the Parson's Pulp and Lumber Company, acquired 35,000 acres of timberland on the reservation of the Eastern Band of the Cherokee Indians in Swain County. The land had been purchased from the Indians several years earlier by a Philadelphia company and was resold in 1909 for $18 an acre, netting a sizable profit for the northern investors. The Parsons Company planned to ship the virgin hemlock, chestnut, and poplar logs by rail to a large mill at Bryson City.[63] In subsequent years, the remote area between Bryson City and Robbinsville took on a boom town spirit, as large companies such as the H.L. Bemis Lumber Company, the Norwood Lumber Company, the Kitchen Lumber Company, and the Montvale Lumber Company moved in to join the West Virginia firms in the removal of the timber resources. The Montvale Lumber Company, which owned 27,000 acres of land on Eagle Creek, was actually a subsidiary of the R.E. Wood Lumber Company of Baltimore, Maryland, one of the largest lumber dealers on the East Coast. At the height of the great timber boom, more than 4,500 people lived within the area. More than 1,000 persons made their home at Proctor, and another 1,000 lived at the headwaters of Hazel Creek.[64]

A similar boom accompanied the construction of a sawmill at Pensacola, in Yancey County, by the Carolina Spruce Company of Philadelphia. The mill was erected to saw the huge native spruce about to be cut off the slopes of Mount Mitchell.[65] The rich forests of the Black Mountains surrounding Mount Mitchell attracted the attention of a number of outside investors, including a group of Chicago capitalists, who purchased a large tract of land in the area in 1911.[66] That same year, a syndicate from Troy, New York, purchased a tract of 40,000 acres in neighboring Madison County, along the Laurel River. Operating as the Laurel River Logging Company, the firm constructed a railroad from Runion up the river to the Tennessee state

63. Lambert, "Logging the Great Smokies," 334; *Manufacturers' Record* 56 (25 Nov. 1909), 53.
64. John Parris, "Nature Regains Land of Sawmills, Trains," Asheville *Citizen*, 25 March, 1965; *Manufacturers' Record* 72 (2 Aug. 1917), 85; Larry Mull, "Bemis Lumber Company and the Graham County Railroad," unpublished MS, n.d., University Archives, Western Carolina Univ.
65. "Timber! Started Railroad Boom" Yancey County *Common Times* 2 (Dec. 1976), 1–2.
66. *Manufacturers' Record* 59 (6 April 1911), 74; *Appalachian Trade Journal* 6 (April 1911), 24.

line and built large lumber mills at Runion and Pounding Mill.[67] Farther north, in Wilkes and Watauga counties, the Grandin Lumber Company was exploiting 70,000 acres of timberland recently tapped by the Watauga and Yadkin River Railroad. By 1913, the company had nearly completed a big sawmill at the new timber town of Grandin.[68]

Across the state line in Tennessee, the most ambitious operations in the Smokies were undertaken by Pennsylvania lumbermen. The Little River Lumber Company, owned by Philadelphia capitalists, logged on about 80,000 acres of choice timberlands in Blount and Sevier counties. Beginning in 1901, the company constructed the Little River Railroad for a distance of eighteen miles into the heart of the Smokies, from a junction with the Southern Railroad, and built a sawmill and company town at Townsend and a timber camp at Elkmont. By 1910, the millsite at Townsend was producing as much as 120,000 board feet a day and was employing hundreds of men.[69] In nearby Tellico Plains, Monroe County, another group of Pennsylvania lumbermen owned about 100,000 acres of land and operated as the Tellico River Lumber Company. This firm, too, constructed a standard-gauge railroad for about thirty miles to its timber properties and employed about 500 men.[70] Together, these two companies controlled most of the lumber production in the Tennessee Smokies.

Throughout the rest of east Tennessee, outside capitalists also controlled the logging industry. A group of West Virginia politicians and businessmen, including John W. Davis, acquired about 40,000 acres of timberland in western North Carolina and east Tennessee, and a similar group from Nashville controlled about 50,000 acres in Morgan, Fentress, and Cumberland counties.[71] New York interests owned the Tennessee Timber Coal and Iron Company, which together developed 80,000 acres of land in Cumberland County and constructed the mill and mining town of Catoosa.[72] A syndicate of

67. *Manufacturers' Record* 59 (9 Feb. 1911), 55.

68. "Developing Mountain Riches," *Manufacturers' Record* 64 (27 Nov. 1913), 49.

69. Robert S. Lambert, "Logging on Little River, 1890–1940," *East Tennessee Historical Society's Publications* 33 (1961), 36–38; Carlos Clinton Campbell, *Birth of a National Park in the Great Smoky Mountains* (Knoxville, 1960), 35.

70. *Appalachian Trade Journal* 7 (Sept. 1911), 22.

71. *Manufacturers' Record* 48 (27 July 1905), 46; *ibid.* 49 (10 May 1906), 472.

72. *Ibid.* 49 (1 March 1906), 174; *ibid* 61 (13 June 1912), 59; *ibid.* 63 (6 March 1913), 67.

English capitalists operated a sawmill on 30,000 acres of virgin timberland in Sevier County, and near Chattanooga, Cincinnati investors organized the Grand View Coal and Timber Company to develop 32,000 acres of land on Walden's Ridge.[73] Another Cincinnati firm, the Conasauga Lumber Company, operated on more than 65,000 acres of white pine and poplar forest in Polk County and in Fannin, Murray, and Gilmer counties, Georgia.[74]

The most spectacular developments of the post-1900 timber boom, however, were associated with the coming of the Champion Fiber Company and the subsequent founding of the town of Canton, North Carolina. No other lumber company had as great or as lasting an impact upon the Blue Ridge and the Smokies. Champion Fiber Company was organized in 1905 by Peter G. Thompson, owner of the Champion Coated Paper Company of Hamilton, Ohio. Thompson had visited western North Carolina in 1904, looking for timberland which would furnish a steady supply of wood pulp for his profitable Ohio paper mill. He found it in the thick forests along the Pigeon River in Haywood County, settling upon a spot five miles from the village of Clyde as the place for his pulp plant. The location was on the site of the defunct Eastern Capitalist Broom Company and offered abundant fresh water and easy access to the railroad and to timber supplies. In 1905, Thompson secured about 300,000 acres of surrounding mountain land, rich in spruce, balsam, and chestnut, and began the construction of a mill and a company town to be named Canton, after Canton, Ohio. Under the direction of his son-in-law, Reuben B. Robertson of Cincinnati, the enterprise expanded rapidly, including the development of massive logging operations on the three prongs of the Pigeon River.[75] "The whole scheme," wrote Carl Alwin Schenck, "was the most gigantic enterprise which western North Carolina had seen."[76]

Along with several other northern capitalists, Thompson organized the Champion Lumber Company in 1911 and, after purchasing an additional 100,000 acres, expanded his logging operations

73. *Ibid.* 57 (20 Jan. 1910), 57; *ibid.* 60 (13 July 1911), 52.
74. *Ibid.* 60 (26 Oct. 1911), 62c.
75. *Manufacturers' Record* 48 (14 Sept. 1905), 219; *ibid.* 48 (21 Sept. 1905), 267; Van Noppen, *Western North Carolina*, 308; Larry Mull, "Early Lumbering In Western North Carolina," unpublished MS, University Archives, Western Carolina Univ., 1–2.
76. Schenck, *Birth of Forestry in America*, 148.

throughout Haywood County and into Swain County and eastern Tennessee.[77] With the help of other subsidiary companies, such as the Suncrest Lumber Company, he constructed logging railroads in some of the most remote parts of the region and built large timber camps at Sunburst, Crestmont, Ravensford, and Smokemont. On the eve of World War I, Champion employed over 7,000 people in its North Carolina operations, including more than 1,000 at its Canton plant.[78] There were at that time some 6,000 people living in Canton and 2,000 more living in the surrounding area. The plant was consuming 300 to 350 cords of wood a day, and the output of wood pulp was 200 tons a day, most of which was shipped to the parent firm in Ohio. By 1930, the Canton factory had begun to develop and produce postcard paper and had grown into the largest paper and pulp mill in the nation.[79]

The coming of Champion Fiber Company to Haywood County coincided with the height of the timber boom in Appalachia. Although Champion continued to thrive, the timber industry as a whole declined rapidly after 1909. The large amounts of capital Thompson and his associates invested in the Champion plant and properties encouraged long-range planning to assure its continued operation. As early as the 1920s, Champion had established a program of reforestation on its cutover woodlands and was developing a process for using the fiber of fast-growing southern pines for making high-quality paper.[80] Most timber companies, however, were less concerned about the future earning value of their forested properties. As one local historian has noted, their attitude was, "All we want here is to get the most we can out of this country, as quick as we can, and then get out."[81] As a result, the cutting of commercial trees was usually

77. *Appalachian Trade Journal* 6 (April 1911), 15; *Manufacturers' Record* 59 (2 Feb. 1911), 74; *ibid.* 59 (6 April 1911), 74; Robert W. Griffith, "The Industrial Development of Western North Carolina," *Southern Tourist* (March 1926), 100–103. Thompson's major partners in the new lumber company included William Whitmer & Sons of Philadelphia, who owned several other logging operations in the area.

78. Mull, "Lumbering in Western North Carolina," 1–4.

79. Van Noppen, *Western North Carolina*, 308; Champion Paper and Fibre Company, *This Is Champion, A Proud Name in American Industry* (Canton, N.C., 1954), 12–13; *Manufacturers' Record* 65 (21 May 1914), 55.

80. Griffith, "Industrial Development of Western North Carolina," 103.

81. John Parris, "Lumber Barons Saw Gold in WNC's Trees," Asheville *Citizen*, 19 May 1978.

carried out with little or no concern for future growth, and the forests of the region were quickly devastated.

The introduction, moreover, of machine logging by the large lumber companies after 1910 added to the destruction of the mountain forests. The utilization of steam-powered equipment such as Shay locomotives, overhead cableway skidders, and giant bandsaws allowed operators to cut more timber at only a fraction of the cost of earlier methods. But when used with log slides, river flumes, and splash dams, the modern techniques destroyed the streambeds and the reproductive capacities of the land. Great woods fires became almost a yearly phenomenon in the Blue Ridge, as lightning or sparks from machinery ignited sawdust and slash piles left by the loggers. The opening of Champion and other pulp mills provided a market for the smallest trees, lending a new meaning to the term "merchantable timber."[82] Entire mountains were clearcut and left to erode with the spring rains. By 1919, these logging practices had begun to take their toll on the Appalachian hardwoods. In that year, timber production in Appalachia fell to 2.4 million board feet, and by 1929 it had dropped to little more than 2 million board feet.[83] After World War I, timber companies increasingly abandoned their southern mountain properties and turned west to the unexploited timberlands of Oregon and Washington. But the marks which they left on the land and people of Appalachia survived for generations to come.

Interviewed in 1910 by the *Manufacturers' Record*, the Reverend Dr. A.E. Brown, superintendent of the mountain school department of the Southern Baptist Convention, lamented the effects of the timber boom upon the Appalachian forests. Dr. Brown had been born and raised in the mountains and had devoted his life to the religious and educational well-being of the mountain people. His travels throughout the region had brought him into close touch with existing conditions and had led him to feel great apprehension for the future of the mountain country, owing to the destruction of the forest areas. "When I first started my work in these mountains, 30 years ago, when the forests were untouched," he noted, "the mountains were full of sparkling brooks and creeks which required a two or three weeks rain to make muddy; today, a few hours' rain will muddy them . . . ; many of the mountain streams are dry throughout the

82. Lambert, "Logging the Great Smokies," 357–59.
83. U.S. Department of Agriculture, *Economic and Social Conditions*, 35.

summer and fall, while in winter, the waters descend in torrents and do vast damage, rendering worthless the bottom lands which used to be the most desirable for farming purposes.''

Nearly all of the large tracts of timberlands, he added, had been bought up by outside companies. ''They have never been timbered by any methods that tend to conserve the forests for the future. These companies cut practically every tree from 12 inches up, and are utterly indifferent to the interest of the natives.'' In removing the timber, loggers had paid no attention to young growth, leaving piles of brush, bark, sawdust, and the tops of trees strewn throughout the forest. This dry brush frequently caught fire, severely burning thousands of acres of woodland, killing mature trees, seedlings, and saplings alike. Lesser fires of the undergrowth had affected at least 80 percent of the forested area. In some places, the young growth itself was now being cut for pulpwood, and the young chestnuts were being cut for the tannic acid they contained, so that between the fire and the pulpwood and tannic acid manufacturers, the remaining forest was being devastated. ''Unfortunately,'' Brown observed,

the men who owned timberlands did not seem to realize they had any other value beyond what they could get for them from the lumbermen, and as the lumbermen had no other interest other than to get out of the timberlands all that was possible, no thought was given to the effect which the cutting of the timber may have on the mountain regions or looking to reforesting the area.

While this work, of course, has given employment to the natives of the mountains since it has been going on, it is destroying the future for them, because the sides of the mountains have been denuded of their top soil and the bottom lands have been overflowed and swept away, thereby destroying their value for agricultural purposes.

I know areas containing hundreds of acres of lands which used to be most fertile and valuable, and which are now practically worthless. This does not apply alone to restricted lands, but can be seen throughout all parts of the Southern Appalachian mountain district.

Moreover, he concluded, the lumbermen had been strongly opposed to the states' passing laws to regulate the manner in which their work should be done, and they had worked strenuously against laws that would tend to curb their operations. ''These are some of the great changes that have taken place, all due to the lack of intelligent cutting of timber in the mountains. Those who have destroyed the forests reaped the only benefit; those left behind, the natives, will have to bear the brunt of this work."[84]

## THE NATIONAL FOREST MOVEMENT

The wanton destruction of Appalachian forests stirred a number of Americans like the Reverend Dr. Brown to push for government action to conserve the remaining mountain timberlands. Several decades earlier, a nascent conservation movement had begun to lobby for protection of the nation's forests, although most of the initial interest was in the protection of public lands in the West. Large timber companies that had acquired thousands of acres in the public domain by subterfuge and fraud had, by unrestrained cutting, begun to turn much of the land into wasteland.[85] In 1875, a group of concerned scientists formed the American Forestry Association (AFA) to look into the destruction of forest resources, and the following year, Congress established the Division of Forestry in the Department of Agriculture to gather statistics and disseminate information on forestry.[86] Pressure from conservation groups such as the AFA finally helped to secure passage in 1891 of the National Forest Reserve Act, which permitted the president to set aside portions of the public domain as "forest reserves" in which the land and resources would be retained permanently in public ownership. On 30 March 1891, President Benjamin Harrison created the first such reserve, the Yellowstone Timberland Reserve, and he later placed an additional thirteen million acres of timberland in Colorado, Wyoming, and California on the list of protected lands.[87] In 1897, Congress enacted the Organic Administration Act establishing guidelines for management of these forest reserves. According to the act, the national forests were to be managed for their own protection and "for the purpose of securing favorable conditions of water flow, and to furnish a continuous supply of timber for the use and necessities of citizens of the United States."[88] By 1900, the conservation movement had acquired significant political influence, and some 35

84. *Manufacturers' Record* 57 (20 Jan. 1910), 52.
85. William E. Shands and Robert G. Healy, *The Lands Nobody Wanted: A Conservation Foundation Report* (Washington, D.C., 1977), 10–11.
86. *Ibid.*, 12; Steen, *The U.S. Forest Service*, 13.
87. Steen, *U.S. Forest Service*, 27–28.
88. Shands and Healy, *Lands Nobody Wanted*, 10–11.

million acres of timberland had been designated for protection. Since federal legislation, however, provided no funds for the acquisition of private property for forest reserves, and since little public land remained in the heavily populated East, all of the land so designated was in the public domain west of the Mississippi. Increasingly, after the turn of the century, therefore, conservationists tended to campaign for the establishment of national forests in the East, especially in Appalachia.

The rapid growth of conservationism after 1890 coincided with the emergence in American politics of what is called the progressive era, and the effect of the conservation movement upon Appalachia was characteristic of many of the political themes of that era. Conservationists were generally members of the new urban middle and upper class—the same group which had begun to use the mountains as a tourist mecca. Most were well educated, and many held professional positions as teachers, scientists, doctors, or technicians. While they deplored the rampant exploitation of the nation's natural resources, most believed ardently in the idea of progress through industrial growth, so long as that growth was orderly, efficient, and controlled by a strong central government. Their faith lay in the development of ambitious federal programs of "scientific management" to regulate the use of natural resources. The political philosophy underlying these programs was that decisions about resource management should be made by "technicians guided by standards of efficiency," that is, by the progressives themselves, rather than by popularly elected politicians at the local level. Their belief in the centralization of power led them to adopt a holistic rather than a particularistic outlook on management practices. Considering resources such as water, timber, minerals, and land to be interrelated elements, they were quick to adopt the idea of efficient "multiple use" planning.[89]

Not all of the conservationists, however, agreed on the proper utilization of the national forest reserves. A small wing of the movement advocated preserving the timberlands in their natural state through the abolition of all commercial activities, including logging and mining. Naturalists like John Muir and other members of the Sierra Club, founded in 1892, hoped that sections of timberland

89. Samuel P. Hays, *The Response to Industrialism, 1885–1914* (Chicago, 1957), 157.

could be set aside for recreational and scenic purposes. In addition to preserving the natural heritage of the country, they argued, the national forests ought to provide an "escape" from the "industrial pace" of urban life.[90] This perspective was later embodied in the creation of national parks, but at the turn of the century, most attention focused on the continued use of the forests for economic purposes. The majority of the leaders of the conservation movement, including its most renowned leaders, Gifford Pinchot and Theodore Roosevelt, perceived the primary purpose of the forest reserves to be the protection and management of timber resources for commercial production. "Forest reserves," wrote Pinchot, chief of the Forest Service, in 1905, "are for the purpose of preserving a perpetual supply of timber for home industries, preventing destruction of the forest cover which regulates the flow of streams, and protecting local residents from unfair competition in the use of forest and range."[91]

Conflict within the conservation movement, between advocates of "scenic preservation" and supporters of "economic forestry," continued to complicate the management of the national forests and subsequently had a major impact upon land use practices in the southern Appalachian region. But common threads which bound the two groups together played an even more important role in shaping the future of the mountains. Both factions approached the issue of conservation from a decidedly nationalistic and predominantly urban perspective. National needs, whether they were those of the tourist, the scientist, or the industrialist, were given priority over local concerns. The popular image of the mountaineer as backward, degenerate, and uncivilized (the very "idea of Appalachia") seemed to justify this attitude, placing power in the hands of those who seemed "best equipped" to bring progress and civilization to the region. For many urban progressives, the creation of national forests in Appalachia became the easiest way to protect the resources they most coveted and the best way also to bring *"Our* Southern Highlanders," as Horace Kephart labeled them, into the modern age.[92]

Efforts to create a national forest reserve in the southern Appalachians—like tourism and the timber industry—began in the 1880s

90. Steen, *U.S. Forest Service*, 113–15.
91. *Ibid.*, 79.
92. Kephart, *Our Southern Highlanders*. Kephart was himself active in the movement to create national forests and later national parks in the southern Appalachians. His book was first published in 1913.

and 1890s. As early as 1885, Dr. Henry O. Marcy of Boston read a paper before an assembly of the American Academy of Medicine in New York City, in which he called for the establishment of a national park in the southern Appalachian Mountains for the climatic treatment of disease. The area's salubrious climate and proximity to the urban Northeast had begun to turn western North Carolina into a major health resort, and Dr. Marcy wished to extend the benefits of the region to larger numbers of Americans.[93] Marcy's proposal attracted little attention, however, until late in the 1890s, when an Asheville physician, Dr. Chase P. Ambler, originally of Ohio, revived the idea. Ironically, Dr. Ambler's concern was not for the construction of a health resort, but for the preservation of the timberlands and trout streams for tourist purposes. Along with a group of Asheville businessmen and lawyers, Ambler organized the Appalachian National Park Association in 1899, to bring the park question before Congress. On 2 January 1900, this group presented a memorial to Congress written by Charles McNamee, a prominent lawyer and cousin of millionare George W. Vanderbilt, calling for the location of a national park and forest reserve in western North Carolina "because of the natural beauty of the area." The memorial urged Congress to act immediately if the magnificent forests of the region were to be saved from the rapid encroachments of lumber interests. At the urging of Senator Jeter C. Pritchard of North Carolina, Congress referred the issue to the Department of Agriculture and authorized five thousand dollars to provide for a preliminary investigation and survey of the timberlands of the entire southern Appalachian region.[94]

The report issued by Secretary of Agriculture James Wilson on 3 January 1901 bore the distinct mark of Chief Forester Gifford Pinchot and recommended the establishment of a national forest reserve in the southern Appalachians to protect the timber resources of that region from indiscriminate cutting. Although the movement for government purchase of a large area of forest land in the East had chiefly contemplated a national park to be administered by the Interior Department, Wilson's recommendation was for the continued utilization of the timberland as a forest reserve under the control of

93. Jesse R. Lankford, Jr., "The Campaign for a National Park in Western North Carolina, 1885–1940" (M.A. thesis, Western Carolina Univ., 1973), 1–2.
94. *Ibid.*, 14–21.

the Department of Agriculture. "The idea of a national park is conservation, not use;" he wrote, "that of a forest reserve, conservation by use. I have therefore to recommend a forest reserve instead of a park. It is fully shown by the investigation that such a reserve would be self-supporting from the sale of timber under wisely directed conservative forestry."[95] Wilson's report struck a blow against efforts to create a national park in western North Carolina. Proponents of a park, especially the tourist industry, were not to see their dream realized until the late 1920s and 1930s, when the government established the Great Smoky Mountains National Park and the Blue Ridge Parkway. But conservationists at the turn of the century were elated with Wilson's recommendation. Even the Appalachian National Park Association shifted its campaign to support the forest reserve movement, maintaining that it had favored both a park and a forest reserve and had never opposed the cutting of mature timber in some areas.[96]

The campaign for a southern Appalachian forest reserve attracted support from a variety of interest groups. Pinchot headed an effective lobby of scientists, foresters, and government technicians, and a number of congressmen, including Senator Pritchard, threw their support behind the cause. The most influential supporter, however, was Theodore Roosevelt himself, who, after becoming president in 1901, made forestry, conservation, and the creation of forest reserves a major theme of his administration. Land companies and, of course, most lumbermen opposed the reserve initially, but some of the more "progressive" large lumber companies increasingly came to favor the idea of federal forest reserves. Acquisition of their timberlands, they reasoned, would not only relieve them of the burden of local taxes but would eliminate their expenses for "timber stand improvement." Having sold the land to the government at a profit, they would still have access to the land for timber cutting and a sustained yield managed at public expense. To the larger, well-capitalized companies, there was a clear, long-range economic advantage. In fact, at their annual conventions in 1902, both the

95. Shands and Healy, *Lands Nobody Wanted*, 13; "Secretary Wilson on National Parks: His Letter Presenting A Preliminary Report," 3 Jan. 1901, quoted in Lankford, "Campaign for a National Park," 22.
96. Lankford, "Campaign for a National Park," 25–28.

National Hardwood Lumber Association and the National Lumber Manufacturers' Association endorsed resolutions favoring the creation of a national forest reserve in the southern Appalachian mountains.[97] Smaller mill operators and independent lumbermen continued to oppose the movement.

Despite the efforts of conservationists, however, Secretary Wilson's recommendations received only limited support in a budget-minded Congress. Legislation authorizing purchase funds for an eastern forest reserve was introduced in 1901 but failed to pass then and in several subsequent Congresses. Resistance to the concept was led by the powerful speaker of the House, Joseph G. Cannon, who vowed to spend "not one cent for scenery."[98] Nevertheless, support grew steadily, as forest conservation was increasingly linked with water problems such as irrigation, navigation, flood control, and hydro-power production. Tragic and costly floods like that which struck the Monongahela River in West Virginia in 1907 stirred further public agitation for watershed protection, and in the election of 1908, both national political parties came out in favor of conservation.[99] Finally, on 1 March 1911, Congress passed the landmark Weeks Act, authorizing the purchase of "such forested, cut-over, or denuded lands within the watersheds of navigable streams as . . . may be necessary to the regulation of the flow of navigable streams . . . ."[100] The act provided $11 million for the acquisition of land and directed the secretary of agriculture to recommend lands for purchase. On 27 March 1911, the Forest Service secured approval for the establishment of the first purchase units of the Appalachian forest reserve—the Mt. Mitchell, Nantahala, Pisgah, and Yadkin areas of western North Carolina.[101]

The passage of the Weeks Act and the subsequent purchase of timberlands initially stirred little popular reaction in the affected areas of the southern mountains. A few business leaders voiced optimism that the forest reserves would boost tourism and insure a

97. *Ibid.*, 35.
98. Shands and Healy, *Lands Nobody Wanted*, 14.
99. Steen, *U.S. Forest Service*, 96.
100. "Weeks Act of March 1, 1911," in U.S. Department of Agriculture, *Forest Service Manual* (Washington, D.C., 1978), 1021–27—1021–30; Shands and Healy, *Lands Nobody Wanted*, 15.
101. Pomeroy and Yoho, *North Carolina Lands*, 211.

perpetual supply of timber, but most local residents reacted indifferently to the legislation.[102] Most of the land being studied for acquisition had already passed out of the hands of local people and into the control of timber companies and other corporations, and, under the new law, these lands would continue to remain open to public access and to use by the timber industry. Not until the late 1920s when the Department of the Interior began to condemn small tracts of farm land for inclusion in national parks—especially for the Blue Ridge Parkway and the Great Smoky Mountains National Park—did mountain residents begin to express opposition to the expansion of government lands. Efforts at that time by the Forest Service to consolidate and expand the national forests were increasingly opposed by local residents.

The initial acquisition of land immediately following the passage of the Weeks Act, however, was limited to large tracts of "high quality" ridgeland located on the headwaters of navigable streams.[103] Such tracts generally did not include farmland or residences and were usually purchased from absentee owners. One of the largest tracts purchased in these years was part of the George W. Vanderbilt estate near Asheville. As early as 1913, Vanderbilt had offered to sell to the government some 87,000 acres of the Pisgah Forest, but negotiations had broken down because of the steep price. Following Vanderbilt's death, Mrs. Vanderbilt agreed to sell the acreage to the government for approximately $5 per acre, but not before selling most of the marketable timber at $12 per acre to a private company.[104]

By 1916, sufficient land had been added to the Vanderbilt tract to create the first eastern national forest, Pisgah National Forest. In 1918, the Pisgah was joined by three more such forests—the Shenandoah in Virginia, the Natural Bridge in Virginia, and the White

102. Albert Phenis, "Southern Appalachian Forest Reserve: Its Practical Bearing Upon the Country's Industrial and Commercial Development," *Manufacturers' Record* 65 (25 June 1914), 41–43. Examination of the Asheville *Citizen* from 1910 to 1920 reveals little local reaction to the creation of the National Forest Reserves; Mary Rose Dullaghan, "The National Forest Service in Contention," unpublished undergraduate paper in author's possession.

103. Pomeroy and Yoho, *North Carolina Lands*, 211–212; Steen, *U.S. Forest Service*, 125.

104. Phenis, "National Forest Reserve," 42. See Contract, George W. Vanderbilt and wife to Louis Carr, 17 Jan. 1913, on file in the U.S. Forest Service Office, Asheville, N.C. Copy in author's possession.

Mountain in New Hampshire. Two years later, five more forests were created in southern Appalachia—the Boone (now part of the Pisgah); the Nantahala in North Carolina, South Carolina, and Georgia; the Cherokee in Tennessee; the Unaka in North Carolina, Tennessee, and Virginia; and the Monongahela in West Virginia. By 1920, the Forest Service had acquired over 250,000 acres of land in western North Carolina alone. This acreage, however, represented only about 13 percent of a two-million-acre program which was planned for the North Carolina mountains.[105]

The greatest growth of national forest acreage in Appalachia came in the 1920s and 1930s, as the Forest Service sought to consolidate its holdings and to expand acquisition to denuded and cutover lands. Initial purchases had concentrated on timberlands of high quality, but the rapid depletion of timber reserves and the high lumber prices prevailing after World War I led industry and government officials to stress the need for reforestation of cutover timberlands. With the passage of the Clarke-McNary Act (1924) and the McNary-Woodruff Act (1928), the Forest Service began a massive effort to acquire and "rehabilitate" devastated forest lands.[106] By 1940, the federal government would control over five million acres of timber-land in the southern Appalachians, including almost 800,000 acres of national forest in western North Carolina.[107]

This rapid growth of government-owned lands would bring the Forest Service and its sister agencies, the Tennessee Valley Author-ity and the National Park Service, into increasing conflict with local mountain people. As greater quantities of land were purchased and as larger numbers of remote farms and ancestral homesteads were ac-quired through condemnation, local hostility to these government agencies continued to grow. The fact, moreover, that the greatest expansion in government lands came during the depression decade of the 1930s made it appear that the federal government was following a well-laid plan to destroy the mountain way of life. In the minds of many local residents, the purchase of mountain land for forests, lakes, and parks had not only contributed to the depression of the local agricultural and timber economy, but it was also depriving a

105. Shands and Healy, *Lands Nobody Wanted*, 15; Pomeroy and Yoho, *North Carolina Lands*, 213, 217.
106. Steen, *U.S. Forest Service*, 182–94.
107. Pomeroy and Yoho, *North Carolina Lands*, 217.

hard-hit people of their last chance at independent survival.[108] During the 1930s, the government's acquisition of large numbers of small farms sold at sheriff's auctions for nonpayment of taxes seemed to support these feelings of suspicion, hostility, and despair.

In fact, the movement of mountain people out of the coves and hollows actually had been a goal put forward by some proponents of the Appalachian Forest Reserve even before the purchase of the first mountain lands. As early as 1914, William L. Hall of the United States Forest Service had argued that the timber and water conservation measures authorized by the Weeks Act created an opportunity "to remake the Appalachians" by replacing the region's subsistence agricultural economy with a more "natural" system of timber culture. The creation of national forest reserves, suggested Hall, would help to eliminate some of the region's social and economic problems by forcing mountaineers to migrate to the cities and mill villages of the New South, where they would enjoy "the advantages of social intercourse, school, and livelihood that village life afforded."[109] Northern missionaries and social reformers had long been engaged in work to "uplift" the mountain people, and many had argued that the major impediment to progress in the region was the isolated and scattered nature of mountain settlements. The migration of the mountaineers to the industrializing centers would be an important step toward the solution of what was called the mountain problem. "As the undertaking actually works out on the ground," wrote Hall, "it is a movement to remake the Appalachians, . . . and set the region to performing the function for which it was clearly intended."[110]

Whether or not the acquisition of mountain land by the federal government reflected a conscious effort to move the mountain people out of the mountains, such policies did contribute to the transformation of mountain society. On the eve of World War II, when the flow of people out of the coves became a rising flood of migration into industrial centers both within and outside of the region, the Forest Service had acquired almost five million acres of forest land in Appalachia, including some 20 percent of the total surface land in the

108. See William G. Davis, "Uncle Sam Ruined Swain's Economy," *Asheville Citizen*, 25 Oct. 1978. Davis was a county commissioner in Swain County, N.C.
109. William L. Hall, "To Remake the Appalachians: A New Order in the Mountains That is Founded on Forestry," *World's Work* 28 (July 1914), 335.
110. Hall, "To Remake the Appalachians," 336. See also Shapiro, "A Strange Land and Peculiar People," 158–65.

eighteen western counties of North Carolina.[111] In some counties, the federal government owned as much as 80 percent of the total surface land.[112] This transition in land ownership played a major role in shaping the structure and nature of mountain society in the mature industrial order of the postwar years. By that time, the federal government had become an inextricable part of mountain life.

## PUBLIC WORK

The remaking of the Appalachians was not limited, of course, to the impact of the timber industry and the emergence of the national forests and other federally owned lands. The arrival of the railroads after 1880 stimulated a variety of nonagricultural developments— including furniture, textile, tourism, oil, chemical, and mineral-related industries—which combined to pull large numbers of mountaineers into the new industrial system. Just as changing land ownership patterns pushed some mountain families off the land and into burgeoning cities and towns, the promise of steady employment and a cash income pulled others into the mines and mills, into what mountain people called "public work." This "push-pull" effect resulted in the transformation of the mountain labor force from a predominantly agrarian to an increasingly industrial or semi-industrial character.

The largest source of nonagricultural employment in the Blue Ridge during these years was the timber industry and its dependent industries—lumber, furniture, leather, and rayon mills. The number of individuals employed in these industries in western North Carolina, for example, increased more than tenfold between 1900 and 1920. While the majority were employed directly in logging operations, others worked in small planing mills and pulp mills, or in the small furniture companies of Asheville.[113] Hundreds of Blue Ridge families migrated to the eastern foothills to find work in the furniture plants of Lenoir, Mount Airy, and Morganton, while others moved to the industrial boom towns of East Tennessee. At Kingsport, Tennessee, wood was used in the manufacture of photographic

111. Based on statistics provided in Si Kahn, *The Forest Service and Appalachia* (New York, 1974), 2, 136.
112. Davis, in Asheville *Citizen*, 25 Oct. 1978.
113. Based upon analysis of the *Reports of the Bureau of Labor Statistics of the State of North Carolina, 1900–1920*. These statistics are incomplete, however, and should be considered to reflect only partial levels of employment.

print stock, and at Elizabethton, Tennessee, wood pulp was used in the production of rayon.[114] In 1928, the American Enka Company, a Dutch-owned corporation, began to produce rayon at a mill near Asheville, and by 1940, it had attracted some 3,000 employees.[115]

A by-product of the timber industry was tannin, a product derived from chestnut and oak bark and used in the manufacture of leather. The growth of the tan-bark industry provided employment for hundreds of mountain residents and gave rise to a thriving leather industry in the region. At the height of the industry's activity in 1916, there were nearly 1,200 people employed in tanning and leather manufacture in western North Carolina alone. The arrival of the chestnut blight, the popularity of the automobile, and the introduction of synthetic fabrics, however, brought about the sudden demise of the mountain leather industry. By 1926, the North Carolina Bureau of Labor Statistics reported less than four hundred individuals working in the leather and tanning trades in the western counties.[116]

For hundreds of mountain families, the movement from agriculture to timber-related employment was also accompanied by migration from the farm to one of the many temporary company towns established throughout the region. Most of the smaller, more remote timber camps provided short-term housing for male employees, but the larger timber towns offered more substantial residences for entire families. One of the largest of these towns was constructed at Sunburst in Haywood County, North Carolina, by the Champion Fiber Company. At the height of the timber boom, Sunburst housed more than 2,000 people and maintained a commissary, a clubhouse, boarding houses, and a church which doubled as a school, a dance hall, and a skating rink.[117] Other towns, such as those at Runion, Smokemont, Ravensford, Townsend, and Crestmont, typically housed from 300 to 1,000 individuals and provided proportionately less in the way of social facilities. Timber towns resembled other company towns of this period, except for their shorter life expectancy. Houses were generally small and of board-and-batten type construction, with no indoor plumbing or sanitary facilities. Companies were usually reluc-

114. U.S. Department of Agriculture, *Economic and Social Conditions*, 85.
115. Van Noppen, *Western North Carolina*, 364.
116. *Reports of the Bureau of Labor Statistics of the State of North Carolina* (Raleigh, 1916, 1926).
117. Interview with Larry Mull, Cullowhee, N.C., 9 April 1975, at the abandoned site of Sunburst; Larry Mull, "Lumbering in Western North Carolina," 3–5.

tant to invest more than a minimal amount of money in communities that were expected to survive only as long as it took to extract the surrounding timber. Residents of these towns had little voice in community affairs and were dependent on the company for maintenance of community health and safety.

With the decline of timber production after World War I, most of the company towns disappeared, and their residents returned to farms or searched for employment elsewhere. For many of the mountaineers of the Blue Ridge and Smoky Mountain country who had been lured to the sawmills, the collapse of the timber industry was disillusioning. On the farm the family had worked together in a disciplined way on common tasks, but the old disciplines had begun to break down under the weight of the new wage system. Gradually, through the years, farm life had begun to deteriorate. Fields went uncultivated and grew up in weeds. Fences went down because the men were working at the lumber mills, and supplies, which before had been grown entirely on the farm, were now bought at the store or commissary. "When the sawmill had finished its work and folded up as suddenly as it had come," remembered Granville Calhoun, "they saw the illusion of permanency by which they had been tricked; their fields overgrown, fences unrepaired, farm tools rusted, young men strangers to the plow and hoe, children demoralized." All of this had happened gradually, he recalled, "and when the people came to realize it, it was out of their control."[118]

As logging in the mountains declined, therefore, thousands of mountaineers began to search for other industries to fill their new dependency upon wage employment. Some found temporary opportunities in mining and smelting operations, which began to expand in the Blue Ridge after the turn of the century. At Ducktown on the Tennessee, North Carolina, and Georgia border, the Tennessee Copper Company began extensive development in 1901 that attracted hundreds of local residents to its copper mines. The open smelting pits of this New York–owned corporation not only consumed all of the fuel wood from the area but also emitted a sulfurous acid gas that denuded the surrounding forests, creating a 23,000-acre barren wasteland. "The entire surroundings," lamented Carl

118. Granville Calhoun, quoted in Rebecca Cushman, "Seed of Fire: The Human Side of History In Our Nation's Southern Highland Region and Its Changing Years," unpublished MS, North Carolina Collection, Univ. of North Carolina, n.d., 143.

Schenck, "had been converted into a desert, dissected by deep gullies and ravines, looking like the landscape of the moon."[119] In nearby Maryville, Tennessee, the Aluminum Company of America completed its sprawling works, and mountaineers flocked to the factory for jobs in the rolling mill or smelting plants.[120]

In North Carolina, the expansion of mica mining operations in Yancey and Mitchell counties and the opening of large kaolin deposits in Jackson, Clay, and other counties provided additional employment opportunities. Between 1906 and 1926, the number of persons employed in mining in western North Carolina jumped from 55 to over 800, with many more employed in transportation and service-related industries.[121] Before the bottom fell out of the mica market in the late 1920s, the mines in Yancey and Mitchell counties produced 75 percent of the mica mined in the United States.[122] Neighboring villages such as Burnsville, Spruce Pine, and Hayesville experienced significant economic growth during these years, as nonfarm employment increased the local demand for consumer goods.

Other mountain families were caught up in the great textile boom that swept the Southeast at the turn of the century. Cotton mills had operated in the South long before the Civil War, but it was not until the 1890s that the rate of new mill construction in the region surpassed that of the old mill districts of New England. Between 1890 and 1897, the number of spindles in the South increased by 151 percent; by 1904, the South had taken the lead over New England in the amount of cotton comsumed by its mills.[123] At the same time that northern capitalists were pouring large amounts of money into Appalachian timber and mineral lands, New England investors were transferring millions of dollars into the construction of cotton mills, primarily in Georgia, South Carolina, Alabama, and North Carolina. This transfer of New England textile capital into southern mills was the result of a number of factors, including the proximity of raw materials, cheap water power, lower taxes, and cheap nonunion

119. Schenck, *Birth of Forestry*, 114. See also North Callahan, *Smoky Mountain Country* (Boston, 1952), 101; *Manufacturers' Record* 39 (21 March 1901), 170.
120. Callahan, *Smoky Mountain Country*, 100.
121. *Reports of Bureau of Labor Statistics*, 1906, 1926.
122. *Manufacturers' Record* 81 (16 Feb. 1922), 55.
123. Woodward, *Origins of the New South*, 306–8.

labor, but the greatest of these attractions was the large untapped source of cheap labor. It was estimated that in 1897 the cost of labor was 40 percent lower in the South than in New England, and the average working day was 24 percent longer.[124]

While the majority of southern cotton mills were constructed in piedmont counties, mountain counties attracted their share of the booming textile industry. Some small mills were constructed in rural communities such as Marshall, Hendersonville, and Swannanoa, but major textile centers emerged in Rutherfordton, Forest City, Lenoir, Marion, Elkin, and Asheville. From 1900 to 1930, thousands of mountaineers left their farms for the mill districts of these towns or for the mill villages of distant cities such as Greenville, Spartanburg, Kingsport, Knoxville, Elizabethton, Chattanooga, Dayton, Bristol, or Rome.[125] After the turn of the century, when labor supplies began to diminish in the piedmont, many of the mill owners actively recruited workers in the mountain districts, sending agents into remote areas to tap what was believed to be an inexhaustable source of cheap labor.[126] Life in the textile mills, the recruiters preached, would be "like heaven" compared to the struggles of living on a small mountain farm.[127] As one supporter of the southern textile industry argued:

> If I were a Carnegie or a Rockefeller seeking to improve the conditions of our poor mountain people, I would build them a cotton-mill. I would gather their children in just as soon as they are big enough to doff and spin, and instead of feeding them on homilies and panegyrics, I would pay them a stipend that would buy them more than "bread and meat." I would teach them with real money what money brings.[128]

124. *Ibid.*, 307.

125. *Manufacturers' Record* 16 (10 Aug. 1889), 13; U.S. Department of Agriculture, *Economic and Social Conditions*, 85–86; Cotton, "Appalachian North Carolina," 65.

126. Broadus Mitchell, *The Rise of Cotton Mills in the South* (Baltimore, 1921), 208; Frank T. DeVyver, "Southern Industry and the Southern Mountaineer," *American Federationist: Official Magazine of the American Federation of Labor* 35 (1928), 1319; Wade H. Harris (ed. of the Charlotte *Observer*), "Abundant American Labor South's Great Asset," *Manufacturers' Record* 90 (28 Oct. 1926), 126–29.

127. See Herbert Francis Sherwood, "Our New Racial Drama," 492–93.

128. Thomas Robinson Dawley, Jr., *The Child that Toileth Not: A Story of a Government Investigation* (New York, 1912), 140.

For over three-quarters of a million mountaineers, the migration from mountain cabin to mill village was a major break with their land, their families, and their culture.[129] The hopes with which they abandoned their farms for life in the mill villages were too often quickly dashed by the realities of the cotton mills.[130] Housing was poor, crowded, and unsanitary, and wages ranged from 35 to 60 cents a day. The typical work day was eleven and a half hours, and men, women, and children worked from 65 to 72 hours a week.[131]

Approximately 80 percent of the workers in most mills were women and children. One investigator from the Department of Labor found that at a typical mill, 60 percent of the employees were females and fully one-half were children between the ages of twelve and sixteen.[132] Under these conditions, for some mountain families the move to the mill village came only as a last resort.[133]

There was an alternative, however, to the mill villages. After the turn of the century, the timber industry in West Virginia and the Cumberland Plateau began to give ground rapidly to the arrival of the coalmen. By the time logging had begun to decline in the Blue Ridge, labor demands were reaching their height in the coal fields. The coal barons were no longer able to fill their labor needs from the local population, and they began to recruit in other areas of the mountains, in the Deep South, and in southern Europe. For many mountaineers, the transition from logging to coal mining was a natural progression, and they poured by the thousands out of the mountains of Tennessee and North Carolina into the nearby coal fields of Kentucky, Virginia, and West Virginia.[134]

The ascendancy of coal marked the end of the lumber era in the mountains. Logging would continue in the Smokies until the last

129. Sherwood, "Our New Racial Drama," 489.
130. An excellent fictional account is Grace Lumpkin's *To Make My Bread* (New York, 1932).
131. *Manufacturers' Record* 32 (22 Oct. 1897), 197.
132. Dawley, *Child that Toileth Not*, 137.
133. The history of the southern textile industry will not be detailed here since the majority of cotton mills were located outside the mountains and thus beyond the scope of this book. See also Benjamin Franklin Lemert, *The Cotton Textile Industry of the Southern Appalachian Piedmont* (Chapel Hill, 1933); Lois MacDonald, *Southern Mill Hills: A Study of Social and Economic Forces in Certain Textile Mill Villages* (New York, 1928); Shapiro, *Appalachia On Our Mind*, 162–85.
134. Statistical information on the amount of migration between the Blue Ridge and the coal fields is not available. This observation, however, is based upon the reading of hundreds of family histories and oral history transcripts from the

great tree was cut or until the federal government quieted the saws by establishing national forests, but the lumbermen would never again reign supreme. In the 1920s, most of the lumber companies abandoned the mountains, leaving behind a land and a people deeply scarred by their operations. The lumbermen's place in the new industrial order was assumed by others who carried forward the modernization process. The timber boom lasted less than thirty years in Appalachia, but in that time it touched the lives of generations of mountaineers. In the end, however, its impact was obscured by events being played out in the coal fields, for it was there that the machine age came to have its most ominous effects.

region. The author's own family migrated from small farms in the Blue Ridge of Virginia and North Carolina to employment in the timber mills and, after 1910, to the coal fields of southern West Virginia.

# CHAPTER FOUR

# THE ASCENDANCY OF COAL

IN THE LATE nineteenth and early twentieth centuries, coal was king of the industrial world. The black dusty mineral not only fired the boilers of locomotives, factories, and ships, but it also fueled the generators of the new electric power plants and warmed the homes of the urban middle class. In its processed form (coke), coal was a critical element in the manufacture of iron and steel. Until it was dethroned by the rise of oil and gas after World War I, coal was the primary source of cheap energy for the United States and much of Europe. Without the ready availability of coal, the American drive for industrial maturity after 1890 would have been considerably slowed.

The fifty million acres or so of coal lands in the Appalachian South was the nation's largest supply of bituminous coal, and in the heyday of industrial expansion it was inevitable that these mountain reserves would be tapped. Railroads had opened up the region in the 1870s and 1880s, but economic conditions had delayed the large-scale development of coal mining. The financial panic of 1893 drove coal prices down, and early in 1894 they reached their lowest point in twenty years.[1] Thereafter, however, the nationwide business recovery and the war with Spain began to generate an increased demand for coal, and the Appalachian fields entered a period of unparalleled growth. By 1900, coal production in the region had tripled, and in the next three decades it multiplied again more than fivefold, coming to account for almost 80 percent of national production.[2]

The penetration of the Great Lakes markets by southern coal companies paved the way for the emergence of the coal boom in the mountains. Prior to the turn of the century, most of the coal used in

1. Joseph T. Lambie, *From Mine to Market*, 59.
2. Compiled from figures in U.S. Bureau of Mines, *Mineral Resources of the United States*, 1900 and 1930.

the upper Midwest was supplied by mines in Illinois, Indiana, Ohio, and Pennsylvania. Southern Appalachian coal was restricted primarily to the eastern markets and the transoceanic trade. By 1898, however, southern operators began to challenge this division of markets and to attempt to capture a share of the lucrative Great Lakes trade. The southern operators had several advantages over their northern competitors. Not only was Appalachian coal of better quality than the northern product, but it could be delivered to the consumer at a lower price. The geological location of mountain coal seams made mining easier and less expensive, and railroads usually charged lower freight rates for long hauls. Above all, the coal operators extracted more work at less pay from mountain miners, and this substantially lowered their cost of production. The labor differential became a major factor after 1897, when a successful United Mine Workers strike forced the northern operators to set mining wage rates by collective bargaining. Southern coal operators bitterly resisted unionization and used their cheaper labor costs as a wedge into the Midwest markets.[3]

The success of the mountain coal barons in gaining entry to the Midwest markets was extraordinary. In 1898, for example, southern West Virginia shipped only about 40,000 tons of coal to the Great Lakes, or less than 1 percent of the total market. But by 1913, its shipments had increased to over 6 million tons, or 23 percent of the total. Nonunion eastern Kentucky entered the lake trade in 1909, and by 1921 it was supplying over 2.6 million tons.[4] The tremendous growth of the coal market resulted in rapid overdevelopment of the industry in the mountains, as more and more operators sought to profit from their competitive advantage by expanding production. After 1900, capital that had previously gone into the northern coal fields was increasingly diverted into the southern mountains, and new mines were opened on the creeks and in the hollows every year.

Another factor contributing to the sudden growth of mining operations in the mountains was the relatively small capital investment needed to open a mine in the region. "All that was required," recalled

3. See Thomas, "Coal Country," 140–44; Cubby, "The Transformation of the Tug and Guyandot Valleys," 267–74; William Graebner, "Great Expectations: The Search for Order in Bituminous Coal, 1890–1917," *Business History Review* 48 (1974), 50.

4. Edward Eyre Hunt, Frederick G. Tryon, and Joseph H. Willitts, *What the Coal Commission Found* (Baltimore, 1925), 233.

a coal operator, "was to build houses for the miners, a store to supply them, and a tipple structure to dump the coal into railway cars."[5] Little machinery was required, and the men provided their own tools. Coal mine leases were easy to obtain at the turn of the century, since land companies and railroads were eager to develop their properties. Many companies were organized with no more than $20,000 to $30,000 subscribed by a few men, with money borrowed from banks or wealthy friends.[6] The ease with which a mine could be opened led to the establishment of hundreds of small mines throughout the region, adding to the competition and instability of the industry.

The development of coal mining facilities was so rapid in the first decades of the new century that many journalists revived the old booster spirit of the 1870s and 1880s, predicting prosperity and industrial greatness for the region. The editor of the newspaper in Beckley, West Virginia, spoke for many local leaders in 1907 when he described his faith in the magic of king coal.

> Towns and cities springing up where before stood dense forests or waving fields of grain; thousands of coke ovens gleaming along the pathway of the iron horse and clouding the noon-day sun with their endless streams of smoke; armies of men collected together from every quarter of the globe to dig his vast treasures from the mines; heavily loaded freight trains plunging through mountain fastnesses, fording great rivers and spanning wide canyons to carry to the world its precious supplies of fuel—these are some of the accomplishments of old king coal, who is working out the miracle daily before our eyes.[7]

These sentiments were shared by other journalists inside and outside of the mountains, but no one more ardently promoted the new age in the region than Richard Hathaway Edmonds, the editor of the *Manufacturers' Record*. From the late 1880s, Edmonds was an outspoken advocate of the industrialization of the Appalachian South. "In this great Appalachian area," he argued, "are great latent resources, awaiting development, resources great enough to enrich empires." The region, he claimed, was like a central bank, "the richest on earth, more feasible of financial development than any-

5. Tams, *Smokeless Coal Fields of West Virginia*, 24.
6. *Ibid.*
7. *Raleigh Register* (Beckley, W.Va.), 7 Nov. 1907, quoted in Thomas, "Coal Country," 272.

thing on the American continent."[8] When he was not using the pages of his Baltimore-based journal to urge capitalists to tap that bank, he was traveling throughout the region and the East Coast speaking to businessmen, commercial clubs, and other groups about the great natural wealth of the mountains. In 1910, he challenged the Appalachian Press Association in Knoxville to lead the way in making known to the world the vast resources of their section, and he urged a meeting of the Appalachian Engineering Association in Washington, D.C., to unlock "by means of the proper keys rightfully in [your] possession vault after vault" of this greatest of all natural banks. "There is probably no other area of its size on earth," he believed, "capable of furnishing so broad a foundation for the support of a dense population under the most advantageous conditions of health and comfort and for the creation of wealth . . . as this Appalachian region of the South."[9]

At least a few of those who read his journal or listened to Edmonds speak took up his advice and moved to the southern mountains to participate in the revolution taking place there. A disproportionately large number of engineers became owners, superintendents, or managers of mines in the Appalachian coal fields, using their skills to overcome the natural barriers which had so long guarded the mountain wealth.[10] In 1908, a number of these engineers and coal operators founded the *Appalachian Trade Journal* to serve as a regional version of the *Manufacturers' Record*. The *Appalachian Trade Journal* was established in Knoxville "to advertise the kinds, quality, and commercial value of the wealth" of Appalachia, and, together with the *Manufacturers' Record*, it became an effective means of communications and propaganda for the outside technicians who organized the transformation of mountain life. In 1910, the *Appalachian Trade Journal* became the official organ of the Southern Appalachian Coal Operators Association.[11]

8. Richard H. Edmonds, "Latent Resources of the South," *Appalachian Trade Journal* 4 (May 1910), 20.
9. *Ibid.*; R.H. Edmonds, "Engineers' Opportunities in Southern Appalachians," *Manufacturers' Record* 56 (18 Nov. 1909), 47. See also "The Future of the Appalachian South," *Manufacturers' Record* 48 (4 Jan. 1906), 207; "Millions for Development in the Appalachian South," *Manufacturers' Record* 50 (3 Jan. 1907), 627.
10. Based upon biographical analysis of a sample of 140 coal operators in the Appalachian South. See ch. 6.
11. *Appalachian Trade Journal* 2 (June 1909) and 4 (Feb. 1910). In the 1920s,

The decades after 1900, therefore, witnessed the final arrival of the industrial age in Appalachia. The ascension of coal to the throne of the region's economic, political, and social life was made possible not only by increased national demand, but also by the penetration of new markets and the ease with which mining operations could be undertaken. While the power of the new order was based upon exploitation of mountain resources and people, the minions of King Coal sought to obscure the terms of his rule with acclamations of "progress" and "unbounded future wealth." The managers and technicians whom the king drew around him established effective control over the expanding empire, and for a time they were the lords of the new regime.

## WEST VIRGINIA

"Medieval West Virginia! With its tent colonies and bleak hills! With its grim men and women! When I get to the other side, I shall tell God Almighty about West Virginia."[12]

No other section of the Appalachian South experienced a more intense transformation with the rise of coal than southern West Virginia. After 1910, eastern Kentucky would become the scene of dramatic and sweeping events, but in the first decade of the twentieth century the greatest assaults of the coal men came in the Mountain State. In the 1870s, the C&O Railroad had opened the New River coal fields in Fayette, Raleigh, and Kanawha counties, and in the 1880s the N&W Railway had begun to ship coal from parts of Mercer and McDowell counties, but it was not until the completion of the N&W's Ohio Branch through Mingo County in 1892 that large-scale development of the area commenced. The extension of the N&W to the Ohio River enabled coal operators in southern West Virginia to introduce their product in the Great Lakes markets, and by 1900 the three counties of Mercer, McDowell, and Mingo were producing

---

the magazine moved its headquarters to Cincinnati and also became the official organ of the Appalachian Logging Congress.

12. Mother Jones, quoted in Neil Pierce, *The Border South States* (New York, 1975), 168. A half-century after Mother Jones made her statement about the Mountain State, journalist Neil Pierce found that the despotic politics and economy of West Virginia continued to make it "The Saddest State" of any in the Union.

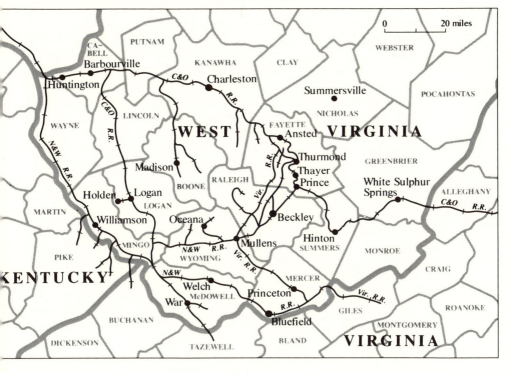

*7. Southern West Virginia*

almost as much coal as the entire state had in 1890. In 1905, McDowell County became the largest coal producer in the state, and over the next two decades coal output in the southern counties ballooned by over 300 percent. By 1920, the nine coal-producing counties south of the New River accounted for about two-thirds of the total production in the state.[13]

The increase in coal output was matched by an equally spectacular rise in the population of the southern counties. In 1890, large portions of southern West Virginia were still unsettled, but with the coming of the coal boom, that area witnessed an inrush of population unparalleled anywhere in the region. Between 1890 and 1920, the population of the area increased more than fourfold and in some counties

13. U.S. Bureau of Mines, *Mineral Resources of the United States*, 1900, 1920.

133

more than ninefold.[14] McDowell County experienced phenomenal growth. In the decade from 1900 to 1910, McDowell's population burgeoned by some 30,000 inhabitants for a rate of 155.3 percent, while the state average for the decade was only 27.4 percent. During that period, six of the nine coal-producing counties of southern West Virginia had population growths of over 50 percent.[15]

A major share of the increased production and population growth in the region resulted from the arrival of hundreds of independent coal operators, who established mines on land leased from the big absentee land companies. In some counties, the proliferation of small, independent mines led to a concentration of coal camps, one after another, for miles along the narrow hollows. Most of these mines employed from 10 to 300 men and produced on the average about 200,000 tons of coal per year.[16]

Despite their numbers, however, the independent operators produced only a fraction of the coal mined in the area. In fact, a few giant coal companies came to dominate the field. As coal production revived after 1900, syndicates of northern bankers, industrialists, and other capitalists again began to acquire vast tracts of coal land in the mountains and to organize new companies or consolidate the interests of smaller firms. The purpose of these enterprises was to control production in a given area or to provide a continuous supply of coal for the parent firm. Mines in the latter category were usually called "captive" mines, since they produced coal for the parent-consumer rather than for the open market.

One of the three largest coal companies to be established in southern West Virginia at this time was the U.S. Coal and Oil Company, the forerunner of the Island Creek Coal Company. Most of the capital behind this venture was provided by Colonel William A. Coolidge, a Boston attorney and financier, and Albert F. Holden,

14. "Southern Appalachian Population Statistics, 1890–1900," Horace Kephart Journals, vol. 1, pp. 90a–90c, Western Carolina Univ; Southern Appalachian Studies (in cooperation with the Univ. of Georgia), *Number of Inhabitants of the Southern Appalachians, 1900–1957*, Population Data Series No. 1, (Athens, Ga., 1959), Table 19.
15. U.S. Department of Commerce, Bureau of the Census, *Thirteenth Census of the United States, 1910*, III, Population (Washington, D.C., 1913), 1013.
16. Compiled from West Virginia Department of Mines, *Annual Reports*, 1900, 1910; U.S. Bureau of Mines, *Mineral Resources of the United States*, 1900, 1909–1910; Tams, *The Smokeless Coal Fields of West Virginia*, 40.

a wealthy engineer whose family owned the Cleveland (Ohio) *Plain Dealer*. In 1901, Coolidge and Holden purchased about 30,000 acres of coal lands along the Middle Fork of Island Creek in Logan County and incorporated the U.S. Coal and Oil Company to develop the property. The company was capitalized at over six million dollars, and the land was estimated to contain more than 500 million tons of high quality coal.[17] At the turn of the century, Logan County was still untouched by railroads, and most of the land acquired by Coolidge and Holden was yet undeveloped. When the two capitalists came to inspect their property in 1902, the town of Logan Court House had a population of only about two hundred. According to a company history, however, the men were undaunted by the "wilderness," and after walking over the property, they "retired to their tent, donned dinner coats, and, gentlemen to the core, ate dinner in isolated elegance."[18]

To reach their new coal properties, Coolidge and Holden organized the Island Creek Railroad Company and began the construction of a line from Logan Court House through the U.S. Coal and Oil lands to connect with the Ohio Branch of the N&W in Mingo County. In 1903, they established the mining town of Holden and by the end of the following year began to ship coal to the Midwest markets.[19] The opening of the U.S. Coal and Oil Company mines stimulated the rapid development of the Logan Coalfield, as other northern companies acquired land and organized mining companies.[20] Overnight, the town of Logan became a boom town, complete with stone sidewalks, electric lights, and a sewage system.[21] By 1910, Logan County mines were producing over two million tons of coal per year and employing almost 2,400 miners.[22] In that year, the U.S. Coal and Coke Company was reorganized as the Island Creek Coal Company, but Albert F. Holden remained the company's president. Island Creek Coal Company later acquired extensive coal lands in neighboring Pike County, Kentucky, and in

17. *Manufacturers' Record* 48 (20 July 1905), 3; Thurmond, *Logan Coal Field,* 54.
18. Raymond E. Salvati, *Island Creek: Saga in Bituminous* (New York, 1957), 9.
19. Cubby, "The Transformation of the Tug and Guyandot Valleys," 232; *Manufacturers' Record* 48 (20 July 1903), 3.
20. Thurmond, *Logan Coal Field*, 31–35, 41.
21. *Manufacturers' Record* 48 (20 July 1905), 2.
22. U.S. Bureau of Mines, *Mineral Resources of the United States*, 1909–1910.

time became the second-largest coal mining and marketing operation in the country.[23]

While the U.S. Coal and Oil Company was shaping the development of the Logan Coalfield, other northern capitalists were investing heavily in the Flat Top–Pocahontas Coalfield, the largest coal-producing district in southern West Virginia. Beginning shortly after the turn of the century, a group of capitalists associated with the United States Steel Corporation and the Pennsylvania Railroad acquired control of a majority of the coal land in the Flat Top–Pocahontas district. By 1910, through a system of interlocking directorates, they dominated production in that important field. Both the U.S. Steel Corporation and the Pennsylvania Railroad were linked to the New York banking firm of J.P. Morgan and Company. The steel corporation was directly controlled by Morgan interests, and the railroad was tied to Morgan and Company through the Girard Trust Company of Philadelphia.[24] Together, U.S. Steel and the Pennsylvania Railroad constituted the most powerful economic force in Appalachia.

The Pennsylvania Railroad acquired an interest in southern West Virginia coal lands in 1898, when the line purchased control of its two major southern competitors, the C&O and the N&W railroads. Through this new "community of interest," the Pennsylvania Railroad sought to stabilize the coal transportation industry by increasing freight rates and dividing coal markets.[25] As part of its acquisition of N&W properties, the Pennsylvania Railroad gained control of the 300,000 acres of coal land belonging to the Flat Top Coal Land Association in the Pocahontas Coalfield. In 1901, a syndicate of New York men led by Elbert H. Gary, chairman of the newly formed U.S. Steel Corporation, exercised an option to buy the Flat Top lands and subsequently organized the Pocahontas Coal and Coke Company. The Gary syndicate hoped to develop these lands in order to provide a continuous supply of fuel for its steel mills. Within two months, however, the N&W reacquired all of the stock of the

23. *Manufacturers' Record* 60 (16 Nov. 1911), 56; Cubby, "The Transformation of the Tug and Guyandot Valleys," 274.

24. U.S. Congress, Senate, *Hearings Before the Committee on Education and Labor*, 67th Cong., 1st sess., Senate Hearings vol. 181, "The West Virginia Coal Fields," vol. 2 (Washington, D.C., 1921), 640.

25. Allen W. Moger, "Railroad Practices and Policies in Virginia After the Civil War," *Virginia Magazine of History and Biography* 59 (1951), 452–57; Thomas, "Coal Country," 137.

Pocahontas Coal and Coke Company, so as to prevent the over-development of mines along its tracks and thus protect the stability of its freight rate structure. The sale was contingent upon the lease of over 50,000 acres of land to the U.S. Steel Corporation.[26]

Having secured mining rights in the Pocahontas field, the steel corporation then organized a subsidiary company, the United States Coal and Coke Company, and began extensive mining operations in McDowell County. The N&W ran a branch line up the Tug River from Welch to the company's new mining town of Gary, and by 1907, U.S. Coal and Coke was operating sixteen different mines within a few miles of Gary, with expectations of fourteen additional mines.[27] By 1918, U.S. Steel's subsidiary had become the largest single producer of coal in the state of West Virginia, putting out nearly five million tons annually and employing almost 3,900 men.[28] The corporation continued to expand its operations in the southern mountains, leasing and acquiring property throughout the region. In 1923, the United States Coal Commission found that the Morgan affiliate and its auxiliary companies controlled over 750,000 acres of Appalachian coal lands.[29]

Other leading coal companies in the Flat Top–Pocahontas field were also tied to the Morgan interests. The second-largest producer in the field was the Pocahontas Fuel Company, which employed about 2,000 miners. The president of this company was Isaac T. Mann, one of three wealthy capitalists in the original Gary syndicate. After 1901, Mann moved to the coal fields, where he became the head of a coterie of men living in Bramwell, West Virginia, who controlled a number of banks and coal companies in the southern part of the state. In addition to his interests in the Pocahontas Fuel Company, Mann was a shareholder in the Red Jacket Consolidated Coal and Coke Company dominated by E.T. Stotesbury, a partner of Morgan and Company and a director of the Girard Trust.[30] The third-largest producer was the New River and Pocahontas Consolidated Coal Company owned by Edward J. Berwind, a member of a

26. *Manufacturers' Record* 40 (17 Oct. 1901), 209; *ibid.* 40 (5 Dec. 1901), 337; *ibid.* 40 (9 Jan. 1902), 422; Lambie, *From Mine to Market*, 237–38.

27. Edward O'Toole, "Pocahontas Coal Field and Operating Methods of the United States Coal and Coke Company," *Coal Age* 23 (8 March 1923), 400.

28. *Manufacturers' Record* 52 (22 Aug. 1907), 147.

29. Hunt, Tryon, and Willitts, *What the Coal Commission Found*, 90–93. See also *Coal Age* 19 (7 April 1921), 634.

30. Senate hearings, "The West Virginia Coal Fields," 643.

wealthy Philadelphia banking family. Berwind not only held large acreages in the New River and Pocahontas districts but had over 100,000 acres of coal lands in Pike County, Kentucky, as well. In Pennsylvania, he had virtual control of sales and coal belonging to the Pennsylvania Railroad. A director of the Girard Trust, in 1907 Berwind had been a large shareholder in the syndicate organized by J.P. Morgan to acquire the Tennessee Coal, Iron and Railroad Company on the behalf of U.S. Steel.[31]

The sudden rush of activity by northern capitalists after the turn of the century launched a general coal land consolidation movement in southern West Virginia. In areas outside the Pocahontas and Logan coal fields, the Morgan interests and other syndicates sought to gain monopolies on coal production by buying out smaller independent firms. A Morgan group, for example, in 1901 acquired 32,000 acres of highly volatile coal in Kanawha County and thereafter operated under the name of the Kanawha and Hocking Coal and Coke Company.[32] Early in 1906, all but two of the coal companies on Paint Creek were purchased by Scranton, Pennsylvania, capitalists and reorganized as the Paint Creek Collieries Company.[33] The following year, Samuel Dixon, with backing from Scranton and Boston financiers, consolidated twelve mines in the New River district, but Dixon's New River Company was itself absorbed in 1913, when English investors created the Ajax Coal Company to operate ninety-six mines on over 550,000 acres of land in Fayette and Raleigh counties.[34] On Cabin Creek in Kanawha County, other absentee capitalists consolidated eleven mines into the Cabin Creek Consolidated Coal Mining Company.[35] Although there were too many collieries and too many interests for complete consolidation to be achieved, by 1915 the consolidation movement had swept most of the mining companies into the control of a few dominant firms. The higher capitalization of the new consolidated companies, however, increased the pressure for high-volume production, adding to competition and creating an oversupply of marketable coal.[36]

31. *Manufacturers' Record* 48 (3 Aug. 1905), 61; *ibid*. 60 (16 Nov. 1911), 56; Senate hearings, "The West Virginia Coal Fields," 643.
32. Thomas, "Coal Country," 151.
33. *Manufacturers' Record* 49 (18 Jan. 1906), 13.
34. *Ibid*. 51 (12 March 1907), 275; "English Investments in West Virginia Coal Properties," in *ibid*. 64 (23 Oct. 1913), 53.
35. *Ibid*., 51 (7 Feb. 1907), 99.
36. See Thomas, "Coal Country," 157–58.

As expansion and consolidation induced greater production in the older coal districts, other forces were working to open up the last remaining coal fields in southern West Virginia. With the C&O controlling coal shipments along the New and Kanawha rivers on the northern flank of the area and the N&W controlling the Flat Top–Pocahontas and Logan County fields to the south, Pennsylvania Railroad interests had established a monopoly on coal transportation in the southern part of the state. Yet, the interior sections of Raleigh, Fayette, and Wyoming counties remained untouched by the railroads, and it was here that the greatest threat to the power of the Pennsylvania capitalists was introduced.

In 1902, Henry Huttleston Rogers, a key figure in John D. Rockefeller's Standard Oil Company, secretly acquired ownership of the tiny Deepwater Railway on the Kanawha River above Charleston and began to extend the road south into the heart of the coal fields. The new railroad left the line of the C&O at Deepwater and traveled up the Guyandot Valley, across Fayette, Raleigh, and Wyoming counties, and to the Virginia line. When the C&O and N&W—not appreciating the competition with the mines along their tracks—refused to give the Deepwater Railway a reduced rate on the coal to be hauled, an angry Rogers constructed his own railroad across Virginia to Norfolk.[37] In 1907, the Deepwater and the new Tidewater Railway were merged to become the Virginian Railway. The completion of the Virginian opened up the extensive coal lands of the Winding Gulf district of Raleigh and Wyoming counties, effectively ending the monopoly of the two older railroads. Within a decade, the independent coal operators of the Winding Gulf were adding millions of tons to the glut of coal pouring out of the Mountain State.[38]

The last of the untapped coal fields of southern West Virginia was reached in 1911, when the C&O completed a branch line up the Little Coal River in Boone County.[39] Land speculation in Boone County had been intense since 1904, when former Governor William A. MacCorkle of West Virginia and Senator William C. Sproul of Pennsylvania bought large tracts of coal and timber lands along the headwaters of the Little Coal River. The two politicians organized a land company and began construction of the Coal River Railroad into

37. Tams, *Smokeless Coal Fields of West Virginia*, 21–22.
38. *Manufacturers' Record* 55 (1 April 1909), 55; Lambie, *From Mine to Market*, 264; Thomas, "Coal Country," 168–72.
39. Thurmond, *Logan Coal Field*, 51.

their properties.[40] Other speculators flocked to the area, including capitalists from Philadelphia and Milwaukee who purchased nearly 60,000 acres of land. But the development of coal-operating companies awaited the arrival of the C&O, which built branch lines up many of the tributaries of the Little Coal.[41] In 1914, the Lackawanna Coal and Lumber Company of Scranton, Pennsylvania, acquired 30,000 acres of land along Laurel Creek and constructed the company mining town of Griffith.[42] Later, the Colonial Timber and Coal Corporation of Chicago began logging and mining operations on large holdings in Boone and Raleigh counties.[43] By 1925, there were more than sixty mines in Boone County, producing over 4.5 million tons. In that year, coal production peaked in West Virginia at 176 million tons; over 66 percent of that production was in the southern part of the state.[44] The nine coal counties of southern West Virginia produced more coal than any other area of the South.

## KENTUCKY

The coal boom was slower to arrive in eastern Kentucky, although that section was destined later to become the second-largest coal-producing area in the mountains. When development did begin to accelerate at the end of the first decade of the twentieth century, the growth was phenomenal. In 1900, for example, most of the coal mined in Kentucky was produced in the western part of the state. Eastern Kentucky produced only 1.3 million tons, or about 38 percent of the state total. By 1910, that percentage had increased to 41.5, but five years later it had jumped to 64.3 percent, and in the following decade it rose to 78.5 percent. By 1925, three-fourths of all the miners in Kentucky were employed in the Cumberland Plateau, working in over 570 mines.[45]

The rapid growth of the eastern Kentucky coal fields after 1910 was made possible by the extension of railroad branch lines into the

40. *Manufacturers' Record* 49 (22 March 1906), 249.
41. *Ibid.* 48 (3 Aug. 1905), 62; Thurmond, *Logan Coal Field*, 51.
42. *Appalachian Trade Journal* 12 (Feb. 1914), 30.
43. *Manufacturers' Record* 75 (15 May 1919), 85.
44. West Virginia Department of Mines, *Annual Report of 1925*, 100.
45. Isadore Frisch, "Twentieth Century Development of the Coal Mining Industry in Eastern Kentucky and Its Influence Upon the Political Behavior of the Area" (M.A. thesis, Univ. of Kentucky, 1938), 15; U.S. Bureau of Mines, *Mineral Resources*, 1900, p. 393.

area's three major coal districts. In the north, the C&O constructed its Levisa Branch from the head of the Big Sandy River into the Elkhorn district of Pike and Letcher counties. From the south, the L&N built the Wasioto and Black Mountain line into Bell and Harlan counties. And from the west, the eastern Kentucky branch of the L&N was extended from Breathitt County into Perry and Letcher counties in the heart of the Hazard Coalfield. Because of the late development of these districts, many of the mining companies and coal operators in eastern Kentucky came from the older coal fields, especially those in West Virginia, and consequently the area experienced a somewhat greater concentration of the large consolidated or captive mines than was the case elsewhere.

Prior to 1910, most of the coal mined in eastern Kentucky was dug in the southeastern portion of the state. Whitley County in the Jellico Coalfield was the second leading county in Kentucky in coal production between 1890 and 1902. The only other significant production in the Cumberlands was in neighboring Knox and Bell counties.[46] With the opening up of the Great Lakes markets after 1898, these counties became the center of great activity. In Knox, a syndicate of Pennsylvania capitalists constructed a short-line railroad into the Brush Creek district, providing connections for a number of new mining companies. By 1906, there were more than forty operations located in the area.[47] The revival of the coal market had a similar effect in Bell County. The "magic" city of Middlesboro was reborn with the new interest in coal mining, and by 1903 it was home to fifteen mining companies and a population of over 3,000. Elsewhere in the county, new mines were established "by the dozens," and for a short time Bell became the third-largest producer in the state.[48]

As was the case in West Virginia at this time, much of the steady rise in coal production resulted from a general consolidation movement. Beginning about 1907, many of the older operations were absorbed by larger, more highly capitalized corporations. In Bell County, one of the largest of the new consolidated companies was the

46. James Hayden Siler, "A History of Jellico, Tennessee," unpublished MS, Mountain Collection, Berea College, 20–21.

47. *Manufacturers' Record* 48 (28 Sept. 1905), 261; Howard, "Chapters in the Economic History of Knox County, Kentucky," 87.

48. *Manufacturers' Record* 43 (12 March 1903), 153; "Magic Middlesboro: The City That Has Come Back," *Appalachian Trade Journal* 7 (Sept. 1911), 32; U.S. Bureau of Mines, *Mineral Resources*, 1909–1910, p. 141.

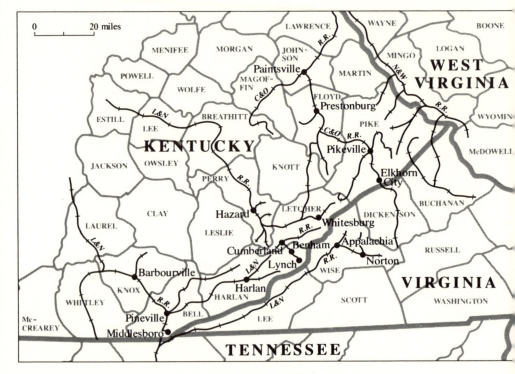

*8. Major Railroads of Eastern Kentucky*

Continental Coal Corporation of Wyoming. Between 1909 and 1913, Continental acquired fifteen mines operating on over 35,000 acres of land leased from the American Association, Inc.[49] Farther north, in Breathitt and Knott counties, capitalists from Ohio and Pennsylvania purchased mines and coal properties around Jackson. And, anticipating the extension of the railroad, G.S. Beckwith and Company of Cleveland acquired nearly 80,000 acres of land in Knott and Letcher counties.[50] In 1911, coal operators from Connellsville,

49. *Manufacturers' Record* 55 (13 May 1909), 48; *ibid.* 57 (11 May 1911), 58; *Appalachian Trade Journal* 10 (April 1913), 17. Continental was itself absorbed in 1911 by Consolidation Coal.

50. *Manufacturers' Record* 52 (15 Aug. 1907), 127; *ibid.* 62 (12 Sept. 1912), 57.

Pennsylvania, consolidated a number of small tracts into a holding of over 175,000 acres in Knott, Perry, and Magoffin counties.[51]

Developments in the older coal districts, however, could not keep pace with the expansion of mining into new areas, and with the arrival of the railroads in the deeper mountain counties, the older fields slipped in the ranks of coal production. The first challenge to the older districts came in 1904, when the C&O began constructing its branch line up the headwaters of the Big Sandy River. The line ran from Louisa in Lawrence County, up the Levisa Fork, and through Johnson, Floyd, and Pike counties to Elkhorn in Letcher County, opening some of the richest coal lands in Kentucky to exploitation. By August 1905, there were already several large operating companies beginning to establish mines along the Levisa Branch.[52] Most of the coal land in the new district—the Elkhorn Coalfield—was controlled by two land companies, the Big Sandy Coal Company and John C.C. Mayo's Northern Coal and Coke Company. The Big Sandy Coal Company was owned by Charles E. Hellier, a Boston attorney who had begun to acquire Elkhorn coal lands in the late 1890s. By consolidating ownership of a number of tracts, Hellier eventually controlled over 130,000 acres.[53] Together, the Hellier and May interests held the title or mineral rights to more than 500,000 acres of Elkhorn land.

The completion of the railroad opened the way for the organization of a large number of mining companies in the Elkhorn field, but the most spectacular developments began with the arrival of the Consolidation Coal Company, a giant Maryland-based corporation with extensive holdings in Pennsylvania and northern West Virginia. In 1909, Consolidation entered the southern coal fields by purchasing 31,000 acres of land along Millers Creek in Johnson, Martin, and Lawrence counties. The following year, the company acquired 100,000 acres of land at the head of Elkhorn Creek in Knott, Letcher, and Pike counties.[54] The Elkhorn land was adjacent to the Hellier properties and to land which Edward J. Berwind had acquired in addition to his southern West Virginia investments.[55] The Millers

51. *Ibid*. 60 (9 Nov. 1911), 55.
52. *Ibid*. 48 (3 Aug. 1905), 60.
53. *Ibid*. 50 (19 July 1906), 3.
54. Beachley, *History of the Consolidation Coal Company*, 54.
55. *Manufacturers' Record* 58 (10 Nov. 1910), 50.

Creek property was purchased from John C.C. Mayo, and the Elkhorn property was acquired from the Northern Coal and Coke Company, of which Mayo was a major shareholder. One of Mayo's associates in the Northern Coal and Coke Company was Senator Clarence W. Watson of West Virginia, chairman of the board of Consolidation Coal.[56]

Soon after gaining control of the Elkhorn coal lands, the Consolidation Company began construction on its own railroad, the Sandy Valley and Elkhorn Railroad, running from its properties to a connection with the C&O above Pikeville. At the headwaters of the Elkhorn Creek, the company built a model mining town called Jenkins to serve as the center of its Kentucky operations. Later, the town of McRoberts was constructed, and by 1922 the company had established additional mining operations on lands in Knox and Bell counties, in Tazewell and Buchanan counties, Virginia, and in McDowell County, West Virginia.[57] Its original expenditures in the Elkhorn field add up to over $40 million, and, according to the *Manufacturers' Record*, they were "planned on a larger scale than any mining undertaking ever projected in this country for an initial development." Consolidation estimated that the Jenkins mines would have an output of more than 25,000 tons a day.[58]

The dominance of the Consolidation Coal Company in the Elkhorn field was assured in 1913 with the incorporation of an affiliated firm, the Elkhorn Fuel Company, to operate on 285,000 acres of land adjacent to the Jenkins property. The president of the new firm was Clarence W. Watson, and its board of directors included Mayo, George W. Fleming of Baltimore, George A. Baird of Chicago, West Virginia Senator Johnson N. Camden, and Virginia Congressman C. Bascom Slemp.[59] The coal lands of the Elkhorn Fuel Company were purchased from the Northern Coal and Coke Company and lay mostly in Letcher and Floyd counties along Beaver Creek. With the outbreak of war in Europe, the Elkhorn Fuel Company was reorganized as the Elkhorn Coal Corporation, and production was increased to full capacity to meet wartime demands. By

56. Beachley, *History of Consolidation Coal Company*, 59; *Manufacturers' Record* 63 (20 March 1913), 54.

57. Beachley, *History of Consolidation Coal Company*, 62–67.

58. *Manufacturers' Record* 63 (13 Feb. 1913), 51.

59. *Ibid.*; *ibid.* 64 (24 July 1913), 57; *Appalachian Trade Journal* 10 (Feb. 1913), 40.

1916, two large company towns had been constructed at Haymond and Wheelwright, and the company was employing hundreds of immigrant miners brought in to work in the Elkhorn mines.[60] Through its own properties and those of the Elkhorn Coal Corporation, the Consolidation interests controlled almost a million acres of southern Appalachian lands, "probably the greatest principality in high-grade coal lands owned by two affiliated interests in the world."[61]

About the time that the Consolidation Coal Company was expanding its operations in the northern part of Letcher County, the L&N Railroad was rushing construction of a branch line from the west into the Hazard Coalfield of Perry and Letcher counties. In 1913, the Lexington and Eastern Kentucky Branch of the L&N was extended from Jackson in Breathitt County to a terminus at McRoberts in Letcher County. As the new line progressed up the North Fork of the Kentucky River, extensive mining operations were undertaken around Hazard, and suddenly the quiet village was transformed into a boom town of 2,000.[62] The first coal was shipped from Perry County in 1912, and by 1916 there were over twenty operations in the Hazard field.[63] The arrival of the railroad in Letcher County brought so many changes between 1913 and 1918 that to one native resident it didn't "seem like the same country. So many new towns, people and coal companies. We have about twenty through freights daily and two locals and four passenger" [trains].[64] By 1920, Letcher and Perry counties ranked third and fourth respectively in coal production in the state.[65]

Unlike the Elkhorn field, no single corporation dominated production in the Hazard district. The largest landholding company was the Kentucky River Coal Corporation, a Virginia company formed by the consolidation of five smaller firms in 1915. The company was

60. *Manufacturers' Record* 70 (24 Aug. 1916), 52; Chapman, "The Influence of Coal in the Big Sandy Valley," 163–72.

61. *Manufacturers' Record* 63 (20 March 1913), 54.

62. B.H. Schockel, "Changing Conditions in the Kentucky Mountains," *Scientific Monthly* 3 (Aug. 1916), 109; Duff, "Government in an Eastern Kentucky Coal Field County," 6–8.

63. *Manufacturers' Record* 69 (9 March 1916), 52; *ibid.* 70 (24 Aug. 1916), 52. *Manufacturers' Record* reported that "a large number" of the operators in this section were from West Virginia, Virginia, and Tennessee coal areas.

64. Whitaker, *History of Corporal Fess Whitaker*, 120.

65. U.S. Bureau of Mines, *Mineral Resouces*, 1920, p. 588.

owned by Congressman C. Bascom Slemp of Virginia, who was also one of the original directors of the Elkhorn Fuel Company. The Kentucky River Corporation controlled over 140,000 acres of rich coal and timber lands and leased to a number of different operating firms.[66] Among the bigger operating companies were the Blue Diamond Coal Company, the Hawey Coal Company, and the Blue-grass Coal Company on First Creek; the Ashless Coal Corporation and the Kentucky Jewel Coal Company at Lowthair, and the Diamond Block Coal Company on Buffalo Creek. The Kentucky River Power Company built a large generating plant at Glowmar to provide electricity for mining and other industrial developments in the area.[67]

The final opening of the eastern Kentucky coal fields came when the Wasiota and Black Mountain Branch of the L&N was completed to the head of the Cumberland River in Harlan County. As early as the turn of the century, northern capitalists were sending land agents into the Harlan Coalfield, but the absence of adequate transportation prevented its early development.[68] In 1907, Thomas Jefferson Asher of Pineville began construction of a short-line railroad up the Cumberland River in Bell County to reach coal lands that he had recently acquired. Three years later, that line was taken over by the L&N and extended some twenty-seven miles to Benham, above the town of Mount Pleasant.[69] The first coal was shipped from Harlan County in 1911, and by 1914 production had reached over a million tons annually. As coal activities increased, the town of Mount Pleasant changed its name to Harlan, and thousands of miners poured into the district from the surrounding hills. Between 1910 and 1920, the population of Harlan County tripled, and it doubled again the next decade. By 1920, Harlan had become the leading coal-producing county in Kentucky.[70]

The largest coal operations in the Harlan Coalfield were estab-

66. *Manufacturers' Record* 67 (25 March 1915), 38; *Coal Age* 23 (3 May 1923), 713.

67. *Manufacturers' Record* 69 (9 March 1916), 52; *ibid.* 69 (24 Aug. 1916), 52.

68. *Manufacturers' Record* 45 (9 June 1904), 462.

69. *Ibid.* 58 (4 Aug. 1910), 69; W.R. Peck and R.J. Sampson, "The Harlan Coal Field of Kentucky," *Coal Age* 3 (24 May 1913), 796.

70. Peck and Sampson, "The Harlan Coal Field," 796; Frisch, "Twentieth Century Development of the Coal Mining Industry," 13; Paul Frederick Cressey, "Social Disorganization and Reorganization in Harlan County, Kentucky," *American Sociological Review* 14 (1949), 390.

lished near the town of Benham. In 1910, the Wisconsin Steel Company, a subsidiary of the Morgan–McCormick International Harvester Company of Chicago, began mining and coking activities on about 20,000 acres of land which it had acquired several years earlier.[71] Benham was constructed "almost over night" from materials hauled in from Virginia before the Wasiota and Black Mountain Branch was completed; by 1915, it contained over two hundred mining houses, a YMCA building, and "other modern conveniences."[72] Two miles east of Benham, at Lynch, another Morgan affiliate, U.S. Coal and Coke, built one of the largest coal-mining plants in the South. Operating on about 60,000 acres of land adjacent to the Wisconsin Steel property, U.S. Coal and Coke constructed some 2,000 buildings to provide for a population that reached 10,000 in 1919. All of the coal produced at the Lynch mines was shipped for coking to the U.S. Steel Corporation's mills in Gary, Indiana.[73]

A second major area of the Harlan field was located along Martin's Fork near the town of Harlan. About 86,000 acres of the mineral land in Martin's Fork was controlled by the Kentenia Land Corporation of New York. The Kentenia Corporation was organized in 1910 by the Davis Estate of Philadelphia, which had acquired the land in the late nineteenth century. Promoters of the Davis property were influential in soliciting the extension of the L&N Railroad into Harlan County, and after 1911 the Kentenia lands became the site of several large mining operations.[74] Other large holdings in the Martin's Fork district were controlled by Judge W.F. Hall, a local politician who owned and leased a nine-foot coal seam—one of the largest in the field.[75]

In 1921, Harlan County produced about 30 percent of all of the coal mined in eastern Kentucky, and together with Pike, Perry, and Letcher counties, accounted for nearly 80 percent of all of the coal

71. *Manufacturers' Record* 45 (9 June 1904), 462; *ibid*. 59 (8 June 1911), 50; *Appalachian Trade Journal* 4 (March 1910), 22.
72. Peck and Sampson, "The Harlan Coal Field," 799; *Manufacturers' Record* 67 (4 Feb. 1915), 52.
73. *Manufacturers' Record* 72 (11 Oct. 1917), 68; *ibid*. 75 (9 Jan. 1919), 77; *ibid*. 75 (10 April 1919), 98.
74. *Manufacturers' Record* 71 (22 March 1917), 60; *Appalachian Trade Journal* 6 (Aug. 1911), 14; John Watts Hevener, "A New Deal for Harlan: The Roosevelt Labor Policies in a Kentucky Coal Field, 1931–1939" (Ph.D. diss., Ohio State Univ., 1971), 5.
75. *Manufacturers' Record* 71 (22 March 1917), 60.

*Lynch, Harlan County, Kentucky, Scene Looking West from East End.*
*Source: Postcard in possession of George Stephenson, Emory, Virginia.*

shipped from the Cumberland Plateau. Over the next decade, the production in Harlan County would more than double, reaching a peak of 15 million tons in 1929.[76]

The increased production of the 1920s, however, came primarily from the expansion of existing mines. The only major new enterprise to be undertaken in that section after 1920 involved the acquisition of coal and timber land in Harlan, Bell, Perry, and Leslie counties by the Ford Motor Company. During the war, Henry Ford had become interested in southern Appalachian coal lands as a source of cheap fuel for his expanding automobile factories in the Midwest. In 1920, he purchased the mining properties of the Banner Fork Coal Corporation in Harlan County. And with his acquisition two years later of the lands of the F.S. Peabody interests of Chicago, Ford came to control more than 165,000 acres of valuable coal lands.[77] Most of the Ford property was in Leslie County and included a number of previously opened mines. With the development of these properties, the last of the great coal fields of eastern Kentucky entered the Industrial Age.

## VIRGINIA AND TENNESSEE

The expansion of the coal industry in southwest Virginia and eastern Tennessee after 1900 was similar to the growth in West Virginia and Kentucky, although on a much smaller scale. Mining had been carried on in parts of Virginia and Tennessee since the 1870s and 1880s; after the turn of the century, production increased rapidly as a result of consolidation and the opening of new and larger mines. By 1910, production in these two states had more than doubled, and in the next decade it increased nearly fivefold. Virginia was the larger coal producer of these two states, having an output of about 45 million tons in 1920 and employing 14,000 men. Tennessee produced 26 million tons and employed 11,000 miners.[78]

The largest coal-producing county in Virginia was Wise County, which consistently produced from 50 to 60 percent of the coal mined in the state. Wise County was opened up in the early 1890s by the Clinch Valley Branch of the N&W Railway, and by 1897 it had

76. U.S. Bureau of Mines, *Mineral Resources*, 1921, Pt. II, 592; Cressey, "Social Disorganization and Reorganization," 390.
77. *Coal Age* 23 (29 March 1923), 534; *Manufacturers' Record* 78 (22 July 1920), 92.
78. U.S. Bureau of Mines, *Mineral Resources*, 1910, 1920.

surpassed Tazewell County in total annual production.[79] The Wise fields continued to be dominated by a few large operations, including the Virginia Iron, Coal, and Coke Company, the Virginia Coal and Iron Company, the Stonega Coal and Coke Company, and George L. Carter's Carter Coal Company. The latter was sold in 1922 to the Consolidation Coal Company, when that multistate firm entered the Wise fields.[80] In 1920, the county contained almost half of all the miners employed in Virginia.[81]

A major factor in the growth of the Virginia coal industry in these years was the penetration of the Clinchfield coal district, which lay between Wise and Tazewell counties. Since the 1880s, promoters had attempted to finance a railroad that would reach the Clinchfield area on a direct route from the Midwest to the coastal cities of the Southeast. The Charleston, Cincinnati, and Chicago Railway was organized to undertake the task, and it completed a portion of the roadbed before succumbing in the financial panic of 1893. After the turn of the century, the project was taken up by George L. Carter, who succeeded in attracting the financial backing of James A. Blair and Company, bankers of New York. In 1902, the Blair interests organized the South and Western Railway and, under Carter's direction, constructed a short line from Dante to St. Paul in Russell County, opening that area to coal mining.[82]

The Blair interests, however, had larger plans for the South and Western. In addition to its control of that road, Blair and Company also controlled the Seaboard Air Line Railway, one of the major trunk lines in the Southeast. Shortly after the completion of the South and Western, the company began to chart the extension of that line to connect with the Seaboard in South Carolina. In 1905, the Blair syndicate established the Clinchfield Coal Corporation and began acquiring coal lands and mining operations in southwest Virginia. The Clinchfield Corporation eventually consolidated over 400,000 acres of coal property in Wise, Dickenson, Russell, and Buchanan counties and gained a virtual monopoly on coal production in the Clinchfield district. One of the directors of the new company was

79. *Ibid.*
80. *Manufacturers' Record* 57 (28 April 1910), 57; *ibid.* 63 (9 Jan. 1913), 61; *ibid.* 81 (16 Feb. 1922), 54; *Coal Age* 17 (4 March 1920), 437.
81. U.S. Bureau of Mines, *Mineral Resources*, 1920.
82. *Manufacturers' Record* 49 (7 June 1906), 579; *ibid.* 52 (1 Aug. 1907), 73; *ibid.* 55 (11 Feb. 1909), 47.

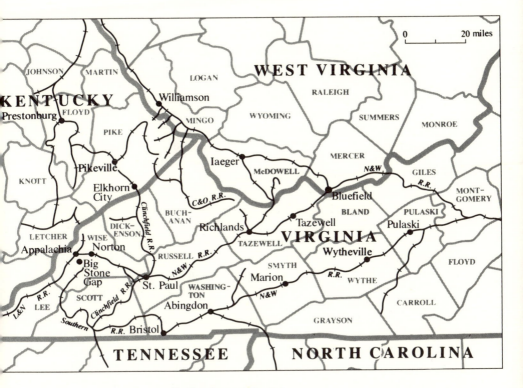

*9. Southwest Virginia*

Isaac T. Mann, president of the Pocahontas Fuel Company in southern West Virginia and associate of the Gary interests at U.S. Steel.[83] Two years after acquiring the Clinchfield coal lands, Blair and Company reorganized the South and Western Railway as the Carolina, Clinchfield, and Ohio Railroad and began construction of that railroad from Spartanburg, South Carolina, to Elkhorn City, Kentucky.[84]

The main objective of the Clinchfield Railroad was to tap the coal reserves owned by the Blair interests and to provide for the transpor-

83. William Way, Jr., *The Clinchfield Railroad: The Story of a Trade Route Across the Blue Ridge Mountains* (Chapel Hill, 1931), 95–97; *Manufacturers' Record* 55 (8 July 1909), 43; *Appalachian Trade Journal* 4 (May 1910), 25.
84. *Manufacturers' Record* 52 (1 Aug. 1907), 73; *ibid.* 55 (11 Feb. 1909), 47.

tation of that coal to the expanding textile mills of the Southeast and the coal piers of the Seaboard Air Line in Charleston. In order to reach the coal fields, the company had to lay its tracks almost three hundred miles over the Blue Ridge Mountains of North Carolina and Virginia. Although construction began in 1907, completion of the line was delayed for several years by the difficulty of building in the rugged mountain country. For eight miles along the Clinch River, the roadbed was hewn out of solid rock from the sides of projecting mountains. Fifty-five tunnels had to be punched through the Blue Ridge, eighteen of them in one 18-mile section.[85] The line finally reached Elkhorn City and the Big Sandy Branch of the C&O in 1915, just in time to meet the rising coal demands of World War I.[86] With the completion of the Clinchfield Railroad, the heart of the coal fields at the headwaters of the Big Sandy River in Kentucky, Virginia, and West Virginia was opened to full development. Over two million acres of coal lands in that area, among the richest in the world, had come under the control of three giant corporations—the Consolidation Coal Company, the Clinchfield Coal Corporation, and the U.S. Steel Corporation.

The completion of new railroad lines also contributed to the steady rise of production in East Tennessee. The extension of the L&N Railroad from Jellico to Knoxville after the turn of the century stimulated mining activities in Campbell and Claiborne counties on the Kentucky border near Middlesboro.[87] For the next three decades, Campbell was the leading coal-producing county in Tennessee, and Claiborne followed, a close second. The Clear Fork section of Claiborne County was opened up in 1906 by an extension of the Southern Railroad, and that district became the location of several large mines. Most of the land in the Clear Fork district—as in much of Bell County, Kentucky—was owned by the American Association, Inc.[88] In 1910, Campbell and Claiborne counties were the only counties in Tennessee producing over a million tons of coal a year.[89] After Campbell and Claiborne counties, the next most important coal-producing areas in Tennessee were in Anderson and Morgan

85. *Ibid.* 55 (11 Feb. 1909), 47; Van Noppen, *Western North Carolina*, 265.
86. *Manufacturers' Record* 68 (8 July 1915), 40.
87. *Ibid.* 48 (27 July 1905), 34–35.
88. *Ibid.* 49 (17 Feb. 1906), 121.
89. U.S. Bureau of Mines, *Mineral Resources*, 1909–1910, p. 198.

counties. The latter county was the home of the only state-owned prison mines in the southern Appalachians. At its two mines on Brushy Mountain, the state of Tennessee employed convicts to produce about 350,000 tons of coal a year.[90]

South of Morgan County, coal production was limited almost entirely to Hamilton and Marion counties in the Walden's Ridge section above Chattanooga. Although the proportion of coal coming from this district declined significantly after the turn of the century, actual production in the field increased, as most of the older mines were consolidated into larger firms. In Marion County, for example, about 300,000 acres of coal land were consolidated in 1906 by the Cumberland Plateau Corporation of New York, which in turn leased its property to several small coal operations near Anderson.[91] In 1910, a group of Baltimore and New York capitalists organized the Durham Coal and Iron Company to operate several mines on more than 66,000 acres of land near Soddy. The Durham Company owned thirteen of the fourteen coal mines in Hamilton County.[92] Like many of the smaller mines of East Tennessee, these operated at peak production during periods of high demand for coal, but they often closed down when the market tightened, unable to compete with the better quality coal and greater production of the mines in other parts of the Cumberland Plateau.

## BOOM AND BUST

The demand for coal increased steadily after 1900, stimulating the rapid growth of the mountain coal industry. Throughout the region the rising trend of production was characterized not only by the arrival of the giant coal corporations like those in the Elkhorn and Pocahontas fields, but also by the proliferation of many smaller producers. Because of the relatively low capital requirements for opening a mine, the number of coal mines in the southern mountains grew in proportion to the rise in market demand. And at times during this period the demand was almost unlimited. Between 1909 and 1919, the total number of coal mines in the United States increased by

90. *Appalachian Trade Journal* 3 (Sept. 1909), 7.
91. *Manufacturers' Record* 50 (1 Nov. 1906), 396.
92. *Ibid.* 58 (17 Nov. 1910), 60; *ibid.* 59 (16 Feb. 1911), 62; *Appalachian Trade Journal* 9 (July 1912), 17.

more than a third, and the largest percentage of that increase came in the South.[93]

Many of the mines opened during the coal boom were marginal operations, often employing only a handful of miners and sometimes working only on a seasonal basis. Such producers might open their mine in the fall months, operate for a few weeks, and then close down, having realized enough profit during that period to pay for their comparatively small investments. These mines were usually called "snow birds," because they ordinarily operated when there was snow on the ground and the demand for coal was at its peak. Other small producers operated all year, competing with the larger companies for markets and coal cars. Profits in coal mining were big, averaging from 15 to 25 percent on investment, and one-fourth of the operators averaged over 25 percent.[94] This prospect helped to entice hundreds of speculators into the field, increasing the competition and instability in the industry as a whole. The largest increases in production and mining operations, moreover, came during the war years, when artificial demands induced the expansion of the industry beyond the limits which the national economy could justify during times of peace.

Beginning in 1915, as American factories geared up to make munitions and other war supplies, coal prices and production rose dramatically. Within a year, coal for steam purposes rose from about eighy cents per ton at the mine to as much as six or seven dollars per ton for prompt shipment. Coal operators in Virginia were getting from ten to twelve dollars per ton for whatever quantities of coke they could produce. A correspondent to the *Manufacturers' Record* reported in 1916 that "this wild chase for enormous profits" was the "greatest prosperity producers [had] ever known," and it was attracting "many operators into the Appalachian fields."[95] Prices were finally stabilized in 1917 when the United States entered the war, but demand remained unlimited. The Federal Fuel Administration set the price for soft coal at $2.58 per ton, "enough to return a profit to any moderately well run mine."[96] The only factor limiting produc-

93. *Manufacturers' Record* 80 (25 Aug. 1921), 62.
94. U.S. Congress, Senate, *Report of the United States Coal Commission*, 2632; E.A. Goldenweiser (Federal Reserve Board), "Incomes of Bituminous Coal Producers," *American Statistical Association* 17 (June 1920), 206–7.
95. *Manufacturers' Record* 70 (14 Dec. 1916), 45.
96. Malcolm Ross, *Machine Age in the Hills* (New York, 1933), 51.

tion was a national shortage of railroad cars. Any operator who could get a supply of cars could sell his coal.[97]

In the intense competition of the war years, southern producers had a number of advantages over their northern counterparts. The Fuel Administration allotted railroad cars on the basis of mine capacity, and the newly opened mines in the mountains shared equally with older northern mines in the daily supply. Most of the increased demand for coal came from the war industries of the Midwest, and the South had been gaining ground in that market since 1898. In fact, the penetration of the Great Lakes markets was a major stimulus in the opening of the eastern Kentucky coal fields, which expanded more rapidly in this period than any other coal field in the country. Southern coal operators were also aided by an already existing freight rate structure that permitted access to the northern markets. Finally, the South had a larger labor reserve than the northern mining districts, where large numbers of miners were departing for urban industrial centers.[98] These factors contributed to the accelerated expansion of coal mining in the southern mountains during the war years, when mines and company towns were constructed by the hundreds, and mountain farmers left their fields in droves to work underground.

The phenomenal growth of coal mining during World War I is best illustrated in eastern Kentucky. In Floyd County, for instance, the number of mines increased from sixteen in 1916 to sixty-two in 1920; the number in Pike County increased from eight to forty-five.[99] In Bell, Harlan, Perry, Letcher, Floyd, and Pike counties, coal mining became the chief means of employment for a majority of the population.[100]

The high prices and unprecedented demand for coal continued until early in 1923. The armistice in Europe and the mild winter of 1918–1919 left large stockpiles of unused coal in the North, causing a drop in demand that lasted into the summer of 1919. Orders began to pick up by the fall, however, and the savage competition in the coal industry resumed. In November of 1919 and again in 1921 and 1922, major strikes hit the union coal fields, just as France and Italy were

97. O.E. Kiessling, "Coal Mining in the South," *Annals of the American Academy of Political and Social Science* 153 (1930), 89.

98. *Ibid*. See also *Manufacturers' Record* 70 (20 July 1916), 62a.

99. Chapman, "The Influence of Coal in the Big Sandy Valley," 221.

100. U.S. Department of Agriculture, *Economic and Social Conditions*, 86–87, 121–24.

beginning to recover from the war and were increasing their demand for American coal. Nonunion southern mines took advantage of the situation and gained a greater share of the market, thus maintaining for a time their expanded level of production.[101] At a point in 1920 when the demand for coal was greatest, moreover, the Fuel Administration withdrew its controls on price, sending coal into a runaway seller's market. Within a few weeks, coal for the Great Lakes was selling at ten dollars a ton, and coal for export brought more than fourteen dollars a ton.[102] The great boom was set back slightly by the recession of 1921--1922, but by the spring of 1923 the coal industry was again producing at such a frantic pace that it taxed the capacity of the railroads to handle the product. In eastern Kentucky, the C&O was hauling 3,500 coal cars per week on its Big Sandy Branch, but the production of the Big Sandy mines was over twice that amount.[103]

Bituminous coal production in the United States reached its height in 1923. In that year there were over 700,000 men working in nearly 12,000 mines, with a possible annual production of nearly a billion tons.[104] Yet, just as coal reached the pinnacle of its power, inherent weaknesses in the industry became apparent and began to take their toll. The first sign of trouble came in the fall of 1923, when orders for winter fuel supplies began to decline. The European mines' return to production and slower growth rates in midwestern industries caused a sharp drop in the demand for American coal. The slump was aggravated in 1924, when coal consumers continued to utilize the large reserves they had accumulated in anticipation of a possible labor strike. The strike was avoided, but the market remained dull throughout 1925.[105]

The effect of the coal depression was to intensify the rivalry between northern and southern producers. The Jacksonville Agreement of 1924 between the union and most of the northern operators tied the latter to a fixed wage scale, whereas the southern operators were free to adjust wages and thereby gain a larger share of the reduced market. As early as the 1890s, southern mine owners had

101. U.S. Congress, Senate, *Report of the U.S. Coal Commission*, 2008–10, 2354–65; Kiessling, "Coal Mining in the South," 89.
102. Ross, *Machine Age in the Hills*, 51.
103. U.S. Congress, Senate, *Report of the U.S. Coal Commission*, 1286.
104. Ross, *Machine Age in the Hills*, 53.
105. Kiessling, "Coal Mining in the South," 90.

followed the practice of lowering production costs by cutting wages. Since labor accounted for about 60 percent of the cost of producing coal, mountain operators frequently pared wages in order to undersell their northern competitors. After the Jacksonville Agreement was signed, most of the nonunion operators reduced wage rates, first to the 1919 level and later to the prewar level and even lower. By the end of 1925, practically all of the mines in southern West Virginia, eastern Kentucky, southwest Virginia, and eastern Tennessee were operating nonunion. Whereas the standard daily wage in the union fields was $7.50, the nonunion mines were paying only about $5.00 per day and were increasing production to unprecedented scales.[106]

In 1926, the coal market revived briefly when a general strike in England threatened a coal shortage, but the increases were temporary and the competitive advantage remained with the nonunion districts. Increasingly, the coal business was diverted from the northern to the southern fields, and in an effort to survive, the union districts sought to reduce their wages as well. Strikes and violence ensued in the North, and the union was eventually defeated in most fields. With the last check on wage reductions removed, the operators slashed prices far below the cost of production and engaged in cut-throat competition. The lower wages and fewer days of employment drove many miners from the northern coal fields to find work in Detroit automobile plants or in the steel mills of Ohio, Illinois, and Pennsylvania. Between 1923 and 1927, over 200,000 miners, mostly from the union districts, left the American coal fields.[107]

The southern Appalachian producers continued to capture a greater share of the production, providing almost 80 percent of the bituminous coal output in 1930, but prices also plummeted.[108] After 1927, production in the mountains commenced a sharp decline, sending the region's once booming coal industry into the abyss of depression. The first mines to close were the smaller operations, the snow birds and those unable to compete with the output and quality of the giant corporations. Hundreds of coal companies in the mountains went bankrupt or simply boarded up their mines, abandoned the company towns, and left the region. Some of the larger companies

106. *Ibid.*, 90–91; Ross, *Machine Age in the Hills*, 54–55; *Manufacturers' Record* 89 (18 March 1926), 91.

107. Ross, *Machine Age in the Hills*, 53.

108. Homer L. Morris, *The Plight of the Bituminous Coal Miner* (Philadelphia, 1934), 14.

continued to make money because of their locations, investments, and the value of their coal, but even they reduced the size of their work force and allowed their facilities to deteriorate. By 1930, unemployment, destitution, and despair stalked the coal fields. Although coal production recovered again with the outbreak of World War II, employment in the Appalachian coal fields never again reached the levels of the halcyon days of the twenties.

In the mountains, the collapse of the coal industry brought the new order to its knees. King Coal had never been entirely healthy in the region, having suffered almost continually from chronic overproduction. The ease of entry, high prices, cheap transportation, and cheap labor costs made mining in the mountains one of the most profitable ventures in that period of capitalist expansion and contributed to the crass overdevelopment of the field. Since no local markets were available, southern mountain coal producers intruded on the markets of other coal districts, generating intense competition in an industry subject to rapidly fluctuating demand. The spurious markets of the war years drove profits higher, stimulating producers to add more capacity than the nation could normally consume. When the inevitable shrinkage of demand came in the early twenties, operators tried to protect their profits by taking losses out of the miners' paychecks, but this resulted only in violence, strikes, and further instability. The fierce competition only drove prices lower. By 1920, the industry was so overexpanded that there were over 6,200 companies actively mining bituminous coal.[109]

Other factors, moreover, came together in the 1920s to complicate the king's illness and to assure his ultimate demise. Prior to 1926, the southern producers had enjoyed a favorable freight rate differential on the long-haul transportation of coal. This differential had allowed them to enter the profitable Great Lakes markets, much to the irritation of northern operators. In 1926, pressured by intense competition, constricted demand, and the Jacksonville wage agreement, the northerners brought suit before the Interstate Commerce Commission (ICC) to alter the existing freight rate structure. Pointing out that the existing rates had deprived them of their former markets in the Midwest, the northern operators requested a 20-cent-per-ton reduction in their freight rates to the lake ports. Southern operators ob-

109. Glen Lawhon Parker, *The Coal Industry: A Study In Social Control* (Washington, D.C., 1940), 12.

jected to any change in the current structure, arguing that the loss of the lake trade would strike a devastating blow to the southern industry and that the "economic ashes" of the northern districts were attributable not to the rate differential but to inefficient management and the "excessive wage scale" of the union mines.[110] On 28 May 1927, the ICC ruled in favor of the northern producers, despite angry protests by the southern coal men.[111] The loss of competitive advantage in the Great Lakes markets came at a critical time for southern production and contributed significantly to the depression of the industry in the mountains.

The problems of overproduction and increased shipping costs were compounded by a general decline in the market demand for coal, as consumers in the postwar period turned increasingly to cheaper fuels such as oil and gas. The inroads of the petroleum industry began to be felt as early as 1919, when a number of northern factories, including several large iron and steel mills, converted to fuel oil.[112] The high price of coal and the uncertainty of supply, due to frequent labor strife, caused many industrial users to switch to fuel oil; moreover, gas and oil were cleaner than coal for household heating. The use of hydroelectric power doubled in the decade from 1917 to 1927, further driving coal from the markets, and research and development on new technology made possible more efficient consumption of coal in industrial boilers and in the generators of electric power plants. For example, the railroads, among the largest users of coal, learned to cut their consumption by millions of tons a year through the introduction of better locomotive fireboxes.[113]

Ironically, technological progress also played a role in overproduction. Not only did science teach industries how to use less coal, but it also invented new ways of mining more coal and of lessening the demand for human labor. The introduction of mining machines and the improvement of underground haulage systems increased the amount of coal that a miner could dig in a day and reduced the number of hands needed on an operation. The mechanization of the southern Appalachian mines proceeded rapidly after 1915, and by 1930 most

110. *Manufacturers' Record* 90 (28 Oct. 1926), 53–54.
111. *Ibid.* 91 (9 June 1927), 60–79; *ibid.* 92 (25 Aug. 1927), 55. The decision was known as the Great Lakes Cargo Freight Rate Case.
112. *Manufacturers' Record* 77 (Jan. 1920), 156.
113. *Manufacturers' Record* 92 (24 Nov. 1927), 79; Ross, *Machine Age in the Hills*, 56–57.

of the larger operations utilized some form of mining machines.[114] During the peak years of production, from 1915 to 1926, much of the growth in total output was due to the introduction of mining machines.[115] After the collapse of 1927, many of the larger companies were able by effective mechanization to continue mining at a profit. At the onset of the Great Depression, the Island Creek Coal Company, for example, decided to abandon the hand loading of coal into mine cars and to install mechanical loading devices. Money to pay for this move was available because the "management of the company had prudently accumulated a very substantial liquid surplus from the profits of the twenties, and this money was now employed to produce further profits."[116] Such practices usually resulted in significant reduction of the work force in a mine at a time when unemployment was already high and many miners had nowhere else to turn.

King Coal, however, had never expressed a deep concern for the mountain people. Like the timber barons before them, the coal men came into the region for the sole purpose of extracting the natural resources of the mountains, as quickly and as profitably as possible. Any benefits that might come to the local population were supplemental. The investors measured success not by any improvement in the quality of life, but by the accumulation of material wealth. The opportunity for great profits had brought them to the mountains, and those profits would have to be maintained, whatever the cost. "Since 1907," wrote the general manager and vice-president of Island Creek Coal Company, "Island Creek . . . has always operated at a profit, and its management holds steadfastly to the determination that its problems must be solved without marring this record. We still live by the precept that profits and progress are inseparable."[117] By 1930, "progress" had been at work in the mountains for over four decades, transforming a "backward" and "primitive" society into an integral part of the modern world. The ascendancy of coal had brought sudden and dramatic changes to the land and people of the hills—changes that would not disappear with the passing of the old king himself. The mountaineers had partaken of progress, but for most, the profits had somehow failed to accrue.

114. Keith Dix, *Work Relations in the Coal Industry: The Hand Loading Era, 1880–1930* (Morgantown, W.Va., 1977), 20–21.
115. *Manufacturers' Record* 80 (25 Aug. 1921), 62; *ibid*. 84 (16 Aug. 1923), 93.
116. Salvati, *Island Creek*, 14.
117. *Ibid*.

# CHAPTER FIVE

# COAL, CULTURE, AND COMMUNITY: LIFE IN THE COMPANY TOWNS

*As you look out of the train window, riding up the Guyan River Valley, through the heart of the Logan County coal field, you see on either side camp after camp in which the houses are little more than shacks to keep the weather out. Some of these houses are propped up on stilts; many of them are unpainted. . . . The camps look like the temporary quarters of some construction gang at work far from civilization. Yet they are permanent residence towns.*

—Winthrop D. Lane, *Civil War in West Virginia*

WINTHROP LANE's graphic account of social conditions in the strike-torn coal fields of southern West Virginia in 1921 was a profound indictment of the new industrial order in Appalachia.[1] The transformation of the region had come quickly. Less than thirty years earlier, the mountains had stood in solitude. Great forests of oak, ash, and poplar covered the hillsides with a rich blanket of deep hues, and clear, sparkling streams rushed along the valley floors. No railroad had yet penetrated the hollows. The mountain people lived in small settlements scattered here and there in the valleys and coves. Life on the whole was simple, quiet, and devoted chiefly to agricultural pursuits.

By the 1920s, however, evidence of change was to be found on every hand. Coal-mining village after coal-mining village dotted the hollows along every creek and stream. The weathered houses of those who worked in the mines lined the creeks and steep slopes, and the black holes themselves gaped from the hillsides like great open wounds. Mine tipples, headhouses, and other buildings straddled the slopes of the mountains. Railroads sent their tracks in all directions, and long lines of coal cars sat on the sidings and disappeared around

---

1. *Civil War in West Virginia: A Story of the Industrial Conflict in the Coal Mines* (New York, 1921), 39.

161

the curves of the hills. The once majestic earth was scarred and ugly, and the streams ran brown with garbage and acid runoff from the mines. A black dust covered everything. Huge mounds of coal and "gob" piles of discarded mine waste lay about. The peaceful quiet of three decades before had been replaced by a cacophony of voices and industrial sounds. "Civilization" had come into the mountains and had caught up the mountain people in the wellspring of progress.

Few aspects of this new order were more symbolic of the transformation than the company towns. Born in the 1880s, the child of necessity and boom, and nourished on the profits of industrial expansion, the company town became for thousands of mountaineers the dominant institution of community life—a vital social center around which the miners' world revolved. Not only was the coal camp the site of one's work, the source of one's income, and the location of one's residence, but for many it also provided an introduction to organized community life and the setting in which new attitudes, values, and social institutions evolved. Completely owned and tightly dominated by the coal companies, the mining towns also reflected the underlying transition in land ownership and social power which had swept the region with the coming of the industrial age. And when they were abandoned by their creators to die and decay in the depression days of the late 1920s, the company towns came to represent in the popular mind the tragic dilemma of Appalachia itself.

Privately owned industrial towns accompanied modernization in other parts of the United States—especially in the northern coal fields and in Ohio, Indiana, and the far West—but in no other area of the country was the influence of the company town more profound and long-lasting than in the soft-coal fields of the southern mountains. Casting its shadow over the lives of almost every mountain family, it directly or indirectly defined the nature of community life in a large part of the region during a critical period of cultural change. At the height of the coal boom, for example, almost four-fifths (78.8 percent) of the mine workers in southern West Virginia and over two-thirds (64.4 percent) of the miners in eastern Kentucky and southwest Virginia lived in company-controlled communities. This compared with 50.7 percent of the miners in the bituminous fields of Pennsylvania, 24.3 percent of those in Ohio, and only 8.5 percent of the miners in Indiana and Illinois. At that time, there were almost five hundred company towns in the southern Appalachian coal fields, but less than one hundred independent incorporated towns.[2]

The preponderance of company towns in the southern coal fields was in part a response to physical and demographic conditions within the region itself. Unlike the northern fields where collieries arose in areas already fairly settled, where villages and towns were already established, and where the coal industry fitted more naturally and normally into community life, mining operations in the mountains commenced in an area of scattered settlements and few organized villages and towns. Good roads were sparse, and miles of rugged forest prevented the daily transportation of large numbers of employees. Pioneer coal operators in the region, therefore, had to develop their own communities to house their labor supply. The company town became a logical and expedient answer to industrial needs. It provided efficient and inexpensive housing for a large labor force, and it contained the added prospect of company control over the activities of the miners themselves.

Opening a mine in the mountains during the early years was often a challenging task. Pioneer operators lacked the financial backing of later town builders and had to manage and direct construction activities themselves. Having secured a lease or—more rarely—purchased the land, the early operator moved to the site of the outcropping and began to build his town. Since most coal seams were located up steep hillsides, in creek valleys, or in inaccessible ravines far from a village or major thoroughfare, the first order of business was to open a tram road on which to transport men and supplies.[3] A work gang then pulled a steam engine and sawmill over this narrow trail and began cutting timber for mine props and colliery buildings. Crews gave first priority to erecting a tipple, administrative offices, and other structures necessary to the operation of the mine and only later considered the construction of miners' houses. Often, the mining plant and the railroad tracks (which arrived soon afterward) consumed all available land in the restricted valley area, and houses

2. U.S. Congress, Senate, *Report of the U.S. Coal Commission*, Table 14, p. 1467; U.S. Department of Commerce, Bureau of the Census, *Thirteenth Census of the United States, 1910: Population*, II, 717–19, 927–28; III, 1023.

3. Branch lines of the railroad usually arrived shortly after mines had been opened, and they were often the only means of communication between the mine and the outside world. Mining camps were often more isolated than independent towns.

*An Early Coal Mine, Miller's Creek, Kentucky. Courtesy of the Appalachian Photographic Archives, Alice Lloyd College.*

had to be strung out along the creek bank or placed on stilts along the mountainside. A hard-working operator could open a mine under these conditions with a small initial investment, and in less than six months he could be producing and selling coal.

Between 1885 and 1927, independent operators and large corporations repeated this pattern of community development in countless hollows and valleys throughout the southern mountains. Expanding slowly at first, the construction of company towns surged after the

164

turn of the century and reached its peak in the years prior to World War I.[4] By 1920, company mining settlements dotted the landscape, having transformed it from an area of small, scattered farms into a region of discrete and isolated self-contained social units.

## THE MINERS

After opening the mine shaft and beginning construction on the company town, the early coal operator then turned to the problem of recruiting a stable labor force. Most of the miners who were attracted to the southern Appalachian coal fields belonged to one of three distinct groups: (1) white Americans from the mountains and from the older coal fields, (2) black Americans primarily from the non-mountain South, and (3) recent immigrants from southern Europe. Although they were initially reluctant to enter the mines, the native mountaineers eventually accounted for the majority of the coal miners employed in the region.

The first coal-mining operations to be established in the mountains were small, and operators initially looked to the surrounding population for labor. In addition to a few resident white miners, the early mines employed a large number of black laborers who had come into the mountains to construct the railroads and who stayed on to work in the burgeoning coal industry. In the 1880s and 1890s, however, the number of mines grew, this local labor supply proved insufficient, and the mine owners began to recruit men from the older coal fields of Pennsylvania, Ohio, and Indiana. When the Norfolk and Western Railroad, for example, opened the Flat Top–Pocahontas coal field after 1883, the mining companies there faced a labor shortage from the outset and regularly turned to the older fields for experienced miners. Most of the latter, moreover, were young and single, and this reduced the need for housing and other facilities in the early coal camps.[5]

Many of the local mountain residents at first were hesitant to leave their farms for work in the mines. Former landowners who had been reduced to tenancy by the acquisition of timber and mineral lands often resented the intrusion of industrialization on their traditional

4. U.S. Department of Labor, Bureau of Labor Statistics, *Housing By Employers in the United States*, Bulletin No. 263 (Washington, D.C. 1920), 56.
5. Tams, *Smokeless Coal Fields of West Virginia*, 61; *Coal Age* 17 (15 April 1920), 779; Thomas, "Coal Country, 175–76.

way of life. Many abhorred the noise, the smoke, the destruction of the land, and the general disturbances created by coal mining. Some regarded industrial life as degrading, and others were frightened by the coal mines themselves.[6] Eventually, however, many were drawn into the mines by necessity or the lure of "big money." As land values rose around the turn of the century, the increase in farm rents drove hundreds of families into the mining camps and mill villages. Later, prior to World War I, the decline of agriculture and the rise of miners' wages enticed young mountaineers into the pits, in the hope of making enough money to buy good land and return to farming.[7]

During the early years of the industry's growth, a few local farmers reluctantly accepted employment in the mines during the winter as a means of supplementing farm income. Such miners were unwilling to live in the company towns because of the congestion and the frequent poor housing conditions, and they abandoned the mines in the summer months for work on their own farms. This practice caused additional problems for the coal operators, who were left with a labor shortage each spring as the farmers returned to their fields.[8] As a result, many operators complained that the local population was unsuited to industrial employment. "They make good woodsmen and guides," wrote one mining engineer, "but their shiftless methods of living have not accustomed them to continuous and sustained labor and very little suffices. In short, they resemble the negro in their desire for frequent periods of 'laying off' . . . never having known or dreamed of anything better than the wretched surroundings of their everyday life, they are supremely unconscious of their own misery."[9]

6. Verhoeff, *The Kentucky Mountains*, 33–35; Herman R. Lantz, "Resignation, Industrialization and the Problem of Social Change," in *Blue Collar World: Studies of the American Worker*, ed. Arthur B. Shostak and William Gomberg (Englewood Cliffs, N.J. 1964), 261; George Fowler, "Social and Industrial Conditions in the Pocohontas Coal Field," *Engineering Magazine* 27 (June 1904), 387; Floyd W. Parsons, "Coal Mining in Southern West Virginia," *Engineering and Mining Journal* 84 (9 Nov. 1907), 883. This reluctance to enter "public work" was also found in noncoal areas; see Sara Evelyn Jackson, "Ashley Weaver: Microcosm of Appalachia" (unpublished paper in author's possession), 40; *Manufacturers' Record* 69 (29 June 1916), 45; Schockel, "Changing Conditions in the Southern Mountains," 130.

7. Watson, "Economic and Cultural Development of Eastern Kentucky," 54–55; Ross, *Machine Age in the Hills*, 15.

8. *Manufacturers' Record* 78 (29 July 1920), 98; *Coal Age* 17 (15 April 1920), 779.

9. Fowler, "Social and Industrial Conditions," 386–87.

Like many other preindustrial workers, the mountaineer found it difficult to adjust to the routines of industrial production.[10] "It has been his wont," an early sociologist observed of the mountaineer, "to work during the favorable time, or when the larder is empty; and to rest during the unfavorable season, or while provisions are at hand." These habits, he added, were not readily broken when the mines, the manufacturing plants, and the lumber mills came to the region, making the local worker "at once the despair and menace of the employer."[11] The tendency of mountain laborers to take off during certain times of the year to participate in farm activities and traditional customs was especially irritating to the mine operators. It was not uncommon for early miners to lay off for planting, harvesting, funerals, and family reunions, and to go hunting and fishing. Occasionally, a miner might work only enough to make sufficient money to keep his family the rest of the month before taking leave of the mine for home. Coal-mine owners found it difficult to reconcile these traditional customs with their own work ethic and the need for continuous production. To many an operator "time was money," and time spent in such "non-productive" activities was a waste of the operator's money.[12]

Absenteeism, however, was only one way that the mountaineers rejected the industrial norms of the mine managers. By ignoring work schedules, mining routines, and other innovations which worked at cross-purposes with their traditional way of life, they sought to maintain their individualism and freedom from authority. In this manner, they hoped to benefit from the economic rewards of industrialization without sacrificing their long-held cultural values.[13] As Ellen Semple noted at the turn of the century, the mountaineer did not easily surrender his independent spirit.

At all times very restive under orders, when they have taken employment under a superior, their service must be politely requested, not

10. See Gutman, *Work, Culture, and Society*, 1–78.
11. Schockel, "Changing Conditions in the Southern Mountains," 130.
12. Semple, "The Anglo-Saxons of the Kentucky Mountains," 581; Douglass, *Christian Reconstruction in the South*, 317; *Manufacturers' Record* 69 (29 June 1916), 45; Leo Joseph Sandman, "Social Effects of the Mining Industry in Eastern Kentucky" (B.A. thesis, Univ. of Kentucky, 1915), 10; Herman Lantz, *People of Coal Town* (Carbondale, Ill., 1958), 37.
13. See Lantz, "Resignation, Industrialization, and the Problem of Social Change," 262.

demanded. If offended, they throw up their job in a moment, and go off regardless of their contract and of the inconvenience they may occasion their employer. Every man is accustomed to be his own master, to do his own work in his own way and his own time. . . . He has little sense of the value of time. If he promises to do a certain thing on a certain date, his conscience is quite satisfied if he does it within three or four days after the appointed time.[14]

Gradually, many of the mountaineers were obliged to adjust to the new industrial system and made their way to the coal camps, but in the highly competitive years after 1900, the mine owners were unwilling to wait for mountain ways to change.[15] Operators increasingly searched for a more permanent labor force that would take no "vacations" and could be relied upon at the mine throughout the year. As many of the miners from the older coal fields, moreover, began to leave the region for higher paying jobs in unionized fields, labor demands became so great that operators cast their nets far afield for workers. Between 1900 and 1920, coal company agents were sent into the South and as far away as Europe to lure potential miners to mountain coal fields. Attracted by glowing descriptions of comfortable housing and steady work at good wages, thousands of southern blacks and European immigrants were brought into the region on railroad labor trains to supplement the local labor supply or to serve as strikebreakers during times of labor strife. The cost of transporting these men was usually charged against them and deducted from their first few months' wages.[16] In this way, the ethnic composition of the mountains began to change again at the turn of the twentieth century, almost as drastically as it had at the turn of the nineteenth.[17]

Blacks had worked in southern Appalachian mines from the opening of the first collieries. As early as the 1850s, slaves were mining coal in the Kanawha Valley, and after the Civil War many of the black laborers who constructed the railroads found employment in

14. Semple, "Anglo-Saxons of the Kentucky Mountains," 581.
15. This cultural change would never be entirely complete, as mountain people continue to cling to many of their traditional values to the present day.
16. Tams, *Smokeless Coal Fields of West Virginia*, 61.
17. See also Phil Conley, *History of the West Virginia Coal Industry* (Charleston, W.Va., 1960), 88–90; Howard B. Lee, *Bloodletting in Appalachia: A Story of West Virginia's Four Major Mine Wars and Other Thrilling Incidents of Its Coal Fields* (Morgantown, W.Va., 1969), 4–8; Nell Pierce, *The Border South States*, 180–81; Thomas, "Coal Country," 177–97.

the mines.[18] Yet the black population was never very large in the mountains until the coal operators began to recruit extensively in the southern states. By 1907, black miners composed about 35 percent of the labor force in the Flat–Top Pocahontas coal field and proportionately less in the other coal fields of the region.[19] In 1920, 43 percent of the black miners employed in the United States worked in West Virginia, and the vast majority of those lived in the southern part of the state.[20] McDowell County, for instance, had the largest concentration of blacks in the Appalachian coal fields. At the height of the coal boom, over 45 percent of the miners in McDowell were black, and one of the major towns of the county, Keystone, was predominantly black.[21] From 1904 until 1913, the black community in McDowell County published its own newspaper, the McDowell *Times*, which reached about 5,000 subscribers.[22]

Most of the nonresident miners who arrived in the mountains after the turn of the century were recruited by labor agents hired by the railroads, a coal company, or a group of companies. Some of the agents were mine guards, and a few were employed directly by the Baldwin-Felts Agency, a leading mine security and strikebreaking firm out of Bluefield, West Virginia.[23] The agents generally traveled in pairs and were well armed and well financed. Those who were sent into the South were usually accompanied by a couple of black "recruiters" who were carefully selected for their eloquence and their willingness to disregard the truth. Once the agents reached their destination, the recruiters went to work in the black community, describing the opportunities to be found in the coal fields. When a sufficient number of volunteers had agreed to make the journey, the

18. Otis K. Rice, "Coal Mining in the Kanawha Valley in 1861: A View of Industrialization in the Old South," *Journal of Southern History* 31 (1965), 415–16.

19. Gillenwater, "Cultural and Historical Geography of Mining Settlements," 35.

20. Sterling Spero and Abram L. Harris, *The Black Worker: The Negro and the Labor Movement* (New York, 1931), 217–19.

21. Thurmond, *Logan Coal Field*, 60; Kenneth R. Bailey, "A Judicious Mixture: Negroes and Immigrants in the West Virginia Mines, 1880–1917," *West Virginia History* 34 (Jan. 1973), 158; West Virginia Department of Mines, *Annual Report*, 1910 and 1920.

22. Thomas, "Coal Country," 184. See also Charles Thomas Davis, *The Autobiography of Charles Thomas Davis and a History of the Town of Pocahontas, Virginia* (Pocahontas, Va., 1948), the account of a black miner who worked in Pocahontas for almost sixty years.

23. Lee, *Bloodletting in Appalachia*, 4n.

new laborers were loaded aboard a train and the doors were sealed and guarded until they reached the mines.[24] Solicitation of black workers was also carried on through the press, with full-page advertisements appearing in some black newspapers. These advertisements typically promised a wide range of opportunities in the mountains, no racial discrimination, and the possibility of earning from two to five dollars a day in the mines.[25] As a result of such efforts, on the eve of World War I black farmers were said to be leaving parts of the South in such large numbers to work in mountain coal mines, that a major southern business journal warned of severe labor problems for white farmers if the trend was not reversed.[26]

Despite this success, however, not all of the southern blacks who came to the mountains arrived voluntarily. In some areas of the Deep South, county and municipal authorities could be enticed with enough funds to open their jail doors for any convict who would board the labor train to the north. During times of extreme labor shortage, agents were known to empty entire jails of their black prisoners. Crowded into boxcars for days with little to eat or drink, some men never made it to the coal fields. Prisoners who demanded to be let off or tried to escape were frequently shot.[27]

Once the new black recruits reached the mining towns, they were quickly confronted with the drudgery of coal-mining life. Coal operators usually segregated the black population into "Colored Towns" consisting of the least desirable houses in the camp. Schools and churches, where provided, were segregated, as were recreational facilities, restaurants, and saloons. Because of the racist attitudes of most mine managers, blacks were never placed in positions of authority, and opportunities for upward mobilty on the job were few. Contemporary white beliefs effectively restricted black workers to the ranks of pick miners and loaders of coal. As George L. Fowler observed from the Pocahontas coal fields,

Here, as elsewhere throughout the South, the negro is the predominating figure, and we find him employed in all grades of labor where cool

24. *Ibid.*, 4–6.
25. Charles Phillips Anson, "A History of the Labor Movement in West Virginia" (Ph.D. diss., Univ. of North Carolina, 1940), 66–67.
26. *Manufacturers' Record* 70 (3 Aug. 1916), 65.
27. See Lee, *Bloodletting in Appalachia*, 7.

judgment, high personal responsibility, or reliability are not required
. . . his shiftlessness, adding thereto the belief that he belongs to an
inferior race—that he ordinarily matured in early manhood and does
not grow after that time. In short, that he is a child in his actions and
ways of thinking, and is an adult in physical strength only. . . .[28]

Notwithstanding such attitudes, the black miners were not totally
unprepared for their experiences in the coal-mining towns, and they
carved out for themselves a place in the life of the coal community.
By 1900, in many parts of the South, black farmers had already
become accustomed to the wage system, the use of "scrip" money,
and purchasing supplies at the plantation store. The evolving patterns
associated with "the factory in the field," as well as the longstanding
forced tradition of overt subservience to white authority, eased the
adjustment to the routines of the company town.[29] Blacks also had
their own churches, dances, and lodges, and in some mining towns,
black lawyers and doctors wielded a degree of political influence.
Blacks in West Virginia, for example, could vote, and the Democrats
often charged the Republican coal operators of southern West Virginia with the colonization of blacks for political purposes.[30]

Social relationships with white miners were often ambiguous.
Incidents of racial violence were not uncommon in the coal fields,
especially during the early years, when lynchings and assaults were
frequently reported in the local newspapers. The fact that many black
workers were brought into the region as strikebreakers did not ease
the tensions. The coal operators also chose to recruit black miners as
a means of creating a "judicious mixture" of whites, blacks, and
immigrants, in order to forestall unionization by segregating the men
and playing one group off against another.[31] Nevertheless, a relatively high degree of harmony existed between the races at a personal
level. Working side by side in the mines, the men came to depend
upon each other for their own safety, and the lack of major differ-

28. Fowler, "Social and Industrial Conditions," 384–85. See also Parsons,
"Coal Mining in Southern West Virginia," 883; Donald T. Barnum, *The Negro in
the Bituminous Coal Industry* (Philadelphia, 1970), 16–17, 45.
29. See George Brown Tindall, *South Carolina Negroes, 1877–1900* (Columbia,
S.C., 1952), 92–123.
30. Bailey, "A Judicious Mixture," 157–59; Thomas, "Coal Country," 90.
31. Bailey, "A Judicious Mixture," 157; Spero and Harris, *Black Worker*,
222–25; Barnum, *The Negro in the Bituminous Coal Industry*, 19.

ences in housing, pay, and living conditions mitigated caste feelings and gave rise to a common consciousness of class. Many of the white mountaineers had never developed a deep prejudice against blacks and had often extended them a measure of social equality. White and black miners freely visited each other's homes, churches, and physicians, and the races mixed openly at rallies, recreational events, and union meetings.[32] In fact, a higher level of racial mistrust existed between blacks and immigrants, whose cultural backgrounds were more clearly diverse.

Immigrants composed the final third of the ethnic mix in the coal fields. Their presence was most noticeable in the newer coal districts of eastern Kentucky, the Logan and Winding Gulf fields of southern West Virginia, and the Clinchfield area of southwest Virginia. Many coal operators preferred immigrant labor to native white or black workers because, they believed, the immigrants would work harder and were more dependable, predictable, and easily controlled.[33] The mine owners of southern West Virginia claimed that their immigrant miners worked from five to ten hours per week longer and produced a substantially higher daily tonnage of coal than any of their American miners.[34] Between 1900 and 1915, the mines of the southern mountains eagerly accepted all of the immigrant laborers they could obtain, and some larger companies predominantly employed foreign-born miners. Almost two-thirds of the work force at the U.S. Coal and Oil Company's mines in southern West Virginia, for example, were recent immigrants.[35] In eastern Kentucky, the U.S. Steel Corporation and the International Harvester Corporation both imported large numbers of foreign miners to their respective facilities at Lynch and Benham.[36]

The methods of recruiting immigrant labor were similar to those used to lure southern blacks. During periods of labor scarcity, the coal companies hired agents to go to Europe and to eastern cities in

32. Ralph D. Minard, "Race Relations in the Pocahontas Coal Field," *Journal of Social Issues* 8 (1952), 31–36; Joseph T. Laing, "The Negro in West Virginia," *Social Forces* 14 (1936), 422; Semple, "The Anglo Saxons of the Kentucky Mountains," 567; Fox, *Blue-Grass and Rhododendron*, 161. Minard found the highest degree of racial prejudice to exist among the management classes.

33. Lantz, *People of Coal Town*, 38.

34. Thomas, "Coal Country," 182.

35. Cubby, "The Transformation of the Tug and Guyandot Valleys," 256.

36. Watson, "Economic and Cultural Development of Eastern Kentucky," 51–52.

the United States to attract potential miners to the region. In the late nineteenth century, expert writers and translators were employed to prepare brochures in several languages, which might be used by European agents contracting laborers for the new world, but this practice became illegal with the passage of new immigration laws.[37] Thereafter, agents concentrated their efforts on Ellis Island, New York, and the ethnic communities of New York City and other northern towns. In West Virginia, coal operators received the help of the state commissioner of immigration when John H. Nugent was appointed to that position in 1907. Although the commissioner of immigration was not given an official salary, Nugent's expenses and salary were provided by the coal companies. In his numerous trips to Europe and England, Nugent carried recruitment propaganda bearing the official endorsement of the state commissioner and testifying to the favorable working and living conditions to be found at the coal mines.[38] When the unsuspecting immigrants arrived at Ellis Island, they would be met in the detention rooms by labor agents and interpreters and rushed on trains to the coal fields. The transportation expenses for the worker and his family, including the agent's fee, were advanced by the company, and upon arrival at the company town, the family was assigned to a house and provided with furniture, tools, and food. All this was charged on credit.[39]

As with black miners, many of the immigrants who arrived in the coal fields were not happy with their new life. Some had been recruited through urban labor brokers or "padrones" who had clearly misled them about the location and nature of the work for which they were being hired. Once they detrained in the coal fields, however, they lived under the constant presence of armed guards until they had "worked out" the cost of their transportation. In some instances, companies hard pressed for labor used extreme levels of intimidation and force to keep the men in the mines. Reports of forced labor conditions in the mountains became so prevalent that in 1903 the New York Society for the Protection of Italian Immigrants sent an agent to the region to investigate complaints of alleged maltreatment. His report, published in the *Outlook* in June 1903, condemned the labor practices and working conditions that he found existing among

37. Lee, *Bloodletting in Appalachia*, 6.
38. Bailey, "A Judicious Mixture," 148–50.
39. Chapman, "The Influence of Coal in the Big Sandy Valley," 166.

Italian miners.[40] Later, after further investigations, the Italian ambassador to the United States complained to Secretary of State Elihu Root that his countrymen were being held against their will in West Virginia. Finally, in 1907, the governor of the Mountain State revealed that Americans and foreigners had been forcibly held by mine owners and the William M. Ritter Lumber Company in the southern part of that state.[41]

The largest ethnic group to immigrate to the mountains were the Italians, although large numbers of Poles, Hungarians, and Slavs arrived as well. The high point of Italian immigration to America was the decade from 1900 to 1910, when over two million Italians arrived in the United States.[42] At the end of that decade, there were 7,600 Italian miners in West Virginia alone.[43] In addition to being recruited for the coal mines, Italian laborers were also consigned to railroad construction crews. The Carolina, Clinchfield, and Ohio Railroad employed hundreds of Italians in the construction of its line through Virginia and North Carolina, and many of the workers remained in the region to become miners in the Clinchfield coal district.[44] Their experience with life in the company towns was, for the most part, similar to that of the native American population. Most of the immigrants had come from rural areas of Europe, and their agricultural backgrounds and traditional culture eased their assimilation into mountain society.[45]

The flow of immigration into the Appalachian coal fields reached its peak in the years before World War I. With the outbreak of hostilities in Europe, thousands of Italian, Hungarian, and Greek miners left the mountains to return to their native countries to fight.[46] Others were attracted to expanding northern steel mills, where they could find higher pay and better living conditions. By 1916, the coal operators were once again faced with a serious labor shortage, and as wartime demand for coal production burgeoned, the companies

40. Gino C. Speranze, "Forced Labor in West Virginia," *Outlook* 74 (13 June 1903), 407–8.

41. Bailey, "A Judicious Mixture," 147.

42. Margaret Ripley Wolfe, "Aliens in Appalachia: The Construction of the Clinchfield Railroad and the Italian Experience," in Emmett M. Essin, ed., *Appalachia: Family Traditions in Transition* (Johnson City, Tenn., 1975), 83.

43. West Virginia Department of Mines, *Annual Report*, 1910, p. 104.

44. Wolfe, "Aliens in Appalachia," 83–88.

45. Thomas, "Coal Country," 197; Wolfe, "Aliens in Appalachia," 87–88.

turned increasingly to southern blacks and to the sons of the mountaineers who had been so hesitant to enter the mines.[47] After 1920, the black mining population also began to decrease in the mountains, as blacks too joined the migration to northern cities.[48] During the boom-and-bust period of the twenties, the population that remained to bear the brunt of the industry's collapse was the native mountaineers, but a few blacks and immigrants stayed on in the region to become a permanent part of mountain life. Today, one can find a sprinkling of Catholic churches and missions in the coal camps and mountaineers with Slavic and Italian sounding names—the last reminders of the thousands of immigrants who once played a major role in the region's history.

## THE MINER'S WORK

For the rural whites, blacks, and immigrants who came to work in the mountain coal mines, the greatest adjustments in their lives came not so much from the nature of their work as from the industrial organization and the feudal living conditions which accompanied that work. Mining, unlike factory employment, continued to provide contact with the land. It required some skill but primarily physical energy, and in the early years the miner enjoyed a high level of independence on the job. The work was dirty and usually tiring, much like that to which they were accustomed on the farm. Yet, the work routines, job discipline, safety conditions, and environment of the company towns were in marked contrast to traditional agricultural life. To a degree, coal mining reinforced old cultural patterns while it introduced new social attitudes, behaviors, and problems.

The most striking fact about the miner's job in the early years of the coal industry was that almost all of the work was done by hand. Mechanical undercutting machines which helped to loosen the coal from the seam were invented as early as the 1870s, but they were slow to gain acceptance in the nation's coal mines. By 1900, only 25 percent of American coal was mined by machines. In 1915, that figure reached 55 percent, but as late as 1930, 20 percent of the U.S.

46. Bailey, "A Judicious Mixture," 151–53.
47. George Wolfe to Justus Collins, 30 July 1916, Justus Collins Papers, West Virignia Univ.; *Manufacturers' Record* 70 (3 Aug. 1916), 65.
48. Chapman, "The Influence of Coal in the Big Sandy Valley," 223.

coal production was still being mined by hand.[49] Many of the smaller mines, of which there were hundreds in the southern mountains, did not begin to mechanize until after World War II. The loading of the coal into the mining cars, which was the most time-consuming part of the miner's job, continued to be done by hand throughout the period from 1880 to 1930. While mules and later locomotives were used to haul the loaded cars to the mouth of the mine, the most arduous and dangerous part of the production process was done at the face of the coal seam by the miner himself.

Most southern Appalachian mines were of the drift-mine variety, which allowed for easy entry and minimized the need for expensive ventilation and transportation equipment. The coal seam of a drift mine was located on a hillside above the valley floor, and the workers entered the mine laterally rather than through the vertical shafts characteristic of other American coal fields. The drift mine not only drained well and was less gaseous, but because it required little machinery, operations could be undertaken with very little initial investment. This low cost contributed significantly to the rapid overexpansion of the industry in the mountains, as well as to the heavy reliance on cheap human labor. During the early years, moreover, the ease of entry into a drift mine gave miners considerable freedom to leave their workplace as they pleased, but as the mines penetrated deeper into the hillside and as company discipline hardened, this advantage was lost.[50]

Once the coal seam had been penetrated, the miners set to work cutting and loading the coal. The mining process was relatively simple. Generally, pairs of miners worked in small rooms off the main entry tunnel. The rooms were separated from each other by pillars of coal left standing to support the roof, and coal car tracks were extended into each of the rooms from the main haulageway. After the coal was removed from the seam and loaded into a coal car, it was pushed to the room entrance, where mules or locomotives gathered the cars and transported them to the loading tipple outside. When all of the rooms in a section had been mined, the pillars were carefully removed as the men retreated toward the main shaft. "Pillar drawing" was extremely dangerous, as it often resulted in the collapse of the overburden in the room, but it was seen as a necessary

49. Dix, *Work Relations*, 20, Table II.
50. *Ibid.*, 1–3; Thomas, "Coal Country," 210.

part of the operation. Proper pillar removal reduced the amount of coal left in the mine and lost to production.[51]

The miner's day started long before daylight and often ended well after dark. In the early morning hours, the miners would set out for the mines carrying their lunch pails and water bottles and wearing lard oil lamps to light their way. The procession, "like fireflies all around the mountain," disappeared into the mine about 6:00 A.M.[52] At the coal face, the miner and his helper or loader began work by undercutting the coal seam. This he accomplished by making a horizontal or wedge-shaped slit with his pick at the bottom of the seam, so that the coal would fall when blasted from above. The miner had to do most of this undercutting lying on his side swinging a short-handled pick into the coal seam. He had to be constantly aware of the condition of the coal he was mining, since there was always danger of coal falling from the face onto the worker below.[53] After taking two or three hours to make an undercut, the miner then drilled holes in the coal, loaded the holes with black powder, and fired them, bringing down the undercut coal. When the dust settled, the men pushed empty mining cars into the room and began the task of loading the coal, being sure to separate out the pieces of rock and slate to prevent being "docked" for loading dirty coal. Several hours after the process began, the miners pushed their loaded cars to the room entrance to be hauled away. Near the bottom of the car the workers placed a brass check bearing the laborers' payroll number. The check was removed by the "check man" at the tipple and the tonnage credited to the proper men.[54]

The miner's job, however, was not finished when the car was removed from the workplace. Wasted rock and debris had to be removed from the room and steel track laid from the main entry to the new facing. In most mines, the miners themselves were responsible for setting their own timber safety props in place to support the roof from falling on the workmen. It often required hours to carry and install these posts, and the procedure was done entirely at the miner's

51. Dix, *Work Relations*, 4–7.

52. Florence Reece, Ellistown, Tenn., quoted in Kathy Kahn, *Hillbilly Women* (New York, 1973), 4.

53. John Brophy, *A Miner's Life* (Madison, Wis., 1964), 43; Dix, *Work Relations*, 8.

54. Tams, *The Smokeless Coal Fields of West Virginia*, 35–36; Dix, *Work Relations*, 8–10.

expense, since he was paid by the ton of coal loaded, not by the time spent on the job. After these preparations were made, the cycle would begin again with undercutting, drilling, blasting, and loading. In mines where drainage was a problem, the miner's clothes often got wet with the first undercutting, and he had to work the remainder of the day in damp clothing.[55] The end of the shift usually came about sundown, and the wet, dust-blackened miners trudged home to a tub of water and a few hours' rest before the next day's work began.

Under these conditions, the average pick miner could earn about two dollars a day at the turn of the century, and an exceptionally hard-working miner might earn as much as three dollars.[56] Wages varied greatly from time to time and from area to area in the mountain coal fields. During the 1920s, some coal operators in southern Appalachia paid wages higher than the national average in an attempt to squelch unionization, but on the whole, the region's wage averages lagged behind those of the rest of the nation. In order to compete with northern coal companies, mine owners in the mountains sought to reduce the price of their coal by cutting miners' wages and other expenses. A pick miner in southern West Virginia, for example, was paid an average of 38.5 cents per ton in 1912 for run-of-the-mine coal, while the statewide average was 48 cents. In the coal fields of Ohio, Indiana, Illinois, and Pennsylvania, miners' wages ranged from 57 cents to $1.27 per ton. Rates in the southern fields, moreover, were based on "long tons" of 2,240 pounds, but those of the northern fields were figured on "short tons" of 2,000 pounds, "hence the wage differential was even greater than it appears."[57] In addition to the marked difference in net wages, a higher percentage of miners in southern Appalachia lived in company towns, and thus a larger share of their wages was returned to the coal company for housing, tools, education, food, and other expenses. The gradual introduction of cutting machines in the years before World War I dramatically increased coal production in the mines, but the miners themselves received only a small share of the gains from increased efficiency.[58]

While wages remained comparatively low in the coal fields, coal

55. Dix, *Work Relations*, 11–12.
56. Tams, *The Smokeless Coal Fields of West Virginia*, 41.
57. Cubby, "The Transformation of the Tug and Guyandot Valleys," 261–62.
58. Thomas, "Coal Country," 202.

mining continued to rank as one of the most dangerous occupations in the United States. In fact, the introduction of machines and electricity actually added to the perils of the mine. Mechanical haulage systems and low-hanging electrical wires became major factors in mine safety, and the higher levels of dust raised by the new cutting machines created new explosion dangers and health hazards.[59] Despite the passage of "progressive" mine safety laws in the first two decades of the twentieth century, the rate of mine fatalities per thousand in the coal industry actually increased steadily after 1906. Over the next thirty years, mine workers in the United States lost their lives in underground accidents at the rate of about 1,600 per year.[60]

The most feared and well-publicized mine accidents were the dramatic explosions that sometimes killed dozens and even hundreds of men. Although most of the southern Appalachian drift mines were relatively free of natural gases, the accumulation of explosive methane gas and coal dust was an unavoidable by-product of coal mining. The gas could be removed from the mine by adequate ventilation, and the coal dust could be rendered nonexplosive by treatment with water or rock dust. But in the hectic days of the coal boom, many of the companies were unwilling to spend additional money on mine safety, and many of the miners were too pressured by the demands of production to spend time on safety precautions. As a result, mine disasters in the mountains increased sharply after 1900.

Prior to the turn of the century, there were only two major explosions in the mountain coal fields. The most tragic occurred at Pocahontas, Virginia, only a year after the railroad reached the mine of the Southwest Virginia Improvement Company. On 13 March 1884, coal dust in the Pocahontas Laurel mine exploded, killing the entire night shift of 114 men. An investigation determined that the disaster was probably caused by an open miner's lamp that ignited a small quantity of fire-damp (methane), which in turn set off a large quantity of coal dust.[61] The second disaster occurred in 1895,

59. Dix, *Work Relations*, 25.
60. *Ibid.*, 67. See also Thomas, "Coal Country," 230, Table VII-A, "Mine Fatalities in West Virginia."
61. J.N. Bramwell, *et al.*, "The Pocahontas Mine Explosions," American Institute of Mining Engineers, *Transactions* 13 (1884–1885), 247–48.

when a gas explosion ripped through the Nelson Mine at Dayton, Tennessee, killing 28 miners.[62]

As mechanization and production accelerated in the next decades, major disasters occurred with shocking frequency. In 1900, the Red Ash Colliery in Fayette County, West Virginia, exploded, killing 57 men and boys. Two years later, 184 miners were killed at the Fraterville Mine in Coal Creek, Tennessee.[63] On 6 December 1907, the largest mine disaster in the United States up to that time occurred in northern West Virginia at Monagah, killing 358 men. Between 1902 and 1927 there were serious mine explosions in the region almost every year and major disasters at Stuart (1907), Switchback (1908 and 1909), Jed (1912), Eccles (1914), Layland (1915), Beckley (1923), Yukon (1924), and Everettsville (1927) in West Virginia; again at Pocahontas, Virginia (1906); at Browder (1910) and Happy (1923) in Kentucky; and at Briceville (1911), Catoosa (1917), and Rockwood (1926) in Tennessee.[64] During these twenty-five years over 2,400 men—an average of nearly 100 workers per year—died in the mountains as a result of mine explosions.[65]

The causes of most of the mine explosions, generally the accumulation of gas and coal dust, were widely known, but coroner's juries impaneled to determine the causes of the disasters almost never ruled against the companies. According to Howard B. Lee, who served as West Virginia's attorney general during the 1920s, out of eleven mine explosions in that state, "in no case was the coal company even censured for its willful neglect or refusal to take necessary safety precautions to prevent the slaughter."[66] Most of the juries ruled that the deaths of the men were "accidental." For example, after the mine at Eccles, West Virginia, exploded twice in 1914 killing 183 miners, the coroner's jury found that the explosion had been caused by a "short circuit of air" which had allowed gas to collect in the mine. "This short circuit," the jury ruled, "was caused without the knowl-

62. U.S. Bureau of Mines, *Historical Summary of Coal Mine Explosions in the United States, 1810–1958*, by Hiram Brown Humphrey, Bulletin No. 586 (Washington, D.C., 1960), 20.
63. William Nelson Page, "The Explosion at the Red Ash Colliery, Fayette County, West Virginia," American Institute of Mining Engineers, *Transactions* 30 (1900); Bureau of Mines, *Summary of Coal Mine Explosions*, 24.
64. Bureau of Mines, *Summary of Coal Mine Explosions*, 24–110.
65. Based on *ibid*. These figures apply only to explosions; the total number of fatalities was higher. See nn. 73 and 74, below.
66. Lee, *Bloodletting in Appalachia*, 83.

edge or consent of the company or any of its operating staff, and . . . the company is in no way to blame for the disaster."[67] Another jury ruled in a similar case that the victims had met their deaths as the result of "an Act of God."[68]

State and federal governments at this time did little more than the coroner's juries to hold the coal companies responsible for mine safety. The U.S. Bureau of Mines was created in 1910, but it served only in an advisory capacity and until 1941 did not have the power to enter upon the property of a mine owner without his consent.[69] Between 1879 and 1912, mine safety laws were passed in all of the coal-mining states, establishing mining codes and creating mine inspection to enforce the codes.[70] The political influence of the coal operators, however, assured that the codes remained weak and ineffective. "Apparently," wrote Howard B. Lee, "their only purpose was to protect the coal operators—the miners were forgotten."[71] The laws generally placed the sole responsibility for mine safety on the miners, and the mining codes simply established regulations for individual work patterns. The codes emphasized one general rule: "Be Careful." Enforcement was almost nonexistent. It was not until the mid-1920s that state and federal mine bureaus began to place any responsibility for mine safety on management, and even then the coal operators were protected from most liability.[72]

Although most of the public outrage that resulted in the passage of mine safety legislation was stirred by the sudden rise in mine explosions, such disasters claimed only a fraction of the total number of miners killed and injured each year. Of the nearly 48,000 fatal mine accidents in the United States from 1906 to 1935, only 16 percent of the victims were killed by gas and dust explosions, while over 71 percent died from roof falls or haulage accidents. Unlike the more highly publicized explosions that killed many miners at once, roof falls and other accidents were solitary killers, and they went unnoticed by the public.[73] Roof falls alone accounted for the majority of

67. R. Dawson Hall, "The Explosion at Eccles, West Virginia," *Coal Age* 5 (23 May 1914), 850.
68. Lee, *Bloodletting in Appalachia*, 83.
69. Dix, *Work Relations*, 80.
70. Bureau of Mines, *Summary of Coal Mine Explosions*, 15.
71. Lee, *Bloodletting in Appalachia*, 103.
72. Dix, *Work Relations*, 80–93.
73. *Ibid.*, 72 and 71, Table III.

mine deaths, claiming an average of about three miners a day.[74] As with other aspects of safety, the responsibility to secure the roof of the workplace with posts was placed upon the miner, and any injury resulting from the failure to "post" was considered to be a product of his own "carelessness." During periods of low wages and management pressure for increased production, miners often waited until the last possible moment to break off from their work to begin posting. If the miner waited too long, weak shale roofs and inadequate supports might bring tons of rock down on the men, crushing them instantly. Each year, roof falls claimed the lives of hundreds of inexperienced miners, but large numbers of veteran laborers were also victims of falling coal and slate.

Low wages and poor health and safety conditions on the job were not the only tribulations of the miner's life. After the turn of the century, coal operators increasingly required their employees to live in the company towns. In many communities there was no alternative to company housing, since the coal and land companies owned all of the land for miles around. The company towns, moreover, were directly related to coal production, in that the mine managers often used forms of off-the-job control to maintain profits and enforce company discipline.

## THE COMPANY TOWNS

Conditions in the company towns, as in the mines, varied greatly from community to community. In some, houses were little more than shanties hastily constructed and thrown up against the hillside with no attention to comfort, appearance, or community plan. In others, they were substantially built structures, carefully designed and fitted into an orderly social scheme. The earliest houses in the region were built of "board and batten" and were generally not ceiled or plastered inside. Running water and other internal improvements were unknown, and according to the U.S. Department of Labor, "often only one well . . . was sunk for 12 or 14 houses and only one privy provided for every three or four houses."[75] Conditions in newer towns improved somewhat with the passage of time—but not markedly. In 1925, forty years after the opening of the region's first

74. Based upon statistics provided in ibid.
75. Bureau of Labor Statistics, *Housing By Employers*, 56.

coal town, the U.S. Coal Commission found that, on the whole, living conditions in the mining camps of the southern mountains were among the worst in the nation.[76]

The typical mining camp was located on the lower slopes and valley floor between two high ridges. Not much more than a crevice in the earth, this natural location provided little space for the necessary structures of a mining town and often contributed to the confined and congested appearance of the camp itself. For many mountaineers, such an environment was a decided contrast to life on the family farm, and this played an important role in their initial reluctance to enter the new mines. Nevertheless, natural location was not the sole determinant of living conditions in a company town, since the Coal Commission found examples of "attractive and well-equipped" communities in areas that seemed distinctly unfavorable for community life.[77]

In most camps, however, operators made little effort to overcome the natural obstacles of location. Houses backed on the railroad tracks and fronted on the creek or squatted on the mountainside like "great drab beetles with their stilt legs braced against the slope."[78] Dwellings nearest the tipple received a daily shower of coal dust, which turned everything a somber gray and frustrated the cleaning efforts of even the most meticulous housewife. There were few surfaced roads, and a layer of mud, black from the run-off waste of the mine, covered the ground during much of the year.[79] The uniformity of housing type, moreover, a characteristic of every company town, added a monotony to the construction-camp atmosphere of the mountain mining town.

The report of the Coal Commission in 1925 clearly documents the substandard quality of company housing in the southern mountains and gives mute testimony to the social ideals of the southern coal barons in the heyday of their prosperity. Examining 713 company-controlled communities in 1922–1923, the commission discovered that one-third of the company dwellings in the southern bituminous fields were still finished on the outside with board and batten—"among the cheapest, if not the cheapest, type of outside finish."[80]

76. U.S. Congress, Senate, *Report of the U.S. Coal Commission*, Pt. III, 1428.
77. *Ibid.*
78. Ross, *Machine Age in the Hills*, 23.
79. Thomas, *Life Among the Hills*, 11.
80. U.S. Congress, Senate, *Report of the U.S. Coal Commission*, Pt. III, 1470.

Among all United States mining areas, the southern fields contained 93 percent of all dwellings of this construction type. Weatherboard and clapboard was the outside finish on most of the houses, but less than one-third were plastered inside, and less than one-tenth had shingled or slated roofs. Wood sheathing covered the interior walls of a majority of company-owned dwellings, and composition paper covered the roof.[81]

The prevalent house style in the region was the "Jenny Lind," a one-story boxlike structure which rested on a post foundation and contained three or four rooms. A pot-bellied stove, centrally located and fired with company coal, provided the building's heat. Overcrowding was always a problem in such dwellings, especially since many miners took in boarders to help pay the rent. Some operators offered a bonus of one dollar a month to every family having over three boarders.[82] Immigrants and blacks suffered more from crowded conditions than whites, since the latter usually received the larger houses. As late as 1920, it was not uncommon to find an immigrant family of three or four keeping from four to ten boarders in a three-room mining house.[83]

Sanitary equipment and other "modern conveniences" were rare in the mountain mining camps. Only about 14 percent of the company houses in Virginia, West Virginia, and Kentucky had indoor running water, while 30 percent of those in Pennsylvania and 90 percent of those in Ohio were equipped with such facilities. Hydrants placed at regular intervals along the street supplied from a tank high up the valley side furnished water in most communities. Investigators found showers, bath tubs, and flush toilets in less than 3 percent of the dwellings surveyed. Outside privies, which often emptied directly into the creek, were the standard means of sewage disposal in both company towns and rural areas of the region, but the greater density of population in the mining camps made sanitary conditions there more hazardous to public health. Although only 2 percent of the company communities had a functioning sewer system, over 70

81. *Ibid.*, 1471, Table 17.
82. Bureau of Labor Statistics, *Housing By Employers*, 58.
83. Tams, *Smokeless Coal Fields of West Virginia*, 67–68; U.S. Department of Labor, Children's Bureau, *The Welfare of Children in Bituminous Coal Mining Communities in West Virginia*, by Nettie P. McGill, Publication No. 117 (Washington, D.C., 1923), 13; Thomas, "Coal Country," 282.

*Company Mining Town, Red Ash, Kentucky. Courtesy of the Appalachian
Photographic Archives, Alice Lloyd College.*

percent of the miners' homes had electric lights.[84] Hung from the
ceiling in the center of the room, these single bare bulbs were one of
the few amenities of coal camp life.

The absence of sanitary facilities in the coal camps and the refuse
from mining operations polluted land and water resources in the coal
districts, causing serious health problems in some areas. Very few
company towns provided for the regular disposal of refuse, and what
could not be fed to the hogs was commonly dumped on the roadsides

84. U.S. Congress, Senate, *Report of the U.S. Coal Commission*, Pt. III, 1473,
Table 19. See also Children's Bureau, *The Welfare of Children in Coal Mining
Communities*, 14–17.

or into the creeks. Investigators found that "garbage, tin cans, broken crockery, and other rubbish littered almost every road in some of the camps; in some, the almost stagnant creeks contained cans, wooden crates, bottles, and even old furniture, shoes, and clothing."[85] Chickens, hogs, ducks, and geese wandered freely in many communities, adding to the general disorder and unhealthiness. In places, sewage from open privies filled the creeks that ran through the center of town or drained into hollows and stood in stagnant pools. "On a hot summer day, the stench was almost unendurable."[86] Children suffered from hookworm, typhoid, and other maladies.[87] The pollution of the creeks and rivers from human waste and from the acid runoff of the mines was so great that around many of the streams the animal life completely disappeared. Yet, the coal companies showed little interest in such problems, arguing that coal could not be mined economically if they concerned themselves with ecology.[88]

The mountaineers had used the streams and forests for both livelihood and recreation, and in the new social order the natural environment continued to play an important, although much reduced, role. According to the Coal Commission, the provision for recreation and amusement in the majority of coal communities was "so meager as to be negligible."[89] A few of the larger companies provided activity centers with moving-picture theaters, gymnasiums, bowling alleys, pool tables, and soda fountains—all available for a small fee—but the average mining town had no such facilities. Most communities had a baseball team, and most miners owned a hunting rifle, but baseball and hunting were seasonal activities, and during most of the year there was little to do in the way of recreation.[90] Almost every camp, however, had its saloon. In those hectic days before World War I, when coal was king and wages were high, the boom-town saloon

85. Children's Bureau, *The Welfare of Children in Coal Mining Communities*, 16–17.

86. Thomas, *Life Among the Hills*, 11.

87. Children's Bureau, *The Welfare of Children in Coal Mining Communities*, 15–16.

88. Thomas, "Coal Country," 304.

89. U.S. Congress, Senate, *Report of the U.S. Coal Commission*, Pt. III, 1432.

90. A semiprofessional league developed among the coal camps in southern West Virginia from 1915 to 1930. See Tams, *The Smokeless Coal Fields of West Virginia*, 55–56; the testimony of C.L. Workman before the "Borah Committee," U.S. Congress, Senate, *Hearings before a Subcommittee of the Committee of Education and Labor*, 63rd Cong., 1st Sess., Senate Hearings vol. 39 (Washington, D.C., 1913), 767–91.

became the focal center of entertainment in the isolated mining towns. Whiskey sold for ten cents a drink and full quart bottles for a dollar. Even during Prohibition, there was always a plentiful supply of moonshine available. On paydays, professional gamblers from Cincinnati, Richmond, and Louisville came to the region, bringing their paraphernalia for faro, roulette, chuck-a-luck, and birdcage, and entire communities became famous (or infamous) for their red-light districts or gaming hotels.[91] Such a wide-open atmosphere was conducive to a high rate of crime, and, as the desire to maintain social order in the mining communities increased, operators began to assert greater control over the activities of the camp saloons.

Churches and schools, traditional institutions for social stability, came late to the mining districts. County school systems, where they existed at all, were poor, understaffed, and scarcely adequate for the educational needs of rural mountaineers, let along those of a large mining population. Early coal operators, moreover, were little inclined to upgrade the educational system, since most of their initial employees were single men. Only as the industry matured and the desire to secure a more permanent and reliable family-based labor force emerged, did companies begin to construct schools or supplement local school funds. Although colliery schools were nominally headed by county superintendents, the coal company usually provided the building and supplies and contacted the teacher—deducting an "education fee" from the miner's monthly wages.[92] The construction of churches followed a similar pattern, with the initiative, however, coming from the miners themselves. Companies matched funds raised by the miners for the purpose of building a church but retained ownership of the property to assure its "proper" use.[93] Despite the potential threat of company control, almost every mining camp had two or three churches of independent denominations. Nationally organized churches, on the other hand, were reluctant to enter the company town.[94]

91. Tams, *The Smokeless Coal Fields of West Virginia*, 55–56. For a fascinating first-hand description of "Cinder Bottom" at Keystone, W. Va., see Lee, *Bloodletting in Appalachia*, App. III, 103–8.

92. George Wolfe to Justus Collins, 23 Aug. 1916, Justus Collins Papers, West Virginia Univ.

93. George Wolfe to Justus Collins, 7 Aug. 1916, *ibid*.

94. John Howard Melish, "The Church and the Company Town," *Survey* 33 (5 Dec. 1914), 263.

At the hub of community life in the isolated mining village was the company store. Usually located near the center of town, this structure housed the commissary, barber shop, post office, and whatever business offices the company required. A convenient place to shop and converse with neighbors and friends, the company store became the focal point of economic and social activity within the mining camp. Most commissaries offered a wide variety of merchandise, from food to home furnishings, all of which could be purchased on credit or with company scrip. Prices in these stores varied with location, but, on the whole, they were "uniformly higher than in independent stores in the same districts."[95] In isolated areas, commissary prices ranged from 5 to 12 percent higher than in areas where independent stores were nearby.[96] Operators, moreover, discouraged competition from independent retailers by refusing to allow outside merchants to set up shop on company land or to deliver goods and services within the company town. "I take the stand," wrote one coal operator, "that our people can trade where and when they please, but no outside team of these merchants . . . can come in on our property and deliver goods."[97] While the miner was not forced to purchase at the company store, subtle means of coercion could be employed where necessary. For the most part, patronage was inevitable, for the local commissary was certainly more convenient, and there was often no practical alternative. Such a system was a constant irritant to mine workers, especially since, as pioneer coal operator W.P. Tams readily admitted, "salaried employees were usually given their store goods at cost."[98]

Although most coal producers viewed the company store as an adjunct to the total mining operation, a few greatly abused the monopoly which the situation afforded. Charging "all the market would bear," they sought to make up from store profits whatever loss they incurred from selling coal below the cost of production.[99] Some

95. U.S. Congress, Senate, *Report of the U.S. Coal Commission*, Pt. III, 1460.

96. *Ibid.*, 1457.

97. George Wolfe to Justus Collins, 4 Oct. 1913, Justus Collins Papers West Virginia Univ. Also see the testimony of C.L. Workman before the "Borah Committee," U.S. Congress, Senate, *Hearings Before a Subcommittee of the Committee of Education and Labor*, 767–91.

98. Tams, *Smokeless Coal Fields of West Virginia*, 28. It should be pointed out that Tams was himself a pioneer coal operator.

99. *Ibid.*, 25, 52; Thomas, "Coal Country," 282–83; M. Michelson,

raked off similar benefits from the miners' burial fund and from deductions for doctors' fees and nurses' salaries. With the passage of state workmen's compensation laws after 1910, the operators sought to reduce their payments into the compensation fund by contracting with private hospitals to serve their employees and then deducting a charge for this "service" from each miner's monthly check. In this way, the workers were made to pay a part of the cost of their own hospitalization for industrial accidents which otherwise would have been free to them under the compensation law.[100]

Not every operator exploited the miners in this way, but even the most paternalistic coal baron balanced the cost of social services and the maintenance of the company town against the primary goal of maximizing profits. As one producer put it, "We are doing this as a business policy. A lot of this welfare work is done with that object in view. We think that it is good business. We have had no strikes in seventeen years."[101]

Repairs and upkeep on company dwellings, the provision for schools and churches, and the maintenance of the company store, therefore, were as much a product of business policy as paternalistic concern. "In places where some pains were taken to keep the houses painted," observed the Coal Commission, "it seemed to be done usually as a measure for preserving the property rather than to increase its attractiveness, for the colors were uniform, and frequently ugly, throughout the entire community."[102]

If aesthetic aspects were a minor consideration in the maintainance of residential dwellings, they were even less important in the planning of the town itself. In fact, systematic town planning as practiced in some of the English coal fields, for example, was almost unknown in the southern bituminous fields.[103] Trade journals and government agencies often urged mine owners to plan their towns with care and

"Feudalism and Civil War in the United States of America," *Everybody's Magazine* 28 (May 1913), 620.

100. Lee, *Bloodletting in Appalachia*, 77–81.

101. J.M. Vest, president and general manager of the Rum Creek Collieries Company, quoted in Arthur Gleason, "Company-owned Americans," *Nation* 110 (12 June 1920), 794.

102. U.S. Congress, Senate, *Report of the U.S. Coal Commission*, Pt. III, 1431.

103. "The 'Company Community' In the American Coal Fields," *New Statesman* 30 (15 Oct. 1927), 7; Philip Nicolas Jones, *Colliery Settlement in the South Wales Coalfield, 1850–1926* (Oxford, England, 1969), 12.

periodically offered suggestions in the techniques of town development, but many early operators lacked the initiative or the capital to employ such techniques.[104] As a result, the average mining town evolved in a random, haphazard manner, reflecting a greater concern for ease and speed of construction and economy of operation than for permanence, comfort, or appearance.

Several company villages, however, did provide alternative models for community development in the region. Usually constructed by large corporations, these "model towns" were the ultimate attempt by southern coal operators to create "an ideal industrial community in which there was perfect harmony between employer and employees and all worked together each for the interest of the other."[105] Towns such as Holden (West Virginia), Widen (West Virginia), Jenkins (Kentucky), and Lynch (Kentucky) combined the best in housing construction, the most recent modern conveniences, and carefully planned streets and parks to produce a surburban atmosphere quite different from that of neighboring mining camps. The Consolidation Coal Company at Jenkins, for example, provided garbage and rubbish collection, a complete sewer system, and a company-owned dairy in its community plan; at Widen, the Elk River Coal Company added a swimming pool, an ice cream parlor, and a "well equipped hospital."[106] Holden, which one enthusiastic observer labeled "the model coal mining operation in the United States, if not the world," had a modern theater building and a clubhouse which included showers, a library, a reading room, two bowling alleys, and even "an up-to-date squash court."[107] Such communities offered a variety of social opportunities for the miner's family and presented a stark contrast to the average mining town. Yet, they typified less than 2

104. See George H. Miller, "Plan Your Town As Carefully As Your Plant," *Coal Age* 8 (20 July 1914), 130; K.B. Lohman, "A New Era for Mining Towns," *Coal Age* 8 (13 Nov. 1915), 799–800; Bureau of Mines, *Housing for Mining Towns*, by Joseph H. White, Bulletin No. 87 (Washington, D.C. 1914), 48f.

105. U.S. Congress, Senate, *Hearings Before the Committee on Education and Labor*, vol. 2, p. 872, testimony of Walter R. Thurmond, president of the Logan County Coal Operators' Association.

106. Alphonse F. Brosky, "Building a Town for a Mountain Community: A Glimpse of Jenkins and Nearby Villages," *Coal Age* 23 (5 April 1923), 560–63; Brosky, "Sociological Works Accomplished by the Consolidation Coal Company," *Coal Age* 15 (9 Jan. 1919), 54–58; Lane, *Civil War In West Virginia*, 33.

107. Lyman, "Coal Mining at Holden, West Virginia."

percent of all the company towns in the southern Appalachian coal fields and touched the lives of only a fraction of the mining population in the mountains.

One alternative, however, not only challenged the idea of the company town but the economic system behind it as well. In 1917, a group of Hungarian immigrants led by Henrich Himler established a model cooperative mining town in Martin County, Kentucky. Himler was an ex-coal miner, visionary, and editor of the *Hungarian Miner's Journal*, who hoped to provide a model community for Hungarian nationals and to test "the ideal of cooperation between labor and capital."[108] He selected a site of 3,200 acres on the Tug Fork of the Big Sandy River upon which to construct his mining town. Most of the houses in Himlerville had five rooms, plastered walls, two fireplaces, gas and electricity, a miner's wash house, and a vegetable garden. Each room in the new houses had two windows, and all of the houses were equipped with a tub and a shower. Miners could purchase the houses or build their own and fix them according to their liking. The town had a hotel, a bake shop, a weekly Hungarian newspaper, a library, an auditorium, and a modern ten-month school. By 1921, Himlerville was a growing community of over a thousand people.[109]

The economic life of the town was the Himler Coal Company— the first known cooperative coal-mining company in the United States.[110] Every employee of the mine was a stockholder in the company and shared in the profits. Himler himself controlled only 2 or 3 percent of the shares, and the rest were held by 1,500 individual stockholders. Of the eleven men on the mine's board of directors, all except President Himler were "common miners" elected by an annual convention. Each of the miners in Himlerville, regardless of his position, shared equally in any stock bonuses distributed by the company.[111] For several years, the unique venture thrived and even acquired additional coal lands, but in the mid-twenties the company became the victim of declining coal prices and competition from larger corporations. In 1927, the company was sold at auction to

108. Chapman, "The Influence of Coal in the Big Sandy Valley," 226.
109. Eugene S. Bagger, "Himler of Himlerville," *Survey* 48 (29 April 1922), 150, 187.
110. *Ibid.*, 146.
111. *Ibid.*, 149.

private capitalists, and the only effort at cooperative mining in the southern mountains came to an end.[112]

While Henrich Himler dreamed and sought to create a more desirable environment for his miners, most coal operators accepted the dismal surroundings of the average mining camp as a matter of course. "The absence of streets, sidewalks, grass, flowers, trees, and gardens," noted the Coal Commission, "is looked upon as a necessary concomitant of coal mining."[113] Some company officials tried to brighten the camp environment by offering prizes for the best gardens, the prettiest flower boxes, and the most attractive yards, but these efforts at community improvement were usually short-lived. Often, however, coal producers simply laid the blame for lawlessness and poor living conditions on the "class" of miners employed in the field—the immigrant from Italy, Hungary, and Poland; the black from the central and deep South; and the native mountaineer, fresh from the backwoods farm. "Unfortunately for him and for all concerned," an industry spokesman complained, "his standard of living is low, and it will take time to educate him out of his present methods." The company town, he admitted, was "no paradise," but the necessities and comforts of life were "well within the reach of the wage earner, if he can only be prevailed upon to take advantage of his opportunities."[114]

The desire to control this transient and undisciplined labor force was a major consideration in the construction of company towns. In a study conducted by the Department of Labor in 1920, mine operators listed a number of grounds for housing men in company dwellings. The need to attract a better class of miners, the advantage of greater efficiency, and the convenience of having men near the mine in case of emergency or accident were reasons most often mentioned by the majority of coal producers. Yet, among operators in the southern districts, a primary reason for company housing was "to give stability to the labor supply." One mine owner emphasized the utility of such housing as a labor-control device and bluntly declared that it had always been his purpose "to have men concentrated so as to have

112. Watson, "Economic and Cultural Development of Eastern Kentucky," 48; Chapman, "The Influence of Coal in the Big Sandy Valley," 234.
113. U.S. Congress, Senate, *Report of the U.S. Coal Commission*, Pt. III, 1442.
114. Fowler, "Social and Industrial Conditions," 396.

proper supervision over them, to better control them in times of labor agitation and threatened strikes."[115]

The problem of labor stability was a major concern for southern coal operators, and this contributed to the degree of social control they wielded over life in the company town. As was indicated earlier, managers of mountain coal mines often bemoaned the irregular work habits and the high turnover rate of the mining population. White mountaineers "laid off" for planting and hunting, and blacks "vacationed" at home in the South during critical times of the year. Drawn from colliery to colliery by higher wages and better living conditions, early miners seldom settled at a mine for more than a year or two. "I have gone over the situation here tonight," wrote a perplexed coal producer in 1916, "and find that we are practically losing men as fast as we bring them in. We pay off every two weeks and after each pay-day there is a bunch that leaves. We will be confronted next week with a loss of from ten to fifteen of our best people."[116]

Operators faced with a constant labor shortage, therefore, made every effort to secure a more permanent, family-based mining force and to encourage "a spirit of contentment with the place." Schools, clubs, theaters, and churches became means not only of attracting a work force but of rendering a degree of stability as well. Even the local saloon—traditionally a disruptive influence on community life—became an instrument of social order and control. By constructing his own saloon, the operator hoped to regulate liquor consumption within the town and thus to assure the miner's presence at the shaft after a long weekend.[117]

As companies expanded their efforts to discipline the labor force, the weight of law enforcement assumed a larger role in colliery life. Operators hired guards to protect the interest and property of the plant and financed additional deputy sheriffs to keep peace in the county and in the mining camps. Under the new system, local officials virtually surrendered their authority to the coal producers, who became the sole arbiters of justice in the company-owned towns.

The power of the mine operator was pervasive, extending over almost every facet of village affairs. If a miner was selling his

115. U.S. Bureau of Labor Statistics, *Housing by Employers*, 21.
116. George Wolfe to Justus Collins, 30 July 1916, Justus Collins Papers, West Virginia Univ.
117. P.J. Riley to Justus Collins, 3 June 1907, *ibid*.

home-brewed wine, or a woman was cheating on her husband, he would "learn of it, give them a warning and, if it continued, send them out of town." He divided the community into an "immigrant town," a "colored town," and an "American town" and enforced the social barriers between the three.[118] He regulated access to the town and restricted movement within it, and he "squelched with a heavy hand" any conduct or activity that hindered the production of coal.[119] His relationship to the miners, according to the courts, was not of landlord to tenant but of master to servant, and he occasionally found the need to exercise the master's right by evicting undesirable visitors or inspecting the miners' homes.[120] Employer, merchant, and master, he sought to apply the principles of business efficiency to the social demands of the mining town. Convinced that the miners' interests were identical to those of the company, he ruled the town as he ruled the mine, without opposition or debate. Under these conditions, the company town was a closed community, and most coal operators were determined that it should remain that way.

The mining settlements of Appalachia, therefore, differed greatly from other small, isolated American towns. Dominated by a single industry, the company town offered few of the amenities of ordinary community life. There were usually no public places and few public roads except the bed of the creek which flowed between the mountain walls. The company controlled or owned the land and furnished the houses, stores, churches, and schools. There were no public agencies to provide for social welfare, and residents had little voice in the management of public affairs. It was a most atypical town, one that strictly limited personal and social liberty and left its residents powerless to control their own destinies.

It was in this setting that many of the mountaineers first confronted the industrial age. While the company town reinforced many old values, it severely altered others and helped to channel the direction of new attitudes and beliefs. Preindustrial mountain society had been based upon a system of small, independent family farms, clustered together in diffuse open-country neighborhoods. There had been few established villages, and the cultural complex of rural life had oper-

118. Laurence Leamer, "Twilight For a Baron: Major William Purviance Tams, Jr.," *Playboy*, May 1973, p. 168.
119. Justus Collins to Jairus Collins, 18 Sept. 1897, Justus Collins Papers, West Virginia Univ.
120. For a discussion of the master-servant relationship, see U.S. Congress, Senate, *Report of the U.S. Coal Commission*, Pt. I, 169.

*Haymond, Kentucky* c *1914. Courtesy of the Appalachian Photographic Archives, Alice Lloyd College.*

ated against the formation of organized communities. The mountaineer's primary responsibility had been to himself and his family, and his relationship to neighbors had usually been informal. His experience in the company town did little to change these traditional values, since miners were highly mobile and had no direct political control of their communities through any town elections.[121] Life on the farm, moreover, had taught him that his future depended not so

121. Even in county elections, candidates were usually "company men."

much upon his own activities as upon the impersonal forces of nature. In the company town, he realized that those impersonal forces lay outside the community—in the decisions of managers in the head office, government policies, and the fluctuations of the coal market. Except for his decision to stay or leave, persons other than himself made the decisions affecting his life. Thus, he was individualistic, fatalistic, and present-oriented, and his powerless situation in the company town augmented these traits.[122]

The impact of the company mining settlement on patterns of social organization in the mountains was predictably disruptive, since it dramatically altered the mountaineer's economic and social status. On the farm, the mountaineer had been master of his own fate, the social equal of any man in his community. In coming to the mining camp, he had exchanged that independence for subordination to the coal company and dependence upon a cash income. Under the new industrial system, he not only worked in the company's mine, digging the company's coal and taking orders from the company bosses, but he also lived in the company's house in the hollow near the tipple along with others of his rank. His "superiors" almost always lived in more comfortable housing separated by considerable distance from the houses of the mining class. Local mine owners often built palatial residences high on the hillsides overlooking the town.[123] Absentee owners and major stockholders were even more remote, economically and geographically, from the workers whose lives they controlled.

In addition to his occupation and the location of his household, the mountaineer's lack of home ownership also defined his new position in the social order. The company owned or leased all of the land in and around the mining town and consistently refused to sell or sublet to individual miners. The mountaineer, whose family and culture tied him to the region, had no opportunity, therefore, to purchase property or acquire a home. This lack of home ownership sorely disturbed many mountain residents, as the testimony of miner C.L. Workman before the Borah Committee in 1913 confirms:

SENATOR KENYON: "There is a home spirit there, is there?"
MR. WORKMAN: "Yes, Sir."

122. See Knipe and Lewis, "The Impact of Coal Mining," 25–37.
123. Gillenwater, "Cultural and Historical Geography of Mining Settlements," 87; Lyman, "Coal Mining at Holden, West Virginia," 1171.

SENATOR KENYON: "What do you say about people, men and women, becoming attached to that country up there?"

MR. WORKMAN: "They are to some extent. They seem to have the idea . . . that they are the men who used to own the land, a great many old settlers and their children, and they built up the mines, and they are living there and have lived there and have their places of residence there, and they think they should have a home there in time of peace or strike until either the coal people or the miners have settled their differences. They look on it as their homes, in the West Virginia hills."[124]

The miner's anomalous position in company housing, moreover, added to the insecurity of his status. Tenancy was conditional upon a man's service to the mine, and when a worker left his job "for any cause whatsoever," he lost the right to occupy his house as well. A sudden altercation with the mine boss might end in discharge and simultaneous loss of shelter for the miner's family.[125]

Miners reacted to this insecurity and expressed their discontent with conditions in the company towns in a variety of ways. Despite the coal operators' efforts at social control, mobility remained high in the southern coal fields throughout the period from 1900 to 1930. Miners constantly drifted from mine to mine searching for higher pay and better living and working conditions. Whereas over 90 percent of the families in the northern coal fields in 1923 had remained in the same district for five years or more, only 26 percent of mining families in southern West Virginia had lived in the same community for that long. After 1915, immigrants and blacks began to leave the mountains in large numbers, as quickly as opportunities arose. Most hoped for a better future in the urban Midwest and East.

When migration was impractical or impossible, miners vented their discontent in almost unceasing efforts to unionize the mountain coal fields. The bloody mine wars that rocked the mountains every decade from 1893 to 1933 reflected the miners' overwhelming desire for greater social freedom. Although wages and working conditions were important factors in these strikes, the elimination of mine guards, overpricing at the company store, assembly and visitation

124. U.S. Congress, Senate, *Hearings before a Subcommittee of the Committee on Education and Labor*, 789–90.
125. U.S. Congress, Senate, *Report of the U.S. Coal Commission*, Pt. III, 1438.

restrictions, and other issues of civil liberty were almost always major areas of concern. Urban journalists commonly attributed the violence of this period in Appalachia to some innate cultural characteristic of the mountaineers, but violence was less a holdover from the frontier than a response to the conditions of industrialism.[126] In fact, the intensity with which the miners fought the more powerful coal companies was an accurate measure of their frustration with a subservient life.

Thus, company towns, as they evolved in the southern mountains, functioned to limit the growth of social freedom and self-determination and to heighten social tensions and insecurities within the region. Unlike the industrial towns of the Northeast, the textile towns of the South, or in fact the majority of American industrial communities, the coal towns of Appalachia were new communities imposed upon a region in which formal social ties were few. They provided an expedient means of urban development but created a system of closed, artificial communities that restricted rather than induced economic growth. By monopolizing almost every aspect of community life, company towns effectively blocked the growth of local retail enterprises and diversified or supporting industries that might have accompanied coal mining. Since the profits from mining went to nonresident owners, the only benefit that might have accrued to the region itself was the miners' wages. But, under the closed company town system, these too flowed largely out of the mountains. The same modernizing forces that oversaw the transition in land ownership and the emergence of a new economic order in the mountains also shaped the new social environment of the region. And like so much accompanying industrialization, that environment was not of the mountaineer's own choosing.

126. See Gordon Bartlett McKinney, "Industrialization and Violence in Appalachia in the 1890's," in *An Appalachian Symposium*, ed. J.W. Williamson (Boone, N.C., 1977), 131–44.

# CHAPTER SIX

# PROFITS AND POWER:
# THE COAL BARONS

*I believe that ambitious men in democracies . . . care much more for success than for fame. What they most ask of men is obedience, what they most convet is empire.*
— Alexis de Tocqueville, *Democracy in America*

FEW American businessmen exemplified de Tocqueville's "ambitious men in democracies" better than the coal barons of the Appalachian South.[1] Carriers of industrialization into an agrarian and sparsely settled land, they were harbingers of a new age, energetic pioneers of an emerging New South. "Men of vision, faith, courage, and skill," in a few short decades they transformed "a veritable wilderness into one of the world's richest coal fields."[2] Yet, as one critic has written, "surely no group of men so symbolized all that was evil and brutalizing about the early years of industrial capitalism as did the coal barons."[3] Entering upon a region of serried hills matted in a dense forest of virgin hemlocks, poplars, oaks, and laurel, they left the land scarred and barren, covered with the black residue of coking ovens, coal tipples, and slag piles. Finding few established communities, they became the feudal lords of closed company towns in which mountaineers exchanged their traditional independence for an existence characterized by "dependency, powerlessness, and a lack of autonomy."[4]

Historians have long recognized the important role which the coal operators played in the drama of Appalachian development. Often the sole ministers of authority within the coal districts, they formed a

1. Alexis de Tocqueville, *Democracy in America* (New York, 1966), 607.
2. Thurmond, *Logan Coal Field*, 84. See also Conley, *History of the West Virginia Coal Industry*; Tams, *Smokeless Coal Fields of West Virginia*.
3. Leamer, "Twilight For a Baron," 114. See also Caudill, *Night Comes to the Cumberlands*, 112–37.
4. Knipe and Lewis, "The Impact of Coal Mining," 35.

powerful interest group that greatly influenced the social, political, and economic evolution of the region. To a marked degree, they reflected many of the attitudes and values of the generation of business leaders who came to power in the mountains with the rise of the new regime. During a critical period of cultural change, these independent entrepreneurs were among the "power elite" of the mountain social system.[5] Despite their importance, however, relatively little is known about the early coal barons. Who were they? Were they outsiders or native mountaineers? What were their social origins? Above all, what were their beliefs, values, and attitudes toward labor and mountain society itself?

Unfortunately, southern mountain coal operators left few records upon which to base any comprehensive analysis of their thought. Like other businessmen of their generation, coal producers seemed to have adhered to one of John D. Rockefeller's favorite aphorisms, "Silence is golden."[6] Most were too busy to bother with literary pursuits. Some were reluctant, no doubt, to put their thoughts in print because of diffidence or aversion to personal publicity. As eminently practical men, moreover, they would have vigorously denied that any ideological system motivated their decisions.

Yet, coal barons were imbued with significant assumptions about the nature of society. Underlying their public statements and behavior was a common ideology, a shared matrix of beliefs, which gave them a certain cohesion as a group and molded their actions toward labor and the surrounding mountain community. Manifestations of this ideology varied with individuals, and over time, business policies themselves changed markedly; but the group value system remained substantially the same. While operators seldom expressed their social beliefs directly, they often revealed much about themselves and their world view incidentally in private correspondence, oral testimony, and professional publications. Such sources, therefore, shed considerable light on the social and economic philosophy of these strategic elites of the mountain social system.

5. For an analysis of the role of mountain elites in the modernization process, see H. Dudley Plunkett and Mary Jean Bowman, *Elites and Change in the Kentucky Mountains* (Lexington, Ky., 1973).

6. Quoted in Edward Chase Kirkland, *Dream and Thought In the Business Community, 1860–1900* (Ithaca, N.Y., 1956), 3.

## SOCIAL BACKGROUNDS

Certainly the most striking fact about the men who pioneered in the development of the southern mountain coal industry was that most were not native mountaineers. Although a few local residents opened small independent mines after the turn of the century, the majority of prominent owners, operators, and superintendents were not of indigenous stock. A survey of 140 individuals who operated mines in southern West Virginia, eastern Kentucky, and southwestern Virginia between 1880 and 1930 revealed that over three-quarters of these southern mountain coal producers were born outside the region itself (See table).[7] Forty-six percent of those surveyed originated in the North, primarily Pennsylvania, and 30 percent were born in the nonmountain South. Fewer than one in four of the group studied were native mountaineers, and most of the latter were small operators or managers for absentee corporations. While the survey is incomplete, it does suggest that, for a large portion of the southern mountains at least, men whose social origins were in areas outside the region were a dominant force in determining the nature and direction of industrial growth.

The migration of outside entrepreneurs into the southern mountains paralleled three major stages of industrial development in the coal fields. The earliest operators entered the coal areas of southeastern West Virginia and southwestern Virginia in the 1870s and 1880s, following the completion of the C&O and the N&W railroads. With little capital and much determination, they opened the thick seams of coal, drove shafts into the mountainsides, and began to ship their product to the expanding markets of the Northeast. Most of these pioneer coal producers had some previous experience in the mining

7. This study is based upon the careers of 140 coal operators for whom some biographical data could be obtained. The survey includes large coal producers and small operators from each state in relative proportion to the amount of coal mined in that state in 1916. There is no assurance that this group is representative, but the list includes most of the prominent coal barons in the region before 1930. Operators from the Alabama and eastern Tennessee fields, which were opened earlier and declined in importance after 1900, were omitted from the survey, but research indicates that approximately 80 percent of these operators were born in the nonmountain South. The principal sources were Arthur M. Hull and Sydney A. Hale, eds., *Coal Men of America* (Chicago, 1918); *National Cyclopedia of American Biography*; Addington, *The Story of Wise County*; Tams, *Smokeless Coal Fields of West Virginia*; Thurmond, *Logan Coal Field*.

Origins of 140 Coal Operators in Southern West Virginia,
Eastern Kentucky, and Southwest Virginia, 1880–1930

| | Southern West Virginia | Eastern Kentucky | Southwest Virginia | Total |
|---|---|---|---|---|
| Operators Surveyed | 73 | 48 | 19 | 140 |
| Place of Origin | | | | |
| Mountain South | 14 | 12 | 5 | 31 (22.1%) |
| Nonmountain South | 19 | 23 | 2 | 44 (31.4%) |
| North | 40 | 13 | 12 | 65 (46.4%) |
| Nonmountain Areas Combined | 59 (80.8%) | 36 (75%) | 14 (73.6%) | 109 (77.8%) |

industry, many having come to the southern bituminous fields from the older anthracite fields of Pennsylvania. A few, such as John Laing, Samuel Dixon, and Jenkin Jones, had immigrated to Pennsylvania from the English coal districts after the Civil War and had worked their way up through the ranks from "trapper boy" to mine foreman before setting out for the virgin coal seams of the South.[8] Although few in number, these early operators paved the way for the tremendous coal boom that swept the region after the turn of the century.

As new coal fields began to open in south-central West Virginia and eastern Kentucky, and as new markets began to emerge in the Midwest, a second and larger wave of coal men penetrated the mountains. Younger and better educated than their precursors, these later arrivals were highly individualistic men who set about turning quiet mountain valleys into bustling coal camps and "black gold" into hard cash. The modest investment required to open a mine attracted many aspiring businessmen, and the number of small companies multiplied rapidly, greatly speeding the development of the field.

8. Many English-born coal operators returned to England after their retirement from the coal business. Author's interview with Maj. William Purviance Tams, Jr., retired coal operator, 8 March, 1975, Southern Oral History Program, Univ. of North Carolina, Transcript, 20–21. Hereinafter cited as the Tams Transcript.

Northern men continued to predominate among the operators who arrived in the mountains at the turn of the century, but a significant number of the new coal barons were southern-born. Men like Justus Collins of Clayton, Alabama, William Purviance Tams of Staunton, Virginia, and George Henry Caperton of Lynchburg, Virginia, joined northern businessmen like John Alfred Renahan of Ohio, Howard Nicholas Eavenson of Pennsylvania, and Richard Morgan Olcott of New York in exploiting the mountain coal reserves. Many of the operators from the South were the sons of prominent planters who had lost money during the Civil War, and they saw in the expanding coal industry an opportunity to recoup the family wealth and prestige. All were ambitious men who thrived on competition, hard work, and the privilege of command. As one operator succinctly recalled, "I came here determined to get enough money so that I could tell any man to go to hell. Several million would do. I didn't want a hundred million."[9]

Not every independent coal producer achieved the ultimate goal of financial success, however. The proliferation of coal companies and the rapid increase in coal production soon left the field overexpanded. Unable to meet the rising competition and growing expenses, many operators began to sell out to larger firms. By 1906, a movement to consolidate the small independent mines into large mining corporations was evident, and an increasing number of mines were coming under the direct control of major coal consumers such as U.S. Steel, International Harvester, and the Ford Motor Company. The rise of consolidated and "captive"mines marked the decline of the era of the independent coal baron and the beginning of the age of the "organization man." As corporate executives gradually replaced owner-operators in the management of the mines, company policies toward business problems and community relations changed as well. With few exceptions, the new generation of professional managers continued to reflect the migration of outside businessmen into the region, but now, more than ever, many of the decisions that affected economic growth and social welfare in the mountains came from nonresident corporation heads.[10]

9. William P. Tams, quoted in Leamer, "Twilight for a Baron," 172.
10. A notable exception was James Draper Francis, a native of Pikeville, Ky., who in 1934 became president and later chairman of the board of Island Creek Coal Company, one of the largest coal companies in the United States. See Thurmond, *Logan Coal Field*, 88–89; Tams, *Smokeless Coal Fields of West Virginia*, 86.

Like most prominent businessmen of their day, the majority of the southern mountain coal operators came from middle- and upper-level socioeconomic backgrounds.[11] A few early operators were clearly "self-made men," but most coal producers were the progeny of established planter, merchant, or manufacturing families. Some had inherited estates of "considerable wealth," and many had valuable contacts among the powerful banking houses of the North. Albert F. Holden, for example, was the son of the owner of the Cleveland *Plain Dealer*; Stephen J. Patterson was the brother of the founder of the American Cash Register Company; and Edward J. Berwind was heir to a coal empire in Pennsylvania. Such men usually had acquired "classical" educations, often at the best universities in the Northeast, and not a few had received graduate training in law or engineering. This pattern was also true of the small number of operators born in the mountains; most were generally not from the lower socioeconomic levels. John Caldwell Calhoun Mayo of eastern Kentucky and Rufus A. Ayers of southwestern Virginia were both members of prominent mountain families.

While data on the social origins of mountain coal barons is indicative only of general tendencies and by no means provides complete explanations for the attitudes and behavior of operators as a group, such information does cast light on the social and intellectual contexts from which labor and community policies in the southern coal industry evolved. On the whole, the men who carried industrialization to the mountains were independent, well-educated, and predominantly upper-middle class. Aspiring entrepreneurs, they were products of the Age of Enterprise and reflected much of the prevailing social philosophy of that era. As much as any other business group, they applied a conservative ideology to business and civic relations, and they defended their interests as coal producers from a shared matrix of traditional values and beliefs.

## SOCIAL ATTITUDES

The relationship between the economic interests and the social attitudes of coal operators was not made explicit in the early years of industrial development in the region. Pioneer operators seldom

11. Analysis of the social backgrounds of mountain coal producers is based upon biographical information gathered on 140 operators. See n. 7, above.

thought about the problems of labor management or about the social responsibilities which they, as businessmen, might have to the surrounding mountain community. The first mines employed only a handful of men, and, as late as the 1890s, most mountain communities were still small and very widely scattered. Only as the industry matured and the number of company towns multiplied did the coal producers begin to formulate policies to meet the ever-growing demands of the new industrial age. These policies reflected not only the dictates of self-interest but also the latent influence of certain underlying assumptions as well.

Two antithetical systems of thought worked to mold the social attitudes of coal producers at the turn of the century. A traditional theory of paternalism exerted considerable influence on the ideas of some individuals, while the newer tenets of Social Darwinism held sway in the minds of others. According to the paternalistic viewpoint, it was the responsibility of the rich and successful to protect the poor and unfortunate from the vicissitudes of life. The laboring poor, the theory suggested, were like children who must do their assigned tasks obediently and with alacrity and must defer in their dependence to the social decisions of their superiors.[12] Operators who subscribed to this opinion regarded themselves as "fathers" to their employees, and they often took "a genuine and paternal interest" in providing good houses, sanitation, safe working conditions, and a variety of amusements for the miners and their families.[13] The impact of the Social Gospel buttressed this belief and helped to encourage paternalistic policies, especially among the more socially sensitive coal barons.

Social Darwinism, on the other hand, emphasized the struggle for existence and the role of laissez faire, the free play of competition, in the social order. Since the rich could not care for the poor without decreasing the national wealth (the ultimate measure of national survival), the successful had no social responsibilities to the less capable members of the community. Riches and poverty were only reflections of differences of ability and effort, and, by abstinence and exertion, the poor could always better their lot.[14] In the application of

12. Reinhard Bendix, *Work and Authority in Industry: Ideologies of Management in the Course of Industrialization* (Berkeley, 1974), 435.
13. Lane, *Civil War in West Virginia*, 80. See also the Tams Transcript, 3–4.
14. Bendix, *Work and Authority in Industry*, 435. See also Richard Hofstadter, *Social Darwinism in American Thought, 1860–1915* (Boston, 1955), 31–66.

this "ethics of the jungle," the relationship between the employer and the employed was reduced to a purely economic level. Labor was "a commodity which the worker has the right to sell and the employer has the right to buy under such conditions as the market offers."[15] Operators who accepted the Social Darwinist faith were principally interested in the technical and commercial aspects of the mining enterprise, and, where matters of labor and community relations were concerned, they often responded only to the exigencies of the time. Primarily engrossed in the production of coal itself, they "were not likely to admit," a contemporary author observed, "the importance of sanitation or comfortable homes."[16]

Few operators, however, were so callous as to be unconcerned with social conditions nor so benevolent as to suppress their design for wealth. Most wavered or made their own private compromises between the two contrasting strains of thought. The nature of their economic interests and the similarity of their backgrounds, moreover, gave the coal producers a broader ideological unity, which tempered the diversity of individual social attitudes. They all shared a view of society, for example, that delegated power and authority to those who had "demonstrated" ability through material success. They valued harmony and order and feared panics and depressions so much that "stability was their watchword," and almost all had a passionate dislike for labor unions.[17] Manifested in a variety of ways, these values and beliefs were the common ground from which expressions of social responsibility emerged.

Central to the shared ideology of the coal operators was the belief that the employer's authority and control over community life was the natural product of his business success. If, as some operators argued, "superiority comes only from struggle, and only hope of reward invites struggle,"[18] the employer's authority was justified by his success, and his success was a sign of both his virtue and his superior ability. Those who failed in the struggle for achievement and acquisition were believed to lack the requisite qualities of leadership, and they were enjoined to obey the men whose success entitled them

15. Robert H. Wiebe, *Businessmen and Reform: A Study of the Progressive Movement* (Cambridge, Mass., 1962), 162.
16. Lane, *Civil War in West Virginia*, 82.
17. Wiebe, *Businessmen and Reform*, 10.
18. Thurmond, *Logan Coal Field*, 105. Walter R. Thurmond was himself a pioneer coal operator in the Logan fields.

to command.[19] This division of men into the "fit" and the "unfit" assigned a subordinate position to the laboring man, because he had "demonstrated" his inability to assume social responsibilities by the paucity of his own achievements. Conflict between capital and labor, therefore, was "an unnatural condition," since "the class possessing the brains, talent, and energies necessary for the accumulation and retention of wealth in this country" was by definition the best judge of community welfare.[20]

The laboring man, of course, had the opportunity to advance in both wealth and power, if he [could] only be prevailed upon to take advantage of his opportunities."[21] This required that he discipline himself to hard work and hard saving and that he accept the "grim reality" of the competitive life. Like other American businessmen, operators believed that idleness and leisure thwarted a man's capacity to achieve and led him to abuse time and increase his debt by developing a taste for "improper amusements and luxuries."[22] Not every man possessed the natural capacity for success, they admitted, but each individual had an obligation to work for the cumulative benefit and material progress of all. "I believe," professed a West Virginia coal baron, "it is the duty of every man to work. And I believe that unless he does work he is not entitled to a living."[23]

Coal operators emphasized the conservative economic virtues of hard work, frugality, and sobriety both in their relations with employees and in their hiring practices. For this reason, many operators preferred immigrant to native mountain white or southern black labor. "Most of the immigrants made excellent miners," recalled one coal producer. "They were accustomed to hard work, were quick to learn and eager to please." Their great ambition was "to save enough money to pay the passage of their wives and children. To that end they worked as hard as possible and spent no more than absolutely

19. Bendix, *Work and Authority in Industry*, 258.

20. William Nelson Page to William E. Sackett, secretary of the United States Industrial Commission, 8 March 1899, William Nelson Page Papers, Southern Historical Collection, Univ. of North Carolina at Chapel Hill, Box 4, folder 77, pp. 8, 25. Page was a coal operator who owned and managed mines in southern West Virginia between 1873 and 1917.

21. Fowler, "Social and Industrial Conditions," 396.

22. James Warren Prothro, *The Dollar Decade: Business Ideas in the 1920's* (Baton Rouge, 1954), 7.

23. U.S. Congress, Senate, *Hearings Before the Committee on Education and Labor*, card 14, p. 923, testimony of William Coolidge, coal operator.

essential on themselves."[24] Negroes and mountain whites, on the other hand, who composed the majority of the labor supply, were "shiftless" and "unreliable." A reporter for the *Engineering and Mining Journal* noted the blacks "would make excellent miners if they could be induced to work regularly; but the darkey thinks it necessary to lay off a couple of days after each pay day and try to spend the money he has earned."[25] Mountain whites were little better, another writer charged, since "they resemble the negro [*sic*] in their desire for frequent periods of laying off."[26] Accustomed to the independent and seasonal work habits of rural life, most blacks and mountain whites were ill prepared to accept the industrial work ethic, and early mine operators continually complained of the thriftlessness, intemperence, and absenteeism of the native work force.[27]

Concerned with the problem of labor instability and with what they felt was the "uncivilized" quality of mountain life, many operators made every effort to assure stability and control within the coal community and to "educate" the miner to his role in the new social order. The company town, with its parallel streets and uniform housing design, became not simply a "coal camp" but an ordered social system that flattered the operator's sense of propriety and offered the promise of labor control. "Company discipline" was the effective jurisprudence within this social system, and the coal baron himself was the sole arbiter of justice. "To use the expression of the Middle Ages," William P. Tams recalled, "I was the high justice, the middle and the low."[28]

Operators differed widely in their attitudes toward the administration of company discipline. The more paternalistic employers applied "something of a military conception of industry" to the social scene. "My mine is a ship," stated one operator who was proud of the clean surroundings and comfortable living quarters of his employees. "I am its captain. My superintendent is the officer on deck. I expect my orders to be obeyed."[29] Such employers often ran a "tight ship"

24. Thurmond, *Logan Coal Field*, 63.
25. Parsons, "Coal Mining in Southern West Virginia," 883. Only about one-fifth of the miners in the southern coal fields were immigrants.
26. Fowler, "Social and Industrial Conditions," 387.
27. See also the testimony of John Laing, coal operator, U.S. Congress, *Hearings Before a Subcommittee of the Committee on Education and Labor*, vol. 39, card 5, 1660.
28. Quoted in Leamer, "Twilight for a Baron," 168.
29. Quoted in Lane, *Civil War in West Virginia*, 82.

and took a "personal interest" in their men to the extent of settling marital disputes, regulating drinking habits, and restricting social contacts.[30] Less paternal coal producers, however, viewed the maintenance of social stability as an annoying but necessary part of the total operation of the mine. "We are not running a Christian Endeavor camp meeting nor a Sunday School," Justus Collins advised his brother Jairus, "yet a certain amount of decency and order must be required of our people. " Any conduct that hampered moneymaking, he added, "should be squelched with a heavy hand."[31]

High on the list of activities forbidden in the company town, of course, was "union agitation," and most coal operators considered this form of "mutiny" to be grounds for immediate dismissal from the mine. Indeed, few American businessmen were more staunchly opposed to unionization than the southern coal barons. An individualistic breed, each of whom was determined to run his own business in his own way, they viewed the union movement as a personal threat not only to their freedom to determine business policies within the mine but to their authority within the company town as well. They found no room for the concept of collective bargaining in their social theory. Men were obliged to obey their "superiors," they argued, both in business and community life. Any "unnatural combination of labor against capital" threatened to disrupt the stable social order and to impede the accumulation of national wealth.[32] It is not surprising, therefore, that mountain coal operators fought unions with such bitter hostility, for labor organization challenged both their economic interests and their world view.

Throughout the period of industrial violence in the coal fields, many mountain operators believed that efforts to unionize their men represented a "genuine bona fide conspiracy" to disrupt the "natural harmony between management and labor" in the region.[33] Early operators located the source of this conspiracy among their business competitors to the north and in the union leaders' personal quest for

30. See Tams Transcript, 14; Leamer, "Twilight for a Baron," 168.
31. Justus Collins to Jairus Collins, 18 Sept. 1896, Justus Collins Papers, West Virginia Univ.
32. William Nelson Page to William E. Sackett, 8 March 1899, Page Papers, Box 4, folder 77, p. 10, Univ. of North Carolina.
33. William Nelson Page to G.W. Atkinson, 3 Feb. 1899, *ibid.*, Box 4, folder 77, p. 8; Justus Collins, "My Experience in the Smokeless Coal Fields of West Virginia," in Maude A. Rucker, ed., *West Virginia: Her Land, Her People, Her Traditions, Her Resources* (New York, 1930), 115.

power, but later coal producers charged that the conspiracy was truly national in scale. According to one mine official, the periodic labor disturbances which plagued the coal fields were "not local or isolated affairs to correct some imaginary wrong, but part of a general movement beginning to take form in this country to destroy the American form of government and American way of life and substitute a socialistic government." That such disturbances were "masterminded far from the actual theater of action was evident," he added, "and those actually engaged were only misguided individuals falling victim to organizations of subversive character."[34] Operators felt that the majority of miners were happy and generally loyal to the company for which they worked; it was only a small group of "outside agitators" who stirred the fires of discontent.[35]

## POLITICS

In order to assure the harmony and order of the coal camps and to protect their little kingdoms from outside interference, the coal barons early established control of the local political systems. Under the guise of law and order, the newcomers defeated the family-clan system and replaced it with a network controlled by economic interests. The mountain people often resisted the new regime. The history of this period is replete with strikes, violence, and other forms of antagonism toward outsiders, but the opposition of the local residents was curbed by the newcomers' effective use of force. The coal developer-novelist John Fox, Jr., described the process whereby "the sternest ideals of good order and law" were set up and maintained when coal mining came to Big Stone Gap, Virginia.

In this town, certain young men—chiefly Virginians and blue-grass Kentuckians—simply formed a volunteer police-guard. They enrolled themselves as county policemen, and each man armed himself— usually with a Winchester, a revolver, a billy, a belt, a badge, and a whistle. . . . They were lawyers, bankers, real-estate brokers, newspaper men, civil and mining engineers, geologists, speculators and several men of leisure. Nearly all were in active business—as long as there was business—and most of them were college graduates repre-

34. Thurmond, *Logan Coal Field*, 102.
35. See Tams Transcript, 17–18; Collins, "My Experience in the Smokeless Coal Fields," 119.

senting Harvard, Yale, Princeton, the University of Virginia, and other Southern colleges. Two were greatgrandsons of Henry Clay, several bore a like relation to Kentucky governors, and, with few exceptions the guard represented the best people of the blue-grass of one State and the tide-water country of the other.[36]

A similar assumption of power occurred in mining communities throughout the region as the newcomers established their authority over town and county governments.[37] Eventually, the native middle class caught "the fever for law and order" and provided an effective internal structure for maintaining control. As local lawyers, merchants, and other businessmen were converted to the industrial faith, they were incorporated into the ranks of the new elite, and the mine owners relied increasingly upon the local officials to protect their interests.

Within the new political system, the coal barons were vitally concerned with the makeup of county government, and they came to dominate the political machines in both Democratic and Republican districts.[38] The mountain Republican party underwent the greater conversion during these years, as the coal producers and other industrialists usurped the power of the native leadership and turned the party into the guardian of the new economic order. In many of the traditionally Democratic counties of southern West Virginia and eastern Kentucky, the arrival of the coal men marked the ascendancy of the Republican party to power, and the GOP maintained its political supremacy until the 1930s.[39] "The levying of property taxes, the locating of county and state highways, the action of the county court in evicting miners from company houses, and the position taken by the county sheriff during labor disputes" were

36. Fox, *Blue-Grass and Rhododendron*, 210–11. For a more detailed analysis of the Big Stone Gap police guard, see Helen Matthews Lewis, Sue Easterling Kobak, and Linda Johnson, "Family, Religion, and Colonialism in Central Appalachia, or Bury My Rifle at Big Stone Gap," in Helen Lewis, *et al.*, eds., *Colonialism in Modern America: The Appalachian Case* (Boone, N.C., 1978), 120–22.

37. See Gaventa, "Power and Powerlessness," 79–83.

38. See Gordon B. McKinney, *Southern Mountain Republicans, 1865–1900: Politics and the Appalachian Community* (Chapel Hill, 1978); Williams, *West Virginia and the Captains of Industry*.

39. William H. Haney, *The Mountain People of Kentucky* (Cincinnati, 1906), 137–56; Williams, *West Virginia and the Captains of Industry*, 110–22; McKinney, *Southern Mountain Republicans*, 190–94.

important to the coal barons, and they used every means available to assure that such functions were carried out to their benefit.[40]

Under these conditions, some counties were little more than industrial autocracies "with every branch of the county government and every phase of the lives of the people dominated by a super-oligarchy of coal operators."[41] The development of coal operators' associations after 1905 provided not only a means of controlling prices and unionization but also a mechanism for political leverage as well. In Harlan County, Kentucky, for example, the secretary of the Harlan County Coal Operators' Association served as county chairman of the dominant Republican party, and the president of the operators' association chaired the county Democratic organization.[42] The membership of the Southern Appalachian Coal Operators' Association, which published the *Appalachian Trade Journal*, included county judges, party chairmen, congressmen, and state senators; in 1914, the president of that association urged its members to take a more active role in politics so as to counteract the growing "taint of Socialism."[43] The leading political bosses in southern West Virginia after the turn of the century were coal operators, including Joseph Beury of Fayette County, Isaac Mann and John Cooper of Mercer County, and Jenkin Jones of McDowell County. One of the most powerful coal operators in southern West Virginia was Samuel Dixon—known by political and business opponents as "King Samuel"—who presided over the Fayette County Republican party and owned the Fayette *Journal*, the Raleigh *Herald*, and the Charleston *Daily Mail*.[44]

The abuses of the new order were apparent throughout local government. There had always been a degree of nepotism in mountian politics, but the traditional political culture had rarely been plagued with serious cases of graft or dishonesty. With power concentrated in the hands of the coal barons, however, reports of corruption, intimidation, ballot fraud, vote-buying, and other scandals

40. Hevener, "New Deal For Harlan," 16.
41. Lee, *Bloodletting in Appalachia*, 65.
42. Hevener, "New Deal For Harlan," 16.
43. John Evander Patton, "Government and Coal," *Appalachian Trade Journal* 12 (March 1914), 13. The editors of this journal printed a biographical sketch of a leading coal operator in almost every issue; see esp. vol. 9–13.
44. Thomas, "Coal Country," 289–90.

became widespread.[45] In many coal camps, the mine owners dictated who the miners should vote for and instructed the company bosses to see that every available man turned out at the polls. Since the operators controlled the local party machinery and selected the candidates, free primary elections were unknown. As Howard B. Lee recalled,

> The operators selected the candidates they thought were most favorably disposed toward their interests and required their miners to vote for them. Under the caption "I want to vote for the following candidates," they printed the names of all approved candidates on slips of paper called "The Slate," and on election mornings company paid deputy sheriffs handed a copy of The Slate to each voter as he approached the polls. The voter in turn passed the list to the election officials, also company employees, who marked his ballot accordingly.[46]

Those voters whom the bosses could not intimidate with threatened loss of employment were kept in line in other ways. Opposition ballots were sometimes "written off" or discarded, and in many districts, vote-buying was prevalent. Party bosses often sent men into the countryside to haul voters to the polls and to inform them of the most lucrative way to vote. When the individual had cast his ballot, he was entitled to five or ten dollars or a liberal quantity of whiskey.[47] In this manner, the coal barons made certain that only company men were elected to county offices.

Locally, the operators focused their attention on the election of county tax assessors and sheriffs. Since the former were responsible for valuating property for tax purposes, controlling the assessors' offices was important in keeping the taxes down on mine properties. Naming the sheriffs insured the use of local authorities in maintaining order in the coal camps and in suppressing union activities.[48]

Sheriffs had the authority to appoint deputy sheriffs, and in many

45. Cressey, "Social Disorganization and Reorganization," 392; E.V. Tadlock, "Coal Camps and Character," *Mountain Life and Work* 4 (Jan. 1929), 23.

46. *Bloodletting in Appalachia*, 9. See also Helen Hall, "Miners Must Eat," *Atlantic Monthly* 152 (1933), 157.

47. See, for example, Henry P. Scalf, Stanville, Ky., interview in "Our Appalachia: An Oral History," by the Appalachian Oral History Project, unpublished typescript, Emory and Henry Oral History Project, 2–32.

48. Lee, *Bloodletting in Appalachia*, 10–11.

*Coal Man and His Sheriff. Courtesy of the Appalachian Photographic Archives, Alice Lloyd College.*

of the coal counties the salaries of "extra" deputy sheriffs were provided by the mine owners. In such cases, the deputies served as official mine guards in the company towns, protecting the company's property and payrolls, collecting rents, overseeing elections, and performing other services.[49] This practice was especially prevalent in southern West Virginia and was one of the leading causes of discontent among the miners. A state investigation in 1919 revealed that the Logan County Coal Operators Association paid $32,700 a year to the sheriff of that county for the salaries of twenty-five deputy sheriffs. These deputies were stationed on various mining properties around the county, carrying out the wishes of the coal operators.[50] They were public officials, nominated by the sheriff and appointed by the county court, but they were paid by the mine owners and served at the pleasure of the coal men.

The sheriff of Logan County at that time was Don Chafin, one of the most notorious native political leaders to reign during the early coal years. Chafin was born in Logan County in 1887, and he came to the throne of the Logan Democratic party just as the coal companies were beginning to enter the county. In 1908, he was elected to the assessor's office, and between that year and 1925 he ruled the "Kingdom of Logan" like a feudal barony, being elected sheriff for two terms. Although a Democrat, Chafin controlled the county on the behalf of the coal operators. All of the mine owners in the county paid tribute to Sheriff Chafin, and in return he protected the county from unionization. At the height of his power, Chafin employed over three hundred deputized mine guards, whose salaries were provided by the Logan County coal operators.[51]

Chafin's private army spent most of its time preventing the infiltration of Logan County by union organizers. The officers met every train that came into the county and interrogated strangers as to their name and business. If the replies were not satisfactory, the stranger was placed back on the train and told not to return. Union sympathizers among the miners were ferreted out, beaten, and removed from the county. Those citizens who objected to such tactics were also ordered to leave, and, according to E.T. England, West Virginia attorney general at that time, "to ignore the warning sometimes

49. Tams, *Smokeless Coal Fields of West Virginia*, 59.
50. Lane, *Civil War in West Virginia*, 52.
51. Lee, *Bloodletting in Appalachia*, 87–90.

meant death or serious injury at the hands of his deputy-thugs, who always killed their man in self-defense, or while the victim was resisting arrest, or attempting to escape."[52] The sheriff also used force and violence to maintain his political supremacy. Opposing politicians were sometimes arrested and jailed; precincts were closed on election days; and ballots were seized and burned after they had been cast. Chafin's reach extended into the county courts, the public schools, the churches, and almost every other aspect of the county's life.[53] Unfavorable publicity and state and federal investigations of Chafin's corrupt kingdom eventually brought an end to his reign and to the deputy-mine-guard system in southern West Virginia, but the coal operators found other ways and other men to sustain their authority in the coal districts.

The power to control local elections and county government provided a base from which the coal barons also extended their influence over state politics. Since the 1870s and 1880s, state politicians had eased the way for the arrival of the coal men by promoting the abundant natural wealth of the mountains and passing favorable taxation and incorporation laws. Many of the leading figures in state government were themselves tied to the coal industry through retainers or direct ownership of mines, and they used their political power to assure that no legislation was passed that was hostile to the coal interests. As West Virginia Governor George W. Atkinson pointed out in his inaugural address, he planned "to do everything in [his] power" to encourage the development of the state's coal and timber resources, and he intended to place no obstacles in the way of corporate success. In fact, he noted, "I have invariably deemed it to be my duty to aid them in all proper undertakings," and he promised to help remove any prejudices against coal companies and other corporations which might exist in the Mountain State. "Instead of fewer corporations in West Virginia," he concluded, "we need more of them."[54]

The pervasive influence of large corporations in state and local politics was a common problem throughout the United States at the turn of the century, but nowhere did absentee corporations have greater control over the political destiny of a region than in Ap-

52. Quoted in *ibid.*, 90.
53. *Ibid.*, 90–92.
54. Quoted in *Manufacturers' Record* 31 (12 March 1879), 115.

palachia. Although the coal industry was a powerful force in every
coal-producing state of the region, it dominated the political system
of the Mountain State, turning "the entire machinery of State government" to the development and protection of the coal business. "In
this respect," commented the *Manufacturers' Record*, "West Virginia holds a unique position not duplicated by the governmental
machinery of any other State in the South."[55] The coal barons of that
state not only had a hand in the selection of governors and congressmen, contributing liberally to the campaign funds of both Republican and Democratic candidates, but they also usually controlled the upper house of the West Virginia legislature and used that
body to protect themselves from unfavorable state laws. Usually,
there was at least one coal operator elected to the state senate during
each term, and he was almost always appointed chairman of the
Committee on Mines and Mining. Several other senators were generally "company men," and those who were not were bribed with
"lavish dinners, free whiskey, payment of hotel bills . . . and other
entertainment."[56] Together, the coal-controlled senators prevented
the passage of most of the tax reform and mine safety laws that came
before the legislature and successfully crippled those that were passed.

The strength of the coal lobby in West Virginia was illustrated by
the failure of the legislature after the turn of the century to tax the
removal of millions of tons of natural wealth from the state every
year. Progressive politicians introduced severance tax bills in each
legislative session from 1905 to 1909, but the measures were consistently defeated by the coal interests.[57] (Similar efforts were also
defeated in the other coal-producing states during the progressive
period, and severance taxes were never passed in the mountain states
until the 1970s.) West Virginia's resources continued to be exploited
and overdeveloped chiefly for the benefit of nonresident corporations, and the state's politicians refused to alter the regressive system
of taxation, despite the compelling need for public revenue.[58] In a

55. *Ibid.*, 50 (18 Oct. 1906), 338. The best account of the role of the coal barons
and other industrial leaders in West Virginia politics is to be found in Williams, *West
Virginia and the Captains of Industry*.
56. Howard B. Lee, *My Appalachia: Pipesterm State Park, Today and Yesterday*
(Parsons, W.Va., 1971), 103–4.
57. *Manufacturers' Record* 55 (25. Feb. 1909), 41.
58. Williams, *West Virginia and the Captains of Industry*, 249.

state where the major portion of the wealth was being siphoned off by absentee corporations, it is ironic that in 1921 West Virginia was the first state in the union to introduce the sales tax. Since the average laborer spent from 60 to 70 percent of his income on taxable commodities, the sales tax naturally bore more heavily upon the poor than the rich.[59] Thus the coal barons—unwilling to pay for improved public services themselves—successfully transferred the burden of the costs of state government to the shoulders of the miners and other mountain residents.

This effort was also carried over into the area of industrial relations, as the coal operators succeeded in limiting or defeating most mine health and safety legislation that was introduced during these years. As early as 1883, West Virginia and the other coal states adopted mining laws aimed at providing a safer workplace for miners, but the bulk of these laws placed the major responsibility for safe working conditions on the laborer rather than on the mine owner. The rise in explosions and other fatal mine accidents after 1900 led to a revision of the West Virginia mining codes in 1907 and the establishment of a state Department of Mines. The new codes contained more exacting standards for ventilation and control of mine dust, prohibited the use of steam locomotives inside the mine, set minimum age limits for mine workers, and gave the department chief the authority to close any mine found in violation of the codes.[60] Enforcement of the mining laws was lax, however, not only because of the understaffed and underfinanced system of mine inspection, but also because district inspectors usually made only "recommendations" for improvements, and the operator-controlled county courts refused to prosecute violations. Moreover, the first man appointed to head the state Department of Mines, John Laing, was himself a prominent coal operator.[61]

In the mountains throughout the progressive period, the coal barons continued to oppose any legislation that might increase production costs and decrease profits. In some cases, they learned to turn the spirit of reform legislation to their own advantage. The passage of workmen's compensation laws after 1910, for example, was sup-

59. Dixon Wecter, *The Age of the Great Depression, 1929–1941* (New York, 1948), 93.
60. Thomas, "Coal Country," 223.
61. Dix, *Work Relations*, 91–92; Thomas, "Coal Country," 223–24.

ported by many coal operators, since the laws reduced the financial responsibilities of employers. Under the compensation codes, miners or their survivors could no longer sue employers for damages from death or injuries incurred on the job.[62] Furthermore, the compensation program was relatively inexpensive for mine owners compared with the rising cost of liability insurance. The average compensation for a death in Kentucky mines in 1912 was about $3,000. In that year the State Compensation Fund paid a total of $156,000 for fifty-two lives. Even when the cost of nonfatal accidents was added to that figure, observed a Harlan County coal operator, "the industry could well afford to meet the bill."[63]


## LABOR MANAGEMENT

As the intensity of public criticism and labor unrest grew, many coal operators began to develop alternative policies toward the problems of industrial relations. Where pioneer operators rejected notions of social responsibility and attempted to solve their labor difficulties by simply dismissing the unacceptable worker, producers after the turn of the century sought increasingly to avoid such problems through careful labor management. The pressure of public opinion and the influence of progressive attitudes toward business reform led to a growing recognition of the social responsibilities of business and prompted many coal barons to reevaluate the relationship between civic conditions and their own economic interests. Operators had always valued a stable and orderly mining community, and, under the new doctrines of scientific management, they came to accept the view that healthy and comfortable surroundings were conducive not only to labor stability but to efficiency and productivity as well. By 1916, coal producers in older areas were beginning to favor policies of community improvement as a means of "producing a spirit of contentment with the place," while those opening mines in newer fields were applying the techniques of management planning to the construction of "model mining towns."[64] A totally planned environment, the latter believed, would create "an ideal industrial com-

62. K.U. Meguire, "Workmen's Compensation," *Appalachian Trade Journal* 11 (July 1913), 16; Dix, *Work Relations*, 88.
63. Meguire, "Workmen's Compensation," 18.
64. George Wolfe to Justus Collins, 7 Aug. 1916, Justus Collins Papers, West Virginia Univ.

munity in which there was perfect harmony between employer and employees and all worked together each for the interest of the other."[65]

Moral considerations undoubtedly played a part in the new emphasis upon community welfare, but there were also sound business reasons for the improvement of social conditions. The desire to attract workers, to resist the encroachment of unions, and to stem the appeal of other "radical" movements pointed in the same direction. As one mine official noted, "the question of sanitation in a mining town is a business proposition. It pays to have healthful conditions."[66] Having almost total responsibility for the "health" of the company town, operators seldom drew sharp distinctions between business and community purposes. They usually viewed "contributions" for good schools, better roads, comfortable housing, and recreational facilities as simply another business expense. "We don't mean to convey the idea that we are more altruistic or have more generosity than any other group of employers," stated a southern coal baron. "We are doing this as a business policy, and feel that that is enough. There is a great deal of competition for labor and we try to do everything possible to make our men contented and satisfied in order to keep them. A lot of this welfare work is done with that object in view. We think it is good business. We have had no strikes in seventeen years."[67]

Many of the larger coal companies that entered the region in the progressive era undertook a two-pronged policy to strengthen their relationships with their own employees and improve their image in the public eye, while continuing to mount an all-out campaign against the union movement. Corporations such as U.S. Steel and Consolidation Coal devised extensive welfare programs to convince labor of

65. U.S. Congress, Senate, *Hearings Before the Committee on Education and Labor*, testimony of Walter R. Thurmond, president of the Logan Coal Operator's Association.

66. Unnamed operator, quoted in American Constitutional Association, *Life in a West Virginia Coal Field* (Charleston, W.V., 1923), 17. See also W.C. Tucker, general manager of Wisconsin Steel Company, Benham, Ky., "Welfare Work and Its Relation to Successful Operation," *Appalachian Trade Journal* 10 (Feb. 1913), 22–23.

67. J.M. Vest, president and general manager of the Rum Creek Collieries Company, quoted in Gleason, "Company-Owned Americans," 794; also quoted in Lane, *Civil War in West Virginia*, 35.

their benevolence and to drive home the idea that employers and employees were really but "one great happy family."[68] Elbert H. Gary, chairman of the board of U.S. Steel, for example, was one of the first business leaders to recognize the value of public respect and confidence in deterring social criticism and government interference. As board chairman, Gary made a conscious effort to present his company in a positive light, and when U.S. Steel and its subsidiaries moved into the southern coal districts, his policy of putting forward a favorable image was applied in the construction of model towns like Gary, Mann, Ennis, and others in the Pocahontas field.[69]

Beginning in 1917 and continuing through the war years, Consolidation Coal Company launched an effort to improve its standing within the coal community by establishing an Employment Relations Department. The purpose of this separate department, the company claimed, was to look into "the health, education, amusement, recreation and other matters connected with the mining population about the company's various plants." In accomplishing its "sociological work," the department hired a force of doctors and nurses, organized Boy Scout companies and sewing circles, sponsored baseball teams and company bands, and published a monthly employees' magazine to encourage an *esprit de corps* among the men. "Our interests being identical," read the slogan of the *Mutual Monthly Magazine*, "we work together for our common good—employer and employed."[70]

Such policies, although often expensive, also attracted a following among many smaller coal companies. Operators constructed moving picture houses, pool halls, and bowling alleys. They awarded prizes for the best gardens and most attractive yards and, in a few cases, instituted profit-sharing plans in order to promote a feeling of mutual interest. "We try to consider our employees and ourselves the same as one large family," remarked the manager of the Logan Mining Company, "realizing that the company must make a reasonable profit if they want to do the best they can for the men in the way of

---

68. See Thomas C. Cochran and William Miller, *The Age of Enterprise: A Social History of Industrial America* (New York, 1961), 336.

69. Morrell Heald, *The Social Responsibilities of Business: Company and Community, 1900–1960* (Cleveland, 1970), 30–31; Fowler, "Social and Industrial Conditions," 386–88.

70. Brosky, "Sociological Works Accomplished by the Consolidation Coal Company," 54.

wages and living conditions."[71] Yet, the language of cooperation and peace increasingly employed by coal producers in the 1920s continued to reflect many of the same assumptions that lay behind the language of combat, struggle, and paternalism that had prevailed in the earlier years of industrial growth. The techniques of labor management were changing, but among the independent coal barons, the concern for order and stability, the desire to retain a degree of authority and control over business and community life, and the determination to oppose the union movement remained substantially the same.

In many respects, however, the new policies of cooperation and the new concern with "public relations" that emerged in the postwar period marked the close of an era in the history of the coal fields. The growth of large-scale mining enterprises, owned by absentee investors and managed by professional personnel, greatly altered the relationship between employer and employee in the region. Where pioneer operators had maintained a close, if not a personal, association with their men and had exercised authority primarily on their own behalf, the superintendents of corporate mines held little or no direct ownership in the enterprise and administered authority on behalf of economic interests far from the scene of production itself. Holding an intermediate position between capital and labor, the managerial leadership developed policies to protect profits and security values and, when possible, to win public approval as well. Unlike their independent counterparts, they viewed labor as a distinct interest group—a "partner" within the corporate system—whose cooperation was necessary for the efficient operation of the mine and whose loyalty "has to be earned by the management."[72] Less interested in protecting a way of life than in maximizing production, the managerial elite were not as concerned with the maintenance of absolute authority within the company town, and thus they played a proportionately smaller role in the life of the coal community.

The rise of consolidated or "captive" mines, moreover, heralded the exodus of the older coal barons themselves from the mountains.

71. J.J. Ross quoted in Gleason, "Company-Owned Americans," 794. See also Tams in Leamer, "Twilight for a Baron," 168; Tams Transcript, 7–9.

72. U.S. Congress, Senate, *Hearings Before the Committee on Education and Labor*, card 15, p. 963, testimony of William Wiley, mine superintendent. For a discussion of the managerial concept of "industrial partnership," see Bendix, *Work and Authority in Industry*, 288–97.

Some operators had begun to leave the company towns for the "pleasant and comfortable" surroundings of the cities in the years before the war, but when expanded wartime production multiplied profits, an ever-increasing number of mine owners left the coal fields. By 1925, "operators rarely if ever resided at the mines."[73] A few paternalistic individuals continued to maintain close supervision over the affairs of the company town, but the majority of independent coal producers sold out or gradually lost touch with the details of production and labor management. With the passing of direct owner involvement in the everyday life of the coal community, therefore, the age of the coal baron came to an end. The impact of this era, however, left a deep and lasting mark on the social history of the region.

The changing economic and social climate of the years after 1900 forced southern mountain coal barons, like other American businessmen, to reexamine and redefine their relationships to labor and the community. Early coal operators seldom faced the question of social responsibility. Later coal producers were almost constantly confronted with the issue. In response to growing labor unrest, competition, and public criticism, operators over the years developed a variety of policies to promote order and stability within the coal community and to improve productivity at the mine. Some took great interest in the affairs of their company towns and worked to maintain clean and comfortable surroundings for their men. Others, more blindly driven by the profit motive and less paternal in their relationships with employees, were not as concerned with the quality of community life. Yet, all sought to apply the principles of business efficiency to the social demands of the mining town. Convinced that the miners' interests were identical to those of the company, they ruled the towns as they ruled the mines, without opposition or debate.

A large number of prominent coal barons migrated to the southern mountains from the North, but there is no evidence to suggest a marked difference in social attitudes between southern-born and northern-born producers. Many operators from the South clearly took a paternalistic attitude toward their employees, but so did many of their counterparts from the North. Almost all seem to have come

73. U.S. Congress, Senate, *Report of the U.S. Coal Commission*, vol. 1, p. 170. See also Tams, *Smokeless Coal Fields of West Virginia*, 74–75.

from similar socioeconomic backgrounds; most were aspiring, educated members of the upper-middle class. Excluding differences of personality and experience, dissimilarities in their professional situations and place of residence contributed most to distinctions between coal producers. Many owner-operators, for example, demonstrated greater concern for maintaining an "ordered social system" within the company town than did individuals sent to manage mines owned by absentee investors. Resident operators were more concerned with social conditions as well. "Those who hustled off to [the cities] and came Monday morning and left Friday night on the night train back," recalled William P. Tams, "had a different attitude from those of us who lived in the company towns." The latter, choosing to remain in the community, wanted "a decent place to live."[74]

In the expression of their social attitudes, Appalachian coal barons were not unlike other industrial entrepreneurs at the turn of the century. They valued order, coveted power, and disdained labor unions. Having entered the mountains solely to exploit the region's vast mineral wealth, they undertook to wield their power over the local community in direct support of their business enterprises. After creating a system of closed company communities, the majority departed from the region—their personal fortunes having been made. Motivated primarily by economic considerations, they had opposed "burdensome" taxes and had often justified civic improvements only as a business expense. During a critical period of social change, they had maintained a personal dominance over the affairs of the coal community which had thwarted the growth of alternative local industries, social services, and public institutions. They carried industrialization to the mountains, but they left the region ill equipped to confront the social and economic problems of the industrial age.

74. Tams Transcript, 8.

# CHAPTER SEVEN

# MODERNIZATION AND THE MOUNTAINEER

In 1933, Lewis Cecil Gray delivered a preliminary report on the social and economic conditions of the southern Appalachians. Gray had been selected by the U.S. Department of Agriculture to head a comprehensive study of the problems in the mountain counties of the southern states, and he had gathered around him an able staff of eighteen researchers and specialists on mountain life. The nation was caught in the grip of depression, and conditions in the South were widely viewed as among the worst in the country. Out of the southern mountains had come appalling reports of poverty, destitution, and despair, and the department hoped that the Gray study would provide a basis for extending some help to the hard-hit mountain people.

Shortly after beginning his research, Gray outlined some of his initial findings at a meeting of the Council of Southern Mountain Workers. The survey, he confided, had uncovered some profound discrepancies between the popular image of the region and reality, discrepancies which would need to be carefully considered in any future economic and social planning for the mountains. Gray noted,

> Our work shows how necessary it is to revise old ideas of the Southern Appalachians as a static region where life goes on unchangingly, a land exclusively occupied by the tall mountaineer with his lanky wife and shock-headed children. The past thirty years have been a time of rapid transformation. Population in the region has increased about 56 percent. This is almost wholly due to great transforming influences—the growth of cities and the development of rural industries, especially mining.[1]

Gray found that the farm population of the region had increased only about 5 percent since 1900, but that the urban population had in-

1. Gray, "Economic Conditions in the Southern Appalachians," 8.

creased more than 300 percent and the rural nonfarm population more than 75 percent. This rapid growth was almost twice that of the non-mountain counties of the Appalachian states, and it reflected a more fundamental transformation in economy and land-use patterns, which had induced dramatic changes throughout the fabric of mountain life.[2]

Two years later, Gray repeated this theme in his final report to the Department of Agriculture, suggesting that no longer could the mountain region be seen "as essentially homogeneous" or pictured "in terms of some of the romantic works of fiction or impressionistic descriptions which have emphasized the striking features of mountain life and customs." The basic problems of the region in the 1930s, he argued, stemmed less from the character of mountain life as depicted in traditional images than from "maladjustments in land use and in the relation of the population to the land." Tangible improvements in the socioeconomic conditions of the mountains, Gray concluded, could not be achieved without the formation of a federal planning agency vested with sufficient power and resources to carry out a rational land-utilization program.[3]

Gray's proposal for an Appalachian planning agency was partially fulfilled with the establishment of the Tennessee Valley Authority in 1933, but it was to be another thirty years before a region-wide development authority was created.[4] The TVA, the U.S. Forest Service, and the U.S. Park Service acted on one of Gray's suggestions—the conversion of "submarginal" land to public ownership—but the report received little public attention.[5] Most Americans continued to see the Appalachians as a "strange land inhabited by a peculiar people," a region which had somehow been passed by in the onrush of the modern world. It was more than a decade later, moreover, that Arnold Toynbee penned his descriptions of the mountaineers as "barbarians," isolated people who had backslid in civilization and existed as living relics of an earlier age.[6] Perhaps such images helped to maintain the sense of progress and superiority so

2. *Ibid.*
3. U.S. Department of Agriculture, *Economic and Social Conditions*, 1–2.
4. The Appalachian Regional Commission was established in 1965.
5. Gray's suggestions for change in the Appalachians included: (1) conversion of land to public ownership; (2) establishment of small, rural, farm-forest communities; (3) development of local manufacturing; (4) combining employment in the mines with part-time work in small factories or on the farm; and (5) emigration.
6. *A Study of History*, II, 312.

vital to the modernizing classes. Perhaps they simply obscured the painful fact that many of the benefits of the new industrial order had been wrung out of the land and the people of the mountains; it was ineffably easier to believe in myths than to confront the inequalities and "maladjustments" of years of greed and exploitation. A few voices challenged the popular "idea of Appalachia," but the Gray report stood as the most comprehensive challenge to the static image.[7]

Most mountaineers, of course, were well aware of the changes that had come over their region in the last half-century. The industrial revolution had touched almost every aspect of mountain society. Traditional patterns of life had been greatly disturbed and in some cases torn asunder, and the mountain residents had increasingly found themselves at the mercy of changing winds of the national economy. Many had benefited in material ways from the prosperity of the boom years. Like other Americans, the mountaineers were quick to take up the advantages of the industrial age: store-bought clothes, furniture, washing machines, radios, and automobiles. In the company towns, food was no longer grown, preserved, and stored for the winter; instead, daily supplies were bought in paper bags and tin cans and acquired "on credit" at the company store.[8] When the collapse of the new economic system came in the mid-twenties, however, the mountain people found that the growing prosperity had bred greater dependence on a system beyond their control. Many were left more destitute than they had been on the independent family farm.

Industrialization had integrated the mountains into the dominant economy of the country as a whole, and it had rendered the region increasingly subject to the fluctuations of the national market system. Prior to the 1880s and 1890s, the Appalachian economy was locally oriented and designed to meet the needs of the resident population. Communities were small and, like the family farms, essentially self-sufficient. The development of railroads, coal mining, timber, textiles, and other industries came about as a result of growing demands in maturing industrial areas outside of the mountains, primarily the urban Midwest and East, and the new commercial order in the region emerged to meet those nonresident needs. Because the

7. See also Ross, *Machine Age in the Hills*.
8. Cressey, "Social Disorganization and Reorganization," 392.

demands of the larger economy were for cheap labor and raw materials, and because outside capitalists quickly acquired most of the natural resources of the region, the bulk of the wealth generated by the new developments flowed out of the mountains. Comparatively little capital was left behind for reinvestment and the building of a self-sustaining local economy. The new mountain economic order, therefore, was highly dependent, labor intensive, and tied to the export of single extractive commodities.

The high concentration of absentee land ownership which accompanied Appalachian industrial development is an element characteristic of advancing industrial capitalism. In Appalachia it served not only to bind the region to the national economy but to hinder the growth of diversified local industries as well. Coal, timber, and land companies were primarily interested in the extraction of the timber and mineral resources, and their land was unavailable for other purposes. In counties where large corporations owned from 50 to 90 percent of the land, there were few opportunities for the development of other enterprises that might have accompanied industrial growth.[9]

The closed company town system further restricted the diversification of the local economic base, since a single company dominated all aspects of community life. Private businesses that might have grown up around the new towns failed to develop, and the native middle class which might have encouraged diversification remained small and tied to the fortunes of the single industry. In normal self-governing communities, the middle class was often responsible for the development of promotional campaigns to attract other types of industry upon which the town's future might rest, but the feudal community structure of the Appalachian coal fields forestalled the emergence of such campaigns.

Alternatives in company town development did exist within the region, including the short-lived cooperative mining town of Himlerville, Kentucky, and the more traditional company community of Rockwood, Tennessee. The latter was built by the Roane Iron Company, but the company's management permitted home ownership, private business development, and eventually self-government through incorporation. Around the turn of the century, local leaders realized that a more diversified economic base was necessary for the

9. Since most coal camps were built in narrow isolated hollows, topography itself also limited the land available for alternative industries.

continued health of the community, and they began a campaign to attract other manufacturers. In time, they succeeded in drawing several textile mills, a lumber mill, a stove works, and other firms to the town, thus providing a broader base from which the community continued to expand after the Roane Iron Company went out of business.[10]

Most of the company towns in the mountains, however, failed to develop an independent business community, and the rural nature of Appalachian industrialization slowed the growth of business in older incorporated towns. In the coal fields, the arrival of industrialization stimulated a rise in the number of banking institutions, but the banks usually served as the private depositories of the coal barons and were reluctant to finance non-coal-related local enterprises. Without local or regional markets, the economic structure of the mountains was solely dependent upon exterior demand. The rapid rise in demand for mineral and timber resources from the 1890s to the early 1920s resulted in substantial economic growth in the region, but very little long-range local development occurred. This condition of growth without development placed the mountains in a highly vulnerable relationship to the larger market system. Slight fluctuations in that system were felt with great intensity throughout the hills. Despite the vast natural wealth within its borders, the southern mountains remained comparatively poor—not because it was backward, but because its wealth enriched the modernizing centers in other parts of the country. Such economic "underdevelopment" is similar to the exploitation experienced by many Third World countries that provide raw materials to larger, more advanced industrial nations.[11]

The extent of the new dependent relationship of the mountain economy was reflected in the decline of agriculture in the region. In 1880, the mountain population was overwhelmingly engaged in agricultural pursuits, making a small but adequate living from full-time farming. By 1930, according to the Gray report, three-fifths of the mountain population was employed off the farm, and many of

10. William H. Moore, "Preoccupied Paternalism: The Roane Iron Company in Her Company Town—Rockwood, Tennessee," *East Tennessee Historical Society Publications* 39 (1967), 56–70.

11. For an excellent description of the "dependency theory" as it is applied to Appalachia, see Douglas O. Arnett, "Counter Power Structure Struggles in Appalachia" (MS based upon the author's Ph.D. diss., Duke Univ., 1978), 7–35. See also Walls, "Internal Colony or Internal Periphery? A Critique" 319–50; Gaventa, "Power and Powerlessness," 1–41; Thomas, "Coal Country," 122–23.

those who were listed as farmers were also engaged in part-time industrial work. In the Cumberland Plateau, almost a third of those gainfully employed worked in coal mining.[12] This rise in the non-farm population was accompanied by a general decrease in the acreage of land in farms, resulting from the absentee corporations' acquisition of farm and forest properties and from the continued division of farms among heirs. Over the period from 1900 to 1930, the amount of land in farms declined almost 25 percent.[13] In many of the coal counties, agriculture was almost wiped out by the impact of industry. Harlan County, Kentucky, for example, witnessed a decline of acreage in farms of more than 50 percent between 1910 and 1925.[14] In 1930, 60 percent of the land area throughout the region remained in farms, compared with 73 percent thirty years earlier.[15]

Industrialization also had a detrimental effect on the nature of farming in the mountains. Whereas the preindustrial farm was largely self-sufficient and engaged in the raising of livestock for local and regional markets, a large portion of the mountain farms of the 1930s were classified as submarginal. Once-thriving cattle and hog industries almost disappeared from the region—victims of changing transportation patterns, the usurpation of pasture for industrial purposes, and the rise of new national markets. Mountaineers had always used the woodlands to graze their sheep, cattle, and hogs, but when the timber was purchased by outside corporations, this part of the mountain farm was lost to production. By the eve of the Great Depression, only about 38 percent of the privately owned timber acreage in the region was in farms. The remaining 62 percent was held by "industrial organizations." This did not, of course, include more than two million acres of timberland that had been acquired by the federal government.[16]

With the woodlands substantially eliminated as a source of income, most farmers turned to raising row crops or maintaining smaller herds on cleared pasture land, but the expanded agricultural markets to sustain these smaller farms, which might have come with industrialization, failed to materialize. The construction of coal camps, timber towns, and other industrial communities, which ordi-

12. U.S. Department of Agriculture, *Economic and Social Conditions*, 3, 16.
13. *Ibid.*
14. Wood, "The Kentucky Mountaineers," 94, Table IV.
15. Gray, "Economic Conditions in the Southern Appalachians," 9.
16. U.S. Department of Agriculture, *Economic and Social Conditions,* 32.

narily would have provided a local market for mountain farms, had little impact on regional production, since transportation patterns and the feudal structure of the company towns worked against their being supplied by local areas. Compared to low-country farms, moreover, mountain farms contained less tillable acreage (only about 10 to 15 acres per farm), and the steep slopes were not appropriate for the use of modern farm machinery. This placed the hillside farms at a competitive disadvantage with their flatland counterparts, and in the growing national market system, mountain farms continued to decline steadily.

As pressure on mountain agriculture increased after the turn of the century, there was a proportionate rise in the percentage of tenancy and part-time farming. The southern Appalachians had for generations been characterized by a high rate of land ownership, but with the coming of industrialization, it became more and more difficult for mountaineers to hold on to their land. Growing property values made land difficult to acquire, and rising taxes made it harder to retain. In approximately one-half of the counties of the mountain region, 30 percent of the farmers were tenants by the outbreak of World War I, and in some counties that figure was more than 50 percent.[17] Many of those who remained on the land were reduced to part-time farming, taking seasonal employment in the mines and logging camps, or other public work. The Gray survey estimated that about 58 percent of the farmers in the region received the bulk of their income from nonfarm sources. On 75 percent of those farms that were self-sufficient, the value of the products sold or used was less than $600.[18] No other area of the United States had as great a concentration of part-time and low-income farms.[19]

While the new order brought hard times to mountain agriculture, it did little more to benefit other aspects of mountain life. Improvement in transportation facilities, for example, not only helped to lower the local value of farm products, but it also increased the geographic insularity of mountain communities. The construction of railroad lines in the region tended to follow geographic contours of the mountain valleys and hollows. Branch lines were usually not connected with each other, and each stopped as it reached the headwaters

17. Campbell, *The Southern Highlander*, 314.
18. Gray, "Economic Conditions in the Southern Appalachians." 10.
19. Williams, "The Southern Mountaineer in Fact and Fiction," 8.

of the valley, leaving many of the new communities isolated one from another. Since the railroads were built primarily to haul natural resources rather than people, railroad executives were reluctant to engage in low-profit passenger traffic and were unwilling to construct branch lines to neighboring communities only for passengers.[20] In the coal fields, the railroads were often the only means of transportation into and out of the camps, since few public highways connected the mining towns.[21] The coal barons, moreover, were unwilling to tax themselves for road projects, and so the public road system remained wretched for decades, further hindering the development of the local economic base. As a result of this limited transportation system, many of the potential benefits of modernization were slow to filter into the rural communities. One researcher in the coal districts estimated that in 1930 "only one farm home in twenty had running water, one in fifty an inside toilet, one in twenty-five electricity, one in thirty a telephone, and one in thirty a radio."[22]

Life in the company towns, of course, was no industrial paradise, despite the greater availability of material comforts. The migration from the family farm to the mining camp or mill village was for many mountaineers a difficult and traumatic move. The noise, congestion, and filth of the industrial communities was in striking contrast to the environment of the mountain farm, and the sultry, thin-walled company houses were hardly an improvement over many mountain cabins. On the farm, the womenfolk had made the cabin bright with coverlets, patchwork quilts, and dried vegetables. Grass and wildflowers grew to the doorway, and trees provided shade from the summer's heat. In the company towns, the house was often dull and lifeless, surrounded by dust and trodden dirt. Cheap metal beds and other furniture replaced the handmade things on the farms, and the women gave up their handicrafts as the family purchased garments and other goods from the company store or mail-order catalogues.[23] The adjustment to the stifling life of the company towns was espe-

20. Thurmond, *Logan Coal Field*, 80.
21. Hunt, Tryon, and Willitts, *What the Coal Commission Found*, 153; Thurmond, *Logan Coal Field*, 80.
22. Gilbert Wheeler Beebe, *Contraception and Fertility in the Southern Appalachians* (Baltimore, 1942), 26.
23. See Thomas, *Life Among the Hills*, 4–5; Wood, "The Kentucky Mountaineers," 29–30; Campbell, *The Southern Highlander*, 196; Ross, *Machine Age in the Hills*, 87; Anne W. Armstrong, "The Southern Mountaineers," *Yale Review* 24 (March 1935), 543–48.

cially hard for mountain women, whose roles and lifestyles changed dramatically with the new order. As Alpha Brackstone lamented in James Still's novel *River of Earth*, "I allus had a mind to live on a hill, not sunk in a holler where fog and dust is damping and blacking. I was raised to like a lonesome place. Can't get used to a mess of womenfolks in and out, borrowing a dab and a pinch of this and that, never paying back. Men tromping sut on the floors, forever talking brash."[24]

Health and social problems which generally accompanied urban life were magnified in the company town. With the movement into crowded and unsanitary coal camps, mountaineers increasingly fell victim to epidemics of smallpox, typhoid fever, and intestinal diseases. Cases of tuberculosis and venereal disease, which were rare in preindustrial days, rose sharply in the congested mining towns, and many children suffered from pellagra and other dietary deficiencies.[25] Accustomed to a diet of milk, vegetables, game, and other natural products on the farm, mountain families "fell into the habit of eating along the line of least resistance, food most easily and quickly prepared."[26] Unbalanced diets of processed and prepackaged foods from which most of the vitamins had been removed contributed markedly to the poor health and the dental problems of the company towns.[27] Alterations in family roles and the decline of communal or family work activities such as house-raisings, quiltings, corn-hoeings, and the like, often increased personal and family tensions and contributed to the rise in divorce, delinquency, and child desertion. In Harlan County, for instance, the divorce rate ballooned by 80 percent between 1922 and 1932.[28]

The company town also symbolized the new social structure of the mountains and the dependent and powerless situation of the working class. Prior to the 1890s, the social distance between the economic

24. (New York, 1940), 51.
25. Children's Bureau, *The Welfare of Children in Coal Mining Communities*, 47–50; Williams, "The Mountaineer In Fact and Fiction," 159–60; Thomas, "Coal Country," 302–3.
26. Sherwood, "Our New Racial Drama," 494.
27. Children's Bureau, *Welfare of Children in Coal Mining Communities*, 52–54.
28. Cressey, "Social Disorganization and Reorganization," 392. See also Armstrong, "The Southern Mountaineers," 551–52; Olive Dame Campbell, "Adjustments to the Rural Industrial Change with Special Reference to Mountain Areas," *National Education Association of the United States: Proceedings* 67 (1929), 484.

classes in rural mountain communities had been small, and there had been considerable social and political contact among groups within the community. Industrialization, however, fragmented the region's social structure, creating a great and growing gulf between the lower-class laboring population and those above them. Lifestyles and physical surroundings began more clearly to delineate social rank, fostering a greater class awareness. The miner or millhand became a man set apart, indeed partly by his own choice but partly because of separate housing and social institutions. As the classes developed their own churches, schools, clubs, and styles of entertainment, contact at any other than a professional level greatly lessened. In the coal fields, the influx of large numbers of immigrants and southern blacks further stratified the social system, adding to the consciousness of class and to tensions in the local community.

One of the striking features of this new order was the emergence of a professional middle class out of the old planter-lawyer-merchant elite of the preindustrial community. Yet the mountain middle class, unlike its counterpart in other American industrial districts, never developed into a large component of the social structure. Absentee-owned extractive industries such as timber and mining did not generate capital for reinvestment in local businesses, and the numbers of middle-level technicians and managers that might have been spawned by local development remained small. Located primarily in the county seat towns, the managerial class of the mountains evolved as an auxiliary to the dominant extractive industries and was tied financially and politically to the outside corporations. When the coal barons and other capitalists left the region, the native managers assumed control of the local political and economic structure and maintained discipline and order on the behalf of the absentee interests.

Most of the region's middle-class lawyers, bankers, doctors, businessmen, and public officials assumed a conservative posture on political and economic issues. They favored change that would yield greater returns from natural resources or enhance their own power, but they gave only limited support to programs of human development.[29] Whereas a large portion of the working class became highly mobile with the coming of industrialization, moving from company town to company town in search of a better life, the middle class

29. See Plunkett and Bowman, *Elites and Change*, 54.

retained a degree of stability that allowed for the crystalization of their power in the local community. Deprived of the opportunity for home ownership and set off in the company towns by their social rank, many of the miners and millhands in the region simply withdrew from active participation in local and county politics, leaving a truncated political system to be controlled by the managerial elite.

A decline in voter participation characterized the new political culture that emerged in the United States after the 1890s. Throughout the country, rural voter turnout dropped sharply, as farmers were alienated from the political system, which they perceived to be increasingly dominated by urban economic interests. In the Appalachian South, as in the rest of the nation, the new political culture was symbolic of the larger changes that had come over mountain life. During most of the nineteenth century, the average mountaineer was relatively well integrated into the local political system, since the kinship network rather than class determined political power. Industrialization not only concentrated power in the hands of the dominant economic group but also made involvement in politics more difficult for the working class. The new "progressive" registration and voting procedures which were passed by most southern states at the turn of the century actually favored those with wealth and education. Laws associated with residence and registration effectively disfranchised many mountain workers who had become semi-migratory and could not meet residency requirements or produce evidence of having paid the poll tax in the previous year. Also, elections were no longer held on Sunday or on specially designated holidays, as had been the custom, and many laborers simply could not take off work to vote— unless the employer was unusually patriotic or desired to control the employee's vote. As a result, mountain people were more and more isolated from the political process, just as they were cut off from other decision-making processes that affected their lives.[30]

The revolutionary changes that swept across the mountains from 1880 to 1930, however, did not touch all parts of the region equally nor permanently destroy Appalachian culture. In fact, many aspects of the traditional culture persisted in the new order, providing a sense

30. For a discussion of the changing political culture in the U.S. from the nineteenth to the twentieth centuries, see Walter Dean Burnham, "The Changing Shape of the American Political Universe," in Joel H. Silbey and Samuel T. McSeveney, eds., *Voters, Parties, and Elections: Quantitative Essays in the History of American Popular Voting Behavior* (Lexington, Mass., 1972), 205–34.

of continuity in a period of rapid change and a foil for social chaos when the new order began to decay. Modernization does not always bring about the immediate destruction of older ways, and in Appalachia the old and the new continued to exist side by side for decades.[31] Several factors contributed to the survival of the old cultural patterns. The uneven penetration of the region by railroads left many hollows and coves relatively untouched by industrialism, and the absence of significant opportunities for education and upward mobility kept the folk culture alive in the mountain working class. But above all, the industrialization of the Appalachians was predominantly a rural phenomenon. The absence of significant urbanization allowed the mountaineers to continue their relationship with the land and enabled them to retain some of their traditional customs, values, and beliefs.

Although the mining camps and timber towns were filled with industrial sights and sounds, the new communities were essentially rural. Most were small and scattered in the remote places of the mountains. Many mountain residents continued to live on the family farm while employed in public work, and others migrated seasonally to the industrial centers. Employment in mining and logging was also more like agriculture than factory work in that laborers still toiled with products of the earth and had greater independence on the job. To a large extent, life continued to revolve around the rhythms of nature, and attachments to the land remained deep and strong.[32]

Despite the high mobility of families in the coal fields, kinship survived as the prime social institution of mountain life. There was some breakdown in the extended family as members left the household to seek employment in the labor market, but the family as a whole remained a close social unit.[33] Loyalty to the family continued to be highly valued, and during the early years of industrialization, the family retained much of its economic function. Children fre-

31. Joseph R. Gusfield, "Tradition and Modernity: Misplaced Polarities in the Study of Social Change," in Jason L. Finkle and Richard W. Gable, eds., *Traditional Societies and Political Development* (New York, 1966), 19; Knipe and Lewis, "The Impact of Coal Mining," 28–30.

32. See Kai T. Erikson, *Everything In Its Path* (New York, 1976), 100–101.

33. Knipe and Lewis, "The Impact of Coal Mining," 33; Neil J. Smelser, "Mechanisms of Change and Adjustment to Change," in Finkle and Gable, *Traditional Societies and Political Development*, 27–42; Harry K. Schwarzweller, "Social Change and the Individual in Rural Appalachia," in Photiadis and Schwarzweller, eds., *Change In Rural Appalachia*, 57.

quently assisted their parents in public work long after the passage of compulsory school attendance and minimum age laws. As late as the 1920s, it was not uncommon to find children from ten to fourteen years old working alongside a parent in the mines and cotton mills.[34] The solidarity of the mountain family proved to be an important cushion against the anxieties, tensions, and frustrations of the new social situation. It provided order, cohesion, and security amid the chaos and helplessness of everyday life. In the industrial districts, the family lost much of its traditional political role, but it assumed a greater emotional importance in the lives of the mountaineers. Under the pressures of modernization, the Appalachian family did not collapse; it simply adjusted and continued to provide strength and a measure of stability—and to connect the mountain folk with their agrarian past.

## EPILOGUE: APPALACHIA IN THE 1930S

In 1930, land and family retained their prominent roles in mountain culture, although in many parts of the region their functions had been altered and in some cases radically changed. The ownership of vast quantities of land had passed out of the hands of local people, and a new industrial economy had replaced the family farm. Agriculture survived as an essential part of the economy, but its health suffered a grievous decline. Increasingly, mountaineers found themselves tied to the national market system and powerless to make many of the decisions affecting their own lives. Having been swept quickly into the modern era, they were then abandoned by the wayside and left to live on their own resourcefulness.

In the mountains, the collapse of the new order did not come with the swiftness associated with the financial crash of 1929—which sent the rest of the country reeling into the Great Depression. As early as 1916 and 1917, the Appalachian timber industry began to waver and eventually fall from too rampant exploitation of forest reserves. As mountain forests deteriorated, more and more companies abandoned their Appalachian lands—usually by selling out to the U.S. Forest Service—and moved on to the virgin wilderness of Oregon and Washington. Employees who did not follow the companies to the

34. See Children's Bureau, *The Welfare of Children in Coal Mining Communities*, 34–36.

Northwest were left without a job. Entire communities disappeared, and in counties that had placed their faith in the lumbermen, the economy plummeted. Following the brief rise in farm prices during World War I, mountain agriculture slipped into permanent decline, leaving many of the recently unemployed loggers with nowhere to turn.

Those who had migrated to the cotton mill villages faced steadily growing hardships in the 1920s, as the loss of foreign markets and intense competition brought hard times to the southern textile industry. Northern owners were quick to reduce wages and to allow poor working conditions to deteriorate still further. Many mills instituted "the stretch-out" system to increase production through longer hours, faster work rates, and elimination of rest periods. Attempts at unionization often resulted in violence and death. By 1930, most of the smaller cotton mills in the mountains had closed their doors, and many of the larger piedmont mills had begun to reduce the size of their labor force.

With the collapse of the minerals industry between 1923 and 1927 and the subsequent decline in transportation and service employment, the loggers and millhands were joined by thousands of other workers displaced by the industrial order. In the coal fields, company after company folded under the pressure of falling prices, and unemployment claimed an ever-growing number of miners. Operators abandoned the worst of the company towns and neglected to maintain the rest. Even the "model towns" soon bore the double yoke of destitution and despair. Finding themselves without work, hundreds of mountain families sought to return to the land to eke out a living on abandoned hillsides or moved in with relatives. Their brief experience with industrialization had left them embittered, their hopes dashed. Thus, long before the rest of the nation experienced the shock of a falling stock market, Appalachia had already entered the depths of the Great Depression. In fact, the three "sick industries" in the United States during the 1920s, a period of general business prosperity, were agriculture, textiles, and bituminous coal—the backbone of the mountain economy.

With the failure of the region's industrial base, mountain families struggled to return to a way of life that they had known prior to the turn of the century. Cratis Williams has estimated that approximately 25 percent of the population had migrated from the mountain farms during the twenties alone, but "untold thousands returned to chink and repair abandoned cabins on the worn-out farms and to live off relief during the 1930's."[35] Although the amount of land in farms remained relatively stable from 1930 to 1940, the number of farms rose significantly during the depression years.[36] As migrants to the industrial centers beyond the mountains returned with larger families, they found that the land which had sustained their ancestors could no longer support the population in a manner even marginally consistent with the demands of modern life. The returned migrants added an extra burden to an already ailing agricultural system.

The depression decade, therefore, was a period of extreme hardship for most mountaineers. Coal production in the region dropped drastically, and the number of miners employed fell to its lowest point in almost twenty-five years. The average per capita earnings of coal miners declined from $851 in 1923 to $588 in 1929, and to the unbelievably low point of $235 in 1933.[37] In that year, a relief worker in eastern Kentucky reported that "cold, hunger, and disease" had taken a tremendous toll, closing in on the coal camps "to an extent almost without parallel in any group in this country."[38] Deaths due to diseases and malnutrition burgeoned in the coal districts. In 1929 in one eastern Kentucky county, for example, fifty-six children died from intestinal disease. The following year, ninety-one children succumbed, and in 1931 there were eighty-four such deaths.[39] The noncoal counties fared only slightly better. In 1929, Olive Dame Campbell reported that the average income of the small farmers in western North Carolina was between $85 and $90 per year.[40]

The spate of federal relief programs passed by the New Deal congresses eased the distress on mountain farms and in the surviving industrial towns. With the aid of the National Industrial Recovery Act, the average earnings of coal diggers were restored to $925 per year in 1935, but unemployment remained high.[41] Conservation programs, price supports, and crop subsidies established by the Agricultural Adjustment Act, the TVA, and other agencies improved conditions on many Appalachian farms. The price support

35. Williams, "The Southern Mountaineer In Fact and Fiction," 9.
36. *Ibid.*, 101.
37. Parker, *The Coal Industry*, 67.
38. Wilmer E. Kenworthy, "First Aid to Soft Coal—Then A Major Operation," *Mountain Life and Work* 9 (April 1933), 1.
39. Hevener, "New Deal For Harlan," 48–49.
40. Campbell, "Adjustments to Rural Industrial Change," 484.
41. Parker, *The Coal Industry*, 67.

system established for tobacco provided a viable cash crop to replace livestock production, and hundreds of mountain farmers turned to the brown leaf as their primary source of income. The production of burley tobacco required low technology and little capital investment, and, being labor-intensive, it well fitted the needs of the large mountain families. Yet its potential as a marketable crop on the small farms of the region depended upon the maintenance of federal quotas and price supports.

Despite these programs, however, many mountaineers were unable to support their families adequately. By 1936, over 47 percent of all mountain families were on federal relief rolls.[42] A gutted economy, an impoverished population, and a growing dependence on federal relief programs increasingly characterized mountain life. Only with the coming of World War II did conditions begin to improve noticeably, and for many Appalachians this improvement came at the expense of mass migration to the booming war industry plants of the North and East Coast.

Ironically, actions taken by the federal government in the 1930s further complicated the desperate conditions in the mountains. Not only did the new social welfare legislation shift the region's dependency onto the federal government, but expanded programs of land acquisition undertaken by the government also displaced hundreds of additional families from the land. When the Forest Service began to consolidate its holdings and when the Park Service and TVA condemned hundreds of family farms for parks and hydroelectric facilities, it appeared to many mountain residents that the government was delivering the final blow to the region's independence and traditional way of life. As the amount of federally owned land increased, the resentment and resistance of the local population grew as well. The frustration at dependence and hard times, and the hopes dashed by the new order, were now vented against the aggressive land policies of the federal government. As more and more families were moved off their ancestral lands, the number of intentionally set "woods fires" rose proportionately. Some families sold willingly; others resisted and passed on to their children a strong bitterness toward the federal agency involved.

The frustration that gripped many mountaineers in the late 1930s

42. Wayne T. Gray, "Mountain Dilemmas: A Study in Mountain Attitudes," *Mountain Life and Work* 12 (April 1936), 1.

*Fontana Dam Construction. Courtesy of the Tennessee Valley Authority.*

as they faced an uncertain future was evident in the correspondence of William Wirt, a mountain farmer from Epperson, Tennessee. In 1938, Wirt wrote a letter to a northern friend in which he described the dramatic events that had descended upon his mountains. The Wirts lived in a remote cove of the Smokies near the North Carolina border, and the family had witnessed the logging boom and now the coming of the TVA. The construction of Fowler Dam near Murphy, North Carolina, he noted, was providing temporary work for many of the local men, but the dam would inundate some of the finest farmland in the county. "What would become of the people," he wondered, and where would the extra revenues come from to pay for county government and for the education of the children? He lamented the arrival of the new age.

> One day we were the happiest people on earth. But like the Indian we are slowly but surely being driven from the homes that we have learned to love, and down to the man we are not a friend of the Government for the simple reason that every move they have made has increased our poverty.
>
> We were told that if we kept the fire out of the forest that we would have plenty of range for our cattle, but we found that after a few years that there is no range left. We were also told that we would have plenty and increasing flow of water in our mountain streams furnishing an abundance of fish for sport and food. But I've found that our streams are drying up and the fish in the ponds that are left are all dying, and at times you can smell them as you pass along the highway. Fifteen years ago you could have seen in the forest here thousands of cattle, sheep and hogs. Today you never see one out of the forest, and if you do his head and horns is the heaviest part about him.
>
> Now what are we going to do, move on and try to fit in where we do not belong or undertake to face the situation and gradually starve to death? In the little mountain churches where we once sat and listened to the preaching of the gospel with nothing to disturb us, we now hear the roar of machinery on the Sabbath day. After all I have come to believe that the real old mountaineer is a thing of the past and what will finally take our place, God only knows.[43]

For William Wirt and millions of other mountaineers, modernization had come like a storm over the ridges, tossing and uprooting the very structure of mountain life. When the storm had passed, what was left was only a shell of what had been before. Suspended halfway between the old society and the new, the mountaineers had lost the independence and self-determination of their ancestors, without becoming full participants in the benefits of the modern world. The vast natural wealth of the region had been swept out of the mountains—into the pockets of outland capitalists and into the expansion of the larger industrial order itself. In return, a deep and lasting depression had settled over the coves.

43. William and Wilma Wirt to Peggy Westerfield, 19 Sept. 1938, Peggy Westerfield Papers, No. 1430, Southern Historical Collection, Univ. of North Carolina.

# BIBLIOGRAPHY

ONLY a handful of scholars have examined the social and economic history of Appalachia. Harry M. Caudill's *Night Comes to the Cumberlands* (1963) remains the standard study of the subject, but this work is undocumented and applies only to eastern Kentucky. Until recently, there have been few depositories of regional manuscripts and other materials from which to write the history of the mountains, and although there is a large body of secondary literature on Appalachia, much of it is superficial and impressionistic. For years, moreover, the popular images and perceptions of the region obscured the historical realities of mountain life, impeding the development of a scholarly historiography.

In recent decades, the awakening of Appalachian regional consciousness and the emergence of Appalachian studies programs have focused new attention on the region's history. Appalachian colleges and universities have established regional archives and oral history programs, and a growing number of historians have begun to turn their efforts toward developing a better understanding of the mountain experience and of the social, economic, and political forces that have shaped that experience. While much research is still in its initial stages, considerable progress has been achieved (see this author's "Toward a New History of the Appalachian South," in *A Guide to Appalachian Studies, Appalachian Journal* 5, no. 1 [Autumn 1977], 74–81).

One of the best of the new studies is John Alexander Williams's *West Virginia and the Captains of Industry* (1976), a powerful examination of the political and economic dynasties established by Henry G. Davis and Stanley B. Elkins in northern West Virginia. The pattern of exploitation followed by Davis and Elkins was repeated at the turn of the century by modernizing elites throughout the southern mountains. The transformation of the mountain Republican party at the hands of the new industrialists is ably described in Gordon B. McKinney's *Southern Mountain Republicans, 1865– 1900* (1978), and the colonization of the Middlesboro area of Bell County, Kentucky, by the British-owned American Association Limited is surveyed in John Gaventa's *Power and Powerlessness* (1980). The response of mountain people to the new order is examined by Gaventa and by John Hevener's *Which Side Are You On?* (1978), a study of labor struggles in Harlan County, Kentucky, in the Great Depression.

Perhaps the most influential of the new works, however, is Henry D. Shapiro's *Appalachia On Our Mind* (1978). Although Shapiro's book is an intellectual history of the formulation of the "idea of Appalachia" in the popular mind, his work provides a critical foundation for understanding the economic exploitation of the region. Not only did the urban middle class in the late nineteenth century come to view Appalachia as a "strange land inhabited by a peculiar people," but it developed a number of "explanations" for this perceived otherness. These explanations were in turn used to justify a plethora of "uplift" programs for Appalachia and to rationalize the exploitation of mountain resources and labor. The idea of Appalachia, therefore, played an important and parallel role with economic and social factors in the modernization of the mountains. This relationship between ideology and economic conditions in the mountains has received increasing attention in the growing literature on Appalachia, including many of the articles and unpublished dissertations listed in this bibliography.

Research on the social and economic history of the southern mountains has been significantly enhanced by the development and expansion of regional archives, but the student will find that the going is still difficult and uncertain. The greatest burden is the paucity of sources reflecting the attitudes and experiences of Appalachian people themselves. Unfortunately, mountain residents have left few diaries, journals, or autobiographical accounts. Those manuscripts which have survived are only now finding their way into archives for scholarly research. The recent popularity of oral history has encouraged the taping of thousands of interviews throughout the region and the publication of an excellent collection of memoirs in Laurel Shackelford's and Bill Weinberg's *Our Appalachia* (1977). The cumulative effect of these oral-history collections is to provide a valuable overview of the common life experiences of mountain folk, but the quality of the transcripts varies greatly and overgeneralization limits their usefulness.

The problem of inadequate sources is less acute with respect to the literature of the economic modernizers. The pages of the *Manufacturers' Record* provide an invaluable compendium of economic undertakings in the southern Appalachians during the period of this study and shed considerable light on the attitudes and expectations of the industrializing elite. A regional trade publication, the *Appalachian Trade Journal*, is also a valuable resource since it was controlled by interest groups within Appalachia itself. Between 1908 and 1921, the *Appalachian Trade Journal* spoke for the Southern Appalachian Coal Operators' Association and thereafter became the official organ of the Appalachian Loggers Congress. Although federal and state documents often do not separate Appalachian from non-Appalachian counties, they too are an important source of information on the region. Especially useful are the 1925 U.S. Senate investigation *Report of the United States Coal Commission* and the 1935 U.S. Department of Agriculture publication *Economic and Social Problems and Conditions of the Southern Appalachians*.

The perspective of the industrialists has been preserved in a small number of manuscript collections and in published memoirs and articles. Early Appalachian industrialists left few records and personal letters, but among useful surviving collections are the Justus Collins Papers at West Virginia University, the William Nelson Page Papers at the University of North Carolina at Chapel Hill, and the Papers of the Burt and Brabb Lumber Company at the University of Kentucky. Local histories such as William P. Tams's *The Smokeless Coal Fields of West Virginia* (1963) and company histories like Raymond E. Salvati's *Island Creek* (1957) are extremely valuable when used with caution, as are the scores of contemporary local color accounts and trade journal articles.

The following bibliography is a list of materials that proved instrumental in the writing of this book. It is not meant to be exhaustive, nor does it include every source or potential source examined during the course of my research. It does not include the countless books, individuals, and experiences which have shaped my life and interpretive eye. But it does contain all but peripheral materials cited in the preceding text, and, I hope, provides thereby a basis for further excursions into the history of the mountains and mountain life.

## Manuscript Collections

Emory and Henry College, Emory, Va. Appalachian Oral History Project, Vertical Files, Bina Lorina Morris-Orr Folder. Vertical files, Gibson P. Vance Folder. "Our Appalachia: An Oral History.

U.S. Forest Service Office. Asheville, N.C. Contract, George W. Vanderbilt and Wife to Louis Carr.

University of Kentucky. Special Collections. King Library. Burt and Brabb Lumber Company Papers. John Fox, Jr., Collection.

University of North Carolina at Chapel Hill. Wilson Library.

North Carolina Collection.

Rebecca Cushman MS. "Seed of Fire: The Human Side of History in Our Nation's Southern Highland Region and Its Changing Years."

Southern Historical Collection.

William Nelson Page Papers.

Peggy Westerfield Papers.

Western Carolina University, Cullowhee, N.C. University Archives, Hunter Library. Horace Kephart Journals.

Map. "North Carolina Portion of the Great Smoky Mountains National Park, Showing Individual Ownership."

West Virginia University. West Virginia Collection. Justus Collins Papers.

## Government Documents

Kentucky, Bureau of Agricultural and Labor Statistics of the State of Kentucky. *Biennial Reports*. Frankfort, Ky.: State Printing Office, 1876–1892.

North Carolina. Bureau of Labor Statistics. *Report of the Bureau of Labor Statistics of the State of North Carolina*. Raleigh, 1900–1926.

United States. Bureau of Education. *A Statistical Study of the Public Schools of the Southern Appalachian Mountains*, by Norman Frost. Bulletin No. 11. Washington, D.C.: Government Printing Office, 1915.

―――. Bureau of Mines. *Housing For Mining Towns*, by Joseph H. White. Bulletin No. 87. Washington, D.C.: Government Printing Office, 1914.

―――. Bureau of Mines. *Historical Summary of Coal Mine Explosions in the United States, 1810–1958*, by Hiram Brown Humphrey. Bulletin No. 586. Washington, D.C.: Government Printing Office, 1960.

―――. Bureau of Mines. *Mineral Resources of the United States*. Washington, D.C.: Government Printing Office, 1891–1930.

―――. Congress. Senate. *Hearings Before a Subcommittee of the Committee on Education and Labor*. 63rd Cong., 1st sess., Senate Hearings Microfiche vols. 38 and 39. Washington, D.C.: Government Printing Office, 1913.

―――. Congress, Senate. *Hearings Before the Committee on Education and Labor*, 67th Cong., 1st sess., Senate Hearings Microfiche vol. 181. "The West Virginia Coal Fields," vol. 2. Washington, D.C.: Government Printing Office, 1921.

———. Congress. Senate. *Report of the United States Coal Commission*, Sen. Doc. 195, 68th Cong., 2nd sess. Washington, D.C.: Government Printing Office, 1925.

——————————. Department of Agriculture. *Economic and Social Problems and Conditions of the Southern Appalachians*. Miscellaneous Publication No. 205. Washington, D.C.: Government Printing Office.

———. Department of Agriculture. *Forest Service Manual*. Washington, D.C.: Government Printing Office, 1978.

———. Department of Agriculture. Forest Service. *Timber Growi.' and Logging Practice in the Southern Appalachian Region*, by E.H. Frothingham. Technical Bulletin No. 250. Washington, D.C.: Government Printing Office, 1931.

———. Department of Interior. Census Office. *Population and Agricultural Statistics* Tenth (1880)–Fifteenth (1930) Census. Washington, D.C.: Government Printing Office.

———. Department of Interior. U.S. Geological Survey. *The Southern Appalachian Forests*, by H.B. Ayers and W.W. Ashe. Professional Paper No. 37. Washington, D.C.: Government Printing Office, 1905.

———. Department of Labor. Bureau of Labor Statistics. *Housing By Employers in the United States*. Bulletin No. 263. Washington, D.C.: Government Printing Office, 1920.

———. Department of Labor. Children's Bureau. *The Welfare of Children In Bituminous Coal Mining Communities in West Virginia*, by Nettie P. McGill. Publication No. 117. Washington, D.C.: Government Printing Office, 1923.

West Virginia. Board of Agriculture. *Biennial Reports of the West Virginia State Board of Agriculture, 1890–1920*, Charleston, W.Va. *Tribune*.

———. Department of Mines. *Annual Reports*. Charleston, W.Va., 1900–1930.

———. Tax Commission. *Second Report, State Development*. Wheeling, W.Va.: Charles Taney, Printer, 1884.

### Periodicals

*Appalachian Trade Journal*. Knoxville, 1908–1923.
*Manufacturers' Record*. Baltimore, 1882–1930.
*The Virginias: A Mining, Industrial, and Scientific Journal*. Staunton, Va., 1880–1885.

### Interviews

Alice Lloyd College, Pippa Passes, Kentucky. Appalachian Oral History Project. Panny Hogg Day. Interview. Transcript no. 155A.

Appalachian State University, Boone, North Carolina. Appalachian Oral History Project. Jim Byrd. Interview. Transcript.

Emory and Henry College, Emory, Virginia. Oral History Project. J. Richard Campbell. Interview. Transcript no. 86.

Dr. C.C. Hatfield, Interview, File 25.

Curry Holmes. Interview. Transcript No. 78.

Marshall University. Appalachian Oral History Project. Special Collections. America Jarrell. Interview.

Mull, Larry. Private Interview. Haywood County, N.C. 9 April 1975.

University of North Carolina at Chapel Hill. Southern Oral History Program. William Purviance Tams, Jr. Author's Interview. 8 March 1975.

*Dissertations and Theses*

Ahrenholg, Gladys T. "Factors Affecting Social Participation in Coal Communities." M.A. thesis, West Virginia Univ., 1951.

Anson, Charles Phillips. "A History of the Labor Movement in West Virginia." Ph.D. diss., Univ. of North Carolina, 1940.

Arnett, Douglas O. "Counter Power Structure Struggles in Appalachia." Ph.D. diss., Duke Univ., 1978.

Chapman, Mary Lucille. "The Influence of Coal in the Big Sandy Valley." Ph.D. diss., Univ. of Kentucky, 1945.

Cotton, William Donaldson. "Appalachian North Carolina: A Political Study 1860–1889." Ph.D. diss., Univ. of North Carolina, 1954.

Cubby, Edwin Albert. "The Transformation of the Tug and Guyandot Valleys: Economic Development and Social Change in West Virginia, 1888–1921." Ph.D. diss., Syracuse Univ., 1962.

Duff, Frank. "Government in an Eastern Kentucky Coal Field County." M.A. thesis, Univ. of Kentucky, 1950.

Eller, Ronald D. "Mountain Road: A Study of the Construction of the Chesapeake and Ohio Railroad in Southern West Virginia, 1867–1873." M.A. thesis, Univ. of North Carolina at Chapel Hill, 1973.

French, Jack. "Segregation Patterns in a Coal Camp." M.A. thesis, Univ. of West Virginia, 1953.

Frisch, Isadore, "Twentieth Century Development of the Coal Mining Industry in Eastern Kentucky and Its Influence Upon the Political Behavior of the Area." M.A. thesis, Univ. of Kentucky, 1938.

Gaventa, John. "Power and Powerlessness: Quiescence and Rebellion in an Appalachian Valley." Ph.D. diss., Oxford Univ., 1975. (Publ. 1980, Univ. of Illinois Press.)

Gibson, Ernest Willis. "The Economic History of Boyd County, Kentucky." M.A. thesis, Univ. of Kentucky, 1929.

Gillenwater, Mack H. "Cultural and Historical Geography of Mining

Settlements in the Pocahontas Coal Fields of Southern West Virginia, 1880 to 1930." Ph.D. diss., Univ. of Tennessee, 1972.

Hevener, John Watts. "A New Deal For Harlan: The Roosevelt Labor Policies in a Kentucky Coal Field, 1931–1939." Ph.D. diss., Ohio State Univ., 1971. (Publ. as *Which Side Are You On?*, 1978, Univ. of Illinois Press.)

Howard, Hugh Asher. "Chapters in the Economic History of Knox County, Kentucky." M.A. thesis, Univ. of Kentucky, 1937.

Laing, James T. "The Negro Miner in West Virginia." Ph.D. diss., Ohio State Univ., 1933.

Lankford, Jesse R., Jr., "The Campaign for a National Park in Western North Carolina, 1885–1940." M.A. thesis, Western Carolina Univ., 1973.

McKinney, Gordon Bartlett. "Mountain Republicanism, 1876–1900." Ph.D. diss., Northwestern Univ., 1971.

Morris, Thomas J. "The Coal Camp: A Pattern of Limited Community Life." M.A. thesis, West Virginia Univ., 1950.

Sandman, Leo Joseph. "Social Effects of the Mining Industry in Eastern Kentucky." B.A. thesis, Univ. of Kentucky, 1915.

Shapiro, Henry David. "A Strange Land and Peculiar People: The Discovery of Appalachia, 1870–1920." Ph.D. diss., Rutgers Univ., 1966.

Thomas, Jerry Bruce. "Coal Country: The Rise of the Southern Smokeless Coal Industry and Its Effect on Area Development, 1872–1910." Ph.D. diss., Univ. of North Carolina at Chapel Hill, 1971.

Watson, Judge. "The Economic and Cultural Development of Eastern Kentucky from 1900 to the Present." Ph.D. diss., Indiana Univ., 1963.

Williams, Cratis Dearl. "The Southern Mountaineer in Fact and Fiction." Ph.D. diss., New York Univ., 1961.

Wood, Harriette. "The Kentucky Mountaineers: A Study of Four Counties of Southeastern Kentucky." M.A. thesis, Univ. of North Carolina, 1930.

*Articles and Unpublished Papers*

Allen, James Lane. "Mountain Passes of the Cumberlands." *Harper's Magazine* 81 (Sept. 1890), 561–76.

———. "Through Cumberland Gap on Horseback." *Harper's New Monthly Magazine* 73 (June 1886), 50–66.

Armstrong, Anne W. "The Southern Mountaineers." *Yale Review* 24 (March 1935), 539–54.

Askins, Donald. "John Fox, Jr.: A Re-Appraisal; or, With Friends Like That, Who Needs Enemies." In Helen Lewis, *et al.*, eds., *Colonialism In Modern America: The Appalachian Case*. Boone, N.C.: Appalachian Consortium Press, 1978, pp. 251–57.

Bagger, Eugene S. "Himler of Himlerville." *Survey* 48 (29 April 1922), 146–50, 187.

Bailey, Kenneth R. "A Judicious Mixture: Negroes and Immigrants in the West Virginia Mines, 1880–1917." *West Virginia History* 34 (Jan. 1973), 141–61.

Banks, Alan J. "The Emergence of a Capitalistic Labor Market in Eastern Kentucky, 1870–1915." Unpublished paper, 1978.

Baron, Hal Seth. "A Case for Appalachian Demographic History." *Appalachian Journal* 4 (Spring–Summer 1977), 208–15.

Beers, Howard W. "Highland Society In Transition." *Mountain Life and Work* 22 (Spring 1946), 1–3, 26.

Belissary, Constantine G. "The Rise of Industry and the Industrial Spirit in Tennessee, 1865–85." *Journal of Southern History* 19 (1953), 193–215.

Billings, Dwight. "Culture and Poverty in Appalachia: A Theoretical Discussion and Empirical Analysis." *Social Forces* 53 (Dec. 1974), 315–23.

Bramwell, J.N. *et al.* "The Pocahontas Mine Explosions." American Institute of Mining Engineers, *Transactions* 13 (1884–1885), 237–49.

Brinksman, Leonard W. "Home Manufacturers as an Indication of an Emerging Appalachian Subculture, 1840–1870." *West Georgia College Studies in the Social Sciences* 12 (June 1973), 50–58.

Brosky, Alphonse F. "Building a Town for a Mountain Community: A Glimpse of Jenkins and Nearby Villages." *Coal Age* 23 (5 April 1923), 560–63.

——. "Sociological Works Accomplished by the Consolidation Coal Company." *Coal Age* 15 (9 Jan. 1919), 54–58.

Buckingham, John E. "John C. Calhoun Mayo." Unpublished paper. Vertical Files. Mountain Collection. Berea College, n.d.

Burnham, Walter Dean. "The Changing Shape of the American Political Universe." In Joel H. Silbey and Samuel T. McSeveney, eds., *Voters, Parties and Elections: Quantitative Essays in the History of American Popular Voting Behavior*. Lexington, Mass.: Xerox College Printing, 1972.

Caldwell, Mary F. "Change Comes to the Appalachian Mountaineer." *Current History* 31 (1930), 961–67.

Campbell, Olive Dame. "Adjustments to Rural Industrial Change With Special Reference to Mountain Areas." *National Education Association of the United States: Proceedings* 67 (1929), 484–88.

Chapman, Maristan. "The Mountain Man." *Century* 117 (Feb. 1929), 505–11.

Collins, Justus. "My Experiences in the Smokeless Coal Fields of West Virginia." In Maude A. Rucker, ed., *West Virginia: Her Land, Her*

*People, Her Traditions, Her Resources.* New York: Walter Neale, 1930, pp. 110–20.

"The Company Community in the American Coal Fields." *New Statesmen* 30 (15 Oct. 1927), 6–8.

Coppock, Paul R. "Huntington's Pacific-to-Atlantic Rails Through Memphis." *West Tennessee Historical Society Papers* 9 (1955), 5–28.

Crawford, Dudley W. "The Coming of the Railroad to Asheville 70 Years Ago." Asheville *Citizen*, 29 Oct. 1950.

Cressey, Paul Frederick. "Social Disorganization and Reorganization in Harlan County, Kentucky." *American Sociological Review* 14 (1949), 389–94.

Davis, D.H. "Changing Role of the Kentucky Mountains and the Passing of the Kentucky Mountaineers." *Journal of Geography* 24 (Feb. 1925), 41–52.

Davis, Rebecca Harding. "By-Paths in the Mountains." *Harper's New Monthly Magazine* 61 (Sept. 1880), 523–47.

Davis, William G. "Uncle Sam Ruined Swain's Economy." Asheville *Citizen*, 25 Oct. 1978.

Dawley, Thomas R. "Our Southern Mountaineers: Removal the Remedy for the Evils That Isolation and Poverty Have Brought." *World's Work* 19 (March 1910), 12704–14.

DeVyver, Frank. T. "Southern Industry and the Southern Mountaineer." *American Federationist: Official Magazine of the American Federation of Labor* 35 (1928), 1319–24.

Duncan, Hannibol. "The Southern Highlanders." *Journal of Applied Sociology* 10 (1926), 556–61.

Estabrook, Arthur H. "Is There a Mountain Problem?" *Mountain Life and Work* 2 (1927).

Everts, C.S. "Modern Methods Invading the Mountains." *Missionary Review* 40 (May 1917), 365–67.

Fisher, Stephen L. "Folk Culture or Folk Tale: Prevailing Assumptions About the Appalachian Personality." In Jerry Williamson, ed., *An Appalachian Symposium: Essays Written in Honor of Cratis D. Williams.* Boone, N.C.: Appalachian State Univ. Press, 1977, pp. 14–25.

Fowler, George. "Social and Industrial Conditions in the Pocahontas Coal Field." *Engineering Magazine* 27 (June 1904), 383–96.

Fox, John Jr. "The Southern Mountaineer." *Scribners* 29 (1901), 387–92, 557–70.

Frost, William Goodell. "Our Contemporary Ancestors in the Southern Mountains." *Atlantic Monthly* 83 (March 1899), 311–19.

Gleason, Arthur. "Company-owned Americans." *Nation* 110 (12 June 1920), 794–95.

Goldenweiser, E.A. "Incomes of Bituminous Coal Producers." *American Statistical Association* 17 (June 1920), 203–9.

Graebner, William. "Great Expectations: The Search for Order in Bituminous Coal, 1890–1917." *Business History Review* 48 (1974), 49–72.

Gray, Lewis Cecil. "Economic Conditions and Tendencies in the Southern Appalachians As Indicated by the Cooperative Survey." *Mountain Life and Work* 9 (July 1933), 7–12.

Gray, Wayne T. "Mountain Dilemmas: A Study in Mountain Attitudes." *Mountain Life and Work* 12 (April 1936), 1–2.

Griffith, Robert W. "The Industrial Development of Western North Carolina." *Southern Tourist* (March 1926), 100–103.

Gusfield, Joseph R. "Tradition and Modernity: Misplaced Polarities in the Study of Social Change." In Jason L. Finkle and Richard W. Gable, eds., *Traditional Societies and Political Development*. New York: John Wiley, 1966.

Hall, Dawson R. "The Explosion at Eccles, West Virginia." *Coal Age* 5 (23 May 1914), 846–50.

Hall, Helen. "Miners Must Eat." *Atlantic Monthly* 152 (1933), 153–62.

Hall, William L. "To Remake the Appalachians; A New Order in the Mountains That is Founded on Forestry." *World's Work* 28 (July 1914), 321–38.

Harney, Will Wallace. "A Strange Land and Peculiar People." *Lippincott's Magazine* 12 (Oct. 1873), 429–38.

Hodge, J.M. "The Big Stone Gap Coal Field." *American Institute of Mining Engineering, Transactions* 31 (1893), 922–38.

Hoffman, Alfred. "The Mountaineer In Industry." *Mountain Life and Work* 5 (Jan. 1930), 2–7.

Kenworthy, Wilmer E. "First Aid to Soft Coal—Then A Major Operation." *Mountain Life and Work* 9 (April 1933), 1–6.

Kiessling, O.E. "Coal Mining in the South." *Annals of the American Academy of Political and Social Science* 153 (1930), 84–93.

Knipe, Edward E., and Helen M. Lewis. "The Impact of Coal Mining on the Traditional Mountain Subculture." In J. Kenneth Moreland, ed., *The Not So Solid South: Anthropological Studies In a Regional Subculture*. Athens: Univ. of Georgia Press, 1971.

Laing, Joseph T. "The Negro in West Virginia." *Social Forces* 14 (1936), 416–22.

Lambert, Robert S. "Logging on Little River, 1890–1940." *East Tennessee Historical Society's Publications* 33 (1961), 32–42.

———. "Logging the Great Smokies, 1880–1930." *Tennessee Historical Quarterly* 21 (Dec. 1961), 350–63.

Lantz, Herman R. "Resignation, Industrialization and the Problem of Social Change." In Arthur B. Shostak and William Gombert, eds., *Blue*

*Collar World: Studies of the American Worker*. Englewood Cliffs, N.J.: Prentice-Hall, 1964.

Lawrence, Randall. "The Mineral Rights Buyer in Pre-Industrial Appalachia: A Study of Richard M. Broas." Unpublished paper, Mountain Collection, Hutchins Library, Berea College, 1975.

Leamer, Lawrence. "Twilight For a Baron: Major William Purviance Tams, Jr." *Playboy*, May 1973, pp. 167–69.

Lewis, Charles D. "Government Forests and the Mountain Problem." *Mountain Life and Work* 6 (Jan. 1931), 2–9.

Lewis, Helen. "Fatalism or the Coal Industry." *Mountain Life and Work* 45 (Dec. 1970), 10–13.

Lewis, Helen Matthews, Sue Easterling Kobak, and Linda Johnson. "Family, Religion, and Colonialism in Central Appalachia, or Bury My Rifle at Big Stone Gap." In Helen Lewis, *et al.*, eds., *Colonialism in Modern America: The Appalachian Case*. Boone, N.C.: Appalachian Consortium Press, 1978.

Lohman, K.B. "A New Era for Mining Towns." *Coal Age* 8 (13 Nov. 1915), 799–800.

Lovejoy, Owen R. "Child Labor in the Soft Coal Mines." *Annals of the American Academy of Political and Social Science* 29 (1907), 26–34.

Lyman, R.G. "Coal Mining At Holden, West Virginia." *Engineering and Mining Journal* 52 (15 Dec. 1906), 1120–23 and (9 Nov. 1907), 1170–73.

Melish, John Howard. "The Church and the Company Town." *Survey* 33 (5 Dec. 1914), 262–64.

Michelson, M. "Feudalism and Civil War in the United States of America." *Everybody's Magazine* 28 (May 1913), 615–28.

Miller, George H. "Plan Your Town As Carefully As Your Plant." *Coal Age* 8 (1914), 130.

Minard, Ralph D. "Race Relations in the Pocahontas Coal Field." *Journal of Social Issues* 8 (1952), 29–44.

Moger, Allen W. "Railroad Practices and Policies in Virginia After the Civil War." *Virginia Magazine of History and Biography* 59 (1951), 423–57.

Moore, William H. "Preoccupied Paternalism: The Roan Iron Company in Her Company Town—Rockwood, Tennessee." *East Tennessee Historical Society Publications* 39 (1967), 56–70.

Mull, Larry. "Bemis Lumber Company and the Graham County Railroad." Unpublished paper. University Archives, Western Carolina Univ., n.d.

———. "Early Lumbering in Western North Carolina." Unpublished paper. University Archives. Western Carolina Univ., n.d.

Murphy, R.E. "A Southern West Virginia Mining Community." *Economic Geography* 9 (1933), 51–59.

McCarthy, Colman. "Going Home to Appalachia." Cleveland *Plain Dealer* 9 Oct. 1975.

McKinney, Gordon Bartlett. "Industrialization and Violence in Appalachia in the 1890's." In J.W. Williamson, ed., *An Appalachian Symposium*. Boone, N.C.: Appalachian State Univ. Press, 1977, pp. 131–44.

Nicholls, W.D. "A Research Approach to the Problems of Appalachia." *Mountain Life and Work* 7 (Jan. 1932), 5–8.

Norton, Helen G. "Feudalism in West Virginia." *Nation* 13 (1931), 154–57.

Obenauer, M.L. "Living Conditions Among Coal Mine Workers in the United States." *Annals 3* (Jan. 1924), 12–23.

O'Toole, Edward. "Pocahontas Coal Field and Operating Methods of the United States Coal and Coke Company." *Coal Age* 23 (8 March 1923), 399–406.

Page, William Nelson. "The Explosion at the Red Ash Colliery, Fayette County, West Virginia." American Institute of Mining Engineers, *Transactions* 30 (1900), 854–63.

Parris, John. "Lumber Barons Saw Gold in WNC's Trees." Asheville *Citizen*, 19 May 1978.

———. "Nature Regains Land of Sawmills, Trains." Asheville *Citizen*, 25 March 1965.

———. "When Buffum's Band Mill Came To Dillsboro." Asheville *Citizen*, 29 July 1978.

Parsons, Floyd W. "Coal Mining in Southern West Virginia." *Engineering and Mining Journal* 84 (9 Nov. 1907), 881–85.

———. "Mining Coal on the Virginian Railroad." *Coal Age* 1 (1911), 1039–43.

Peck, W.R. and R.J. Sampson. "The Harlan Coal Field of Kentucky. *Coal Age* 3 (24 May 1913), 796–800.

Pearsall, Marion. "Some Frontier Origins of Southern Appalachian Culture." *Kentucky Folklore Record* 8 (1962), 41–45.

"Pocahontas No. 1 Retires." *Norfolk and Western Magazine* 33 (1955), 520–24.

Pultz, John Leggett. "The Big Stone Gap Coal-Field of Virginia and Kentucky." *Engineering Magazine* 27 (Oct. 1904), 71–85.

Raine, J. "The West Virginia Lumber Industry." *West Virginia Review* 4 (1927), 226–28.

Ralph, Julian. "Our Appalachian Americans." *Harper's Magazine* 107 (1903), 32–41.

Rambo, Marion V. "The Submerged Tenth Among the Southern Mountaineers." *Methodist Review* 87 (July 1905), 565–75.

Rice, Otis K. "Coal Mining in the Kanawha Valley in 1861: A View of Industrialization in the Old South." *Journal of Southern History* 31 (1965), 393–416.

Robinson, Neil. "The Mineral Man." *President's Address to the West Virginia Coal Mining Institute*. Charleston, West Virginia Coal Mining Institute, 1913.

Ross, Edward Alsworth. "Pocketed Americans." *New Republic* 37 (9 Jan. 1924), 170–72.

Schockel, B.H. "Changing Conditions in the Kentucky Mountains." *Scientific Monthly* 3 (Aug. 1916), 105–31.

Schulman, Steven A. "The Lumber Industry of the Upper Cumberland River Valley." *Tennessee Historical Quarterly* 32 (Fall 1973), 255–64.

Semple, Ellen Churchill. "The Anglo-Saxons of the Kentucky Mountains: A Study in Anthropogeography." *Bulletin of the American Geographical Society* 42, no. 8 (1910), 561–94.

Sherwood, Herbert Francis. "Our New Racial Drama: Southern Mountaineers in the Textile Industry." *North American Review* 216 (Oct. 1922), 489–96.

Siler, James Hayden. "A History of Jellico, Tennessee." Unpublished Paper. Mountain Collection. Berea College, n.d.

Silver, James W. "Hardwood Producers Come of Age." *Journal of Southern History* 23 (1957), 427–53.

Smelser, Neil J. "Mechanisms of Change and Adjustments to Change." In Jason L. Finkle and Richard W. Gable, eds., *Traditional Societies and Political Development*. New York: John Wiley, 1966.

Speranza, Gino C. "Forced Labor in West Virginia." *Outlook* 74 (13 June 1903), 407–10.

Stephenson, John B. "Appalachia and the Third Century in America: On the Eve of an Astonishing Development—Again." *Appalachian Journal* 4 (Autumn 1976), 34–38.

Stow, Audley H. "Mining in the Pocahontas Field." *Coal Age* 3 (1913), 594–600.

Tadlock, E.V. "Coal Camps and Character." *Mountain Life and Work* 4 (Jan. 1929), 20–23.

Thornborough, Laura. "Americans the Twentieth Century Forgot." *Travel* 50 (April 1928), 25–28, 42.

"Timber! Started Railroad Boom." Yancey County *Common Times* 2 (Dec. 1976), 1–2.

Vance, Gibson P. "Logging and Lumbering in Washington County, Virginia." Unpublished paper, Vertical Files. Oral History Project. Emory and Henry College, 1965.

Walls, David S. "Internal Colony or Internal Periphery? A Critique of Current Models and an Alternative Formulation." In Helen Lewis, *et al.*, eds., *Colonialism in Modern America: The Appalachian Case*. Boone, N.C.: Appalachian Consortium Press, 1978, 319–50.

Warner, Charles Dudley. "Comments on Kentucky." *Harper's New Monthly Magazine* 78 (Dec. 1888–May 1889), 255–71.

————. "On Horseback." *Atlantic Monthly* 56 (July–Oct. 1885), 88–100, 194–207, 388–98, 540–54.

Wilhelm, Gene, Jr. "Appalachian Isolation: Fact or Fiction?" In Jerry Williamson, ed., *An Appalachian Symposium*. Boone, N.C.: Appalachian State Univ. Press, 1977.

————. "Folk Settlements in the Blue Ridge Mountains." *Appalachian Journal* 5 (Winter 1978), 204–45.

Williams, Cratis Dearl. "Heritage of Appalachia." In Southern Appalachian Regional Conference, *The Future of Appalachia*. Boone, N.C.: Appalachian Consortium Press, 1975, pp. 128–32.

Williams, John Alexander. "The New Dominion and the Old: Antebellum and Statehood Politics as the Background of West Virginia's 'Bourbon Democracy.' " *West Virginia History* 33 (July 1972).

Wilson, E.B. "Middlesborough: The Magic City." In Bell County Centennial Commission, eds., *The Bell County Story*, 1867–1967. Pineville, Ky.: Bell County Centennial Commission, 1967.

Wilson, Woodrow. "Our Last Frontier." *Berea Quarterly* 4, no. 2 (May 1899), 5–6.

Wolfe, Margaret Ripley. "Aliens in Appalachia: The Construction of the Clinchfield Railroad and the Italian Experience." In Emmett M. Essin, ed., *Appalachia: Family Traditions in Transition*. Johnson City: East Tennessee State University Press, 1975.

Woodson, Carter G. "Freedom and Slavery in Appalachian America." *Journal of Negro History* 1 (April 1916).

Wright, Warren. "The Big Steal." In Helen Lewis, *et al.*, eds., *Colonialism in Modern America: The Appalachian Case* Boone, N.C.: Appalachian Consortium Press, 1978, pp. 161–75.

## *Books*

Addington, Luther F. *The Story of Wise County, Virginia*. Wise County: Centennial Committee, 1956.

American Constitutional Association. *Life in a West Virginia Coal Field*. Charleston, W.Va.: American Constitutional Association, 1923.

Arthur, John P. *Western North Carolina: A History From 1730 to 1913*. Raleigh: Edwards and Broughton, 1914.

Barnum, Donald T. *The Negro in the Bituminous Coal Industry*. Philadelphia: Univ. of Pennsylvania Press, 1970.

Barthes, Roland, *Mythologies*, trans. Annette Lavers. New York: Hill and Wang, 1972.

Beachley, Charles E. *History of the Consolidated Coal Company, 1864–1934*. New York: Consolidation Coal, 1934.

Beebe, Gilbert Wheeler. *Contraception and Fertility in the Southern Appalachians*. Baltimore: Williams and Wilkins, 1942.

Bendix, Reinhard. *Work and Authority in Industry: Ideologies of Management in the Course of Industrialization*. Berkeley: Univ. of California Press, 1974.

Berglund, Abraham, George T. Starnes, and Frank T. DeVyver. *Labor in the Industrial South: A Survey of Wages and Living Conditions in Three Major Industries of the New Industries of the New Industrial South*. Charlottesville: Institute for Research in the Social Sciences, Univ. of Virginia, 1930.

Bowman, Elizabeth Skaggs. *Land of High Horizons*. Kingsport, Tenn.: Southern Publishers, 1938.

Brophy, John. *A Miner's Life*. Madison: Univ. of Wisconsin Press, 1964.

Callahan, North. *Smoky Mountain Country*. Boston: Little, Brown, 1952.

Campbell, Carlos Clinton. *Birth of a National Park in the Great Smoky Mountains*. Knoxville: Univ. of Tennessee Press, 1960.

Campbell, John C. *The Southern Highlander and His Homeland*. New York: Russell Sage Foundation, 1921. Rpt., Lexington: Univ. of Kentucky Press, 1969.

Caudill, Harry Monroe. *Night Comes to the Cumberlands: A Biography of a Depressed Area*. Boston: Little, Brown, 1963.

Champion Paper and Fibre Company. *This Is Champion, A Proud Name in American Industry*. Canton, N.C.: Champion Paper and Fibre, 1954.

Chappell, Louis Watson. *John Henry: A Folk Study*. Jena, Germany: Frommannsche, 1933.

Chataigne, J.H. *Chataigne's North Carolina State Directory and Gazetteer, 1883–1884*. Raleigh: Alfred Williams, 1883.

————. *Chataigne's Virginia Business Directory and Gazetteer, 1880–81*. Richmond, Baughman Brothers, 1880.

Clarkson, Roy B. *Tumult on the Mountain: Lumbering in West Virginia, 1770–1920*. Parsons, W.Va.: McClain Printing, 1964.

Cochran, Thomas C., and William Miller. *The Age of Enterprise: A Social History of Industrial America*. New York: Macmillan, 1961.

Conley, Phil. *History of the West Virginia Coal Industry*. Charleston, W.Va.: Education Foundation, 1960.

Craddock, Charles Egbert (Mary Noailles Murfree). *In the Tennessee Mountains*. Boston: Houghton Mifflin, 1892. Rpt., Knoxville: Univ. of Tennessee Press, 1970.

Dawley, Thomas Robinson, Jr. *The Child That Toileth Not: A Story of a Government Investigation*. New York: Gracia Publishing, 1912.

Debar, Joseph H. Diss. *The West Virginia Handbook and Immigrant's Guide*. Parkersburg, W.Va.: Gibbens Brothers, 1870.

Dix, Keith. *Work Relations in the Coal Industry: The Hand Loading Era, 1880–1930*. Morgantown, W.Va.: Institute for Labor Studies, 1977.

Douglass, H. Paul. *Christian Reconstruction in the South*. Boston: Pilgrim Press, 1909.

257

Erikson, Kai. *Everything In Its Path*. New York: Simon and Schuster, 1976.

Evans, Cerinda W. *Collis Potter Huntington*. Newport News, Va.: Mariner's Museum, 1954.

Ford, Thomas R., ed. *The Southern Appalachian Region: A Survey*. Lexington: Univ. of Kentucky Press, 1967.

Fox, John, Jr. *Blue-Grass and Rhododendron*. New York: Scribner's, 1906.

Fuson, Henry Harvey. *History of Bell County, Kentucky*. II. New York: Hobson Book Press, 1947.

Graebner, William. *Coal Mining Safety in the Progressive Period: The Political Economy of Reform*. Lexington: Univ. Press of Kentucky, 1974.

Gray, Lewis Cecil. *History of Agriculture in the Southern United States to 1860*. II. Gloucester, Mass: Peter Smith, 1958.

Gutman, Herbert G. *Work, Culture and Society in Industrializing America: Essays in American Working-Class and Social History*. New York: Vintage, 1977.

Haney, William H. *The Mountain People of Kentucky*. Cincinnati: Robert Clarke, 1906.

Hays, Samuel P. *The Response To Industrialism, 1885–1914*. Chicago: Univ. of Chicago Press, 1957.

Heald, Morrell. *The Social Responsibilities of Business: Company and Community, 1900–1960*. Cleveland: Press of Case Western Reserve Univ., 1970.

Hicks, George L. *Appalachian Valley*. New York: Holt, Rinehart, 1976.

Hofstadter, Richard. *Social Darwinism in American Thought, 1860–1915*. Boston: Beacon Press, 1955.

Hooker, Elizabeth R. *Religion in the Highlands*. New York: Home Missions Council, 1933.

Hull, Arthur M., and Sydney A. Hale, eds. *Coal Men of America*. Chicago: Retail Coalman, 1918.

Hunt, Edward Eyre, Frederick G. Tryon, and Joseph H. Willitts. *What the Coal Commission Found*. Baltimore: Williams and Wilkins, 1925.

Ireland, Robert M. *Little Kingdoms: The Counties of Kentucky, 1850–1891*. Lexington: Univ. Press of Kentucky, 1977.

Jillson, Willard Rouse. *The Coal Industry In Kentucky: An Historical Sketch*. Frankfort, Ky.: State Journal, 1922.

Johnson, Guy Benton. *John Henry: Tracking Down a Negro Legend*. Chapel Hill: Univ. of North Carolina Press, 1929.

Johnston, David Emmons. *A History of Middle New River Settlements and Contiguous Territory*. Huntington, W.Va.,: Standard Printing, 1906.

Kahn, Kathy. *Hillbilly Women*. New York: Doubleday, 1973.

Kahn, Si. *The Forest Service and Appalachia*. New York: John Hay Whitney Foundation, 1974.

Kephart, Horace. *Our Southern Highlanders*. New York: Macmillan, 1921. Rpt., Knoxville: Univ. of Tennessee Press, 1976.

Kirkland, Edward Chase. *Dream and Thought in the Business Community, 1860–1900*. Ithaca, N.Y.: Cornell Univ. Press, 1956.

Lambie, Joseph T. *From Mine to Market: The History of Coal Transportation on the Norfolk and Western Railway*. New York: New York Univ. Press, 1954.

Lane, Winthrop D. *Civil War In West Virginia: A Story of the Industrial Conflict in the Coal Mines*. New York: B.W. Huebsch, 1921.

Lantz, Herman. *People of Coal Town*. Carbondale: Southern Illinois Univ. Press, 1958.

Lee, Howard B. *Bloodletting In Appalachia: A Story of West Virginia's Four Major Mine Wars and Other Thrilling Incidents of Its Coal Fields*. Morgantown: West Virginia Univ., 1969.

————. *My Appalachia: Pipestem State Park, Today and Yesterday*. Parsons, W.Va.: McClain Printing, 1971.

Looff, David H. *Appalachia's Children: The Challenge of Mental Health*. Lexington: Univ. Press of Kentucky, 1971.

Lumpkin, Grace. *To Make My Bread*. New York: Macaulay, 1932.

Matthews, Elmora Messer. *Neighbor and Kin: Life in a Tennessee Ridge Community*. Nashville: Vanderbilt Univ. Press, 1965.

McCague, James. *The Cumberland*. New York: Holt, Rinehart, and Winston, 1973.

McKinney, Gordon Bartlett. *Southern Mountain Republicans, 1865–1900: Politics and the Appalachian Community*. Chapel Hill: Univ. of North Carolina Press, 1978.

Miles, Emma Bell. *The Spirit of the Mountains*. New York: James Pott, 1905. Rpt., Knoxville: Univ. of Tennessee Press, 1975.

Miller, Nora. *The Girl in the Rural Family*. Chapel Hill: Univ. of North Carolina Press, 1935.

Mitchell, Broadus. *The Rise of Cotton Mills in the South*. Baltimore: Johns Hopkins Univ. Press, 1921.

Montell, William Lynwood. *The Saga of Coe Ridge: A Study in Oral History*. Knoxville: Univ. of Tennessee Press, 1970.

Morris, Homer L. *The Plight of the Bituminous Coal Miner*. Philadelphia: Univ. of Pennsylvania Press, 1934.

Munn, Robert F. *The Coal Industry in America: A Bibliography and Guide to Studies*. Morgantown: West Virginia Univ. Library, 1965.

Nelson, James Poyntz. *The History of the Chesapeake and Ohio Railway Company: Its Antecedents and Subsidiaries*. Richmond: Lewis Printing, 1927.

Nevins, Allan. *Abram S. Hewitt, With Some Account of Peter Cooper*. New York: Harper, 1935.

Owsley, Frank Lawrence. *Plain Folk of the Old South*. Baton Rouge: Louisiana State Univ. Press, 1949. Rpt., Chicago: Quadrangle, 1965.

Parker, Blen Lawhon. *The Coal Industry: A Study In Social Control*. Washington, D.C.: American Council on Public Affairs, 1940.

Photiadis, John D., and Harry K. Schwarzweller, eds. *Change in Rural Appalachia: Implications for Action Programs*. Philadelphia: Univ. of Pennsylvania Press, 1970.

Pierce, Neil. *The Border South States: People, Politics, and Power in the Five States of the Border South*. New York: Norton, 1975.

Plunkett, H. Dudley, and Mary Jean Bowman. *Elites and Change in the Kentucky Mountains*. Lexington: Univ. of Kentucky Press, 1973.

Pomeroy, Kenneth B., and James G. Yoho. *North Carolina Lands: Ownership, Use, and Management of Forest and Related Lands*. Washington, D.C.: American Forestry Association, 1964.

Prescott, E.J. *The Story of the Virginia Coal and Iron Company*. Big Stone Gap: Virginia Coal and Iron Co., 1946.

Prothro, James Warren. *The Dollar Decade: Business Ideas in the 1920's*. Baton Rouge: Louisiana State Univ. Press, 1954.

Raine, James Watt. *The Land of Saddle-Bags: A Study of the Mountain People of Appalachia*. New York: Council of Women for Home Missions and Missionary Education Movement of the United States and Canada, 1924.

————. *Saddlebag Folk: The Way of Life in the Kentucky Mountains*. Evanston: Row, Peterson, 1942.

Redfield, Robert. *Peasant Society and Culture*. Chicago: Univ. of Chicago Press, 1973.

Ritter Lumber Company, William M. *The Romance of Appalachian Hardwood Lumber*. Columbus, Ohio: W.M. Ritter Lumber Co., 1940.

Roberts, Bruce and Nancy. *Where Time Stood Still: A Portrait of Appalachia*. New York: Macmillan, 1970.

Ross, Malcolm. *Machine Age in the Hills*. New York: Macmillan, 1933.

Salvati, Raymond E. *Island Creek: Saga in Bituminous*. New York: Newcomen Society in North America, 1957.

Scalf, Henry P. *Kentucky's Last Frontier*. Pikeville, Ky.: Pikeville College Press, 1972.

Schenck, Carl Alwin. *The Birth of Forestry in America: The Biltmore Forest School, 1898–1913*. Boone, N.C.: Appalachian Consortium Press, 1974.

Schwarzweller, Harry K., James S. Brown, and J.J. Managalam. *Mountain Families in Transition: A Case Study of Appalachian Migration*. University Park: Pennsylvania State Univ. Press, 1971.

Shackleford, Laurel, and Bill Weinberg. *Our Appalachia: An Oral History*. New York: Hill and Wang, 1977.

Shands, William E., and Robert G. Healy. *The Lands Nobody Wanted: A Conservation Foundation Report*. Washington, D.C.: Conservation Foundation, 1977.

Shapiro, Henry David. *Appalachia On Our Mind: The Southern Mountains and Mountaineers in the American Consciousness*. Chapel Hill: Univ. of North Carolina Press, 1978.

Sheppard, Muriel Earley. *Cabins in the Laurel*. Chapel Hill: Univ. of North Carolina Press, 1935.

Sondley, F.A. *A History of Buncombe County, North Carolina*. Asheville, N.C.: Advocate Printing, 1930.

Sorokin, Pitirim A., Carle C. Zimmerman, and Charles J. Galpin. *A Systematic Source Book in Rural Sociology*. Minneapolis: Univ. of Minnesota Press, 1931.

Southern Appalachian Studies. *Number of Inhabitants of the Southern Appalachians, 1900–1957*. Population Data Series No. 1. Athens: Univ. of Georgia Press, 1957.

Spero, Sterling, and Abram L. Harris. *The Black Worker: The Negro and the Labor Movement*. New York: Columbia Univ. Press, 1931.

Steen, Harold K. *The U.S. Forest Service: A History*. Seattle: Univ. of Washington Press, 1976.

Stephenson, John B. *Shiloh: A Mountain Commmunity*. Lexington: Univ. of Kentucky Press, 1968.

Still, James. *River of Earth*. New York: Viking, 1940.

Stover, John Ford. *The Railroads of the South, 1865–1900: A Study in Finance and Control*. Chapel Hill: Univ. of North Carolina Press, 1955.

Tams, William Purviance, Jr. *The Smokeless Coal Fields of West Virginia: A Brief History*. Morgantown: West Virginia Univ. Library, 1963.

Terpenning, Walter A. *Village and Open Country Neighborhoods*. New York: Century, 1931.

Thomas, Jean. *Big Sandy*. New York: Henry Holt, 1940.

Thomas, W.R. *Life Among the Hills and Mountains of Kentucky*. Louisville: Standard Printing, 1926.

Thurmond, Walter R. *The Logan Coal Field of West Virginia: A Brief History*. Morgantown: West Virginia Univ. Library, 1964.

Tindall, George Brown. *The Emergence of the New South, 1913–1945*. Baton Rouge: Louisiana State Univ. Press, 1967.

―――. *South Carolina Negroes, 1877–1900*. Columbia: Univ. of South Carolina Press, 1952.

Tipton, J.C. *The Cumberland Coal Field and Its Creators*. Middlesborough, Ky.: Pinnacle Printing, 1905.

Titus, Warren I. *John Fox, Jr*. New York: Twayne, 1971.

Tocqueville, Alexis de. *Democracy in America*. New York: Harper, 1966.

Toynbee, Arnold. *A Study of History*. II. New York: Oxford Univ. Press, 1947.

Turner, Charles Wilson. *Chessie's Road*. Richmond: Garrett and Massie, 1956.

Van Noppen, Ina Woestemeyer, and John J. Van Noppen. *Western North Carolina Since the Civil War*. Boone, N.C.: Appalachian Consortium Press, 1973.

Vatter, Harold G. *The Drive to Industrial Maturity: The U.S. Economy, 1860 to 1914*. Westport, Conn.: Greenwood, 1975.

Verhoeff, Mary. *The Kentucky Mountains, Transportation and Commerce, 1750–1911: A Study in the Economic History of a Coal Field*. Filson Club Publication No. 26, Vol. I. Louisville: Filson Club, 1911.

Way, William, Jr. *The Clinchfield Railroad: The Story of a Trade Route Across the Blue Ridge Mountains*. Chapel Hill: Univ. of North Carolina Press, 1931.

Wecter, Dixon. The Age of the Great Depression, 1929—1941. New York: Macmillan, 1948.

Weller, Jack E. *Yesterday's People: Life in Contemporary Appalachia*. Lexington: Univ. of Kentucky Press, 1965.

Whitaker, Corporal Fess. *History of Corporal Fess Whitaker: Life in the Kentucky Mountains, Mexico and Texas*. Louiville: Standard Printing Co., 1918.

Wiebe, Robert H. *Businessmen and Reform: A Study of the Progressive Movement*. Cambridge, Mass.: Harvard University Press, 1962.

Williams, John Alexander. *West Virginia and the Captains of Industry*. Morgantown: West Virginia Univ. Library, 1976.

Wolfe, Thomas. *The Hills Beyond*. New York: Harper, 1941.

Woodward, Comer Vann. *Origins of the New South, 1877–1913*. Baton Rouge: Louisiana State University Press, 1951.

# INDEX

267

Virginia-Carolina Railroad, 99
Virginia Coal and Iron Company, 57, 75–76, 150
Virginia Iron, Coal, and Coke Company, 75, 76, 150
Virginia, Tennessee and Carolina Steel and Iron Company, 59
Virginia and Southwestern Railroad, 75
Virginia and Tennessee Railroad, 13, 65
Virginian Railway, 139
*The Virginias* journal, 51
Vivian, Gray and Company, 72

Walbridge interests, 53
Walker, Thomas, 44
Warner, Charles Dudley, 39–42, 85; "On Horseback," 39
Washington College, 50
Washington County, Va., 98
Watauga and Yadkin River Railroad, 107
Watauga County, N.C., 107
Watson, Sen. Clarence W., 144
Watterson, Henry, 45
Watts, Edgar and Frank, 82, 84
Watts Steel and Iron Company, 82
Wayne County, Ky., 95
Waynesville, N.C., 89, 100, 104
Weeks Act, 117–18, 120
Welch, Capt. Isaiah, 51
Welch, W.Va., 137
West Jefferson, N.C., 98
West Virginia: coal industry, 132–40; industrial development, 46–47, 49–52, 67–70, 73–75; population growth (1890–1920), 133–34; timber industry, 95–96
West Virginia, state of: Board of Agriculture, xxi–xxii, 96; Committee on Mines and Mining, 216; Commission on Immigration, 46, 173; Department of Mines, 218; Tax Commission, 64

*West Virginia Handbook and Immigrants' Guide,* 46
Western North Carolina Railroad, 48, 89, 99, 101
Wetzell, H.B., 53
Wheelwright, Ky., 145
Whitaker, Cpl. Fess, 60
Whitcomb, Henry, 67
White Mountain National Forest, 118
White Top Mountain (Va.), 98
Whitehouse, Ky., 78
Whitehouse Cannel Coal Company, 78
Whitley County, Ky., 60, 79, 94, 95, 141
Widen, W.Va., 190
Wilderness Road, 14, 39
Wilkes County, N.C., 107
Williams, Cratis, 238
Wilson, James, 115–17
Wilson Creek Lumber Company, 104
Winchester, Ky., 79
Wirt, Willard, 241–42
Wisconsin Steel Company, 147
Wise County, Va., 49, 59, 75–77, 98, 149–50
Wise Terminal Railway, 59
Wolfe, Thomas: *The Hills Beyond,* xxiv
Women: in company towns, 232–33; in pre-industrial society, 31–32; in textile mills, 126
Wood, Ky., 95
Wood, R.E., Lumber Company, 106
Wood, Stuart, 52
Workman, C.L., 196–97
Workmen's Compensation laws, 218–19
Wyoming County, W.Va., 51, 71, 72, 96, 139

Yadkin National Forest, 117
Yancey County, N.C., 101, 106, 124
Yellow Poplar Lumber Company, 93, 96

*Twentieth-Century America Series*

DEWEY W. GRANTHAM, GENERAL EDITOR

Each volume in this series focuses on some aspect of the politics of social change in recent American history, utilizing new approaches to clarify the response of Americans to the dislocating forces of our own day—economic, technological, racial, demographic, and administrative.

VOLUMES PUBLISHED:

THE UNIVERSITY OF TENNESSEE PRESS : KNOXVILLE